Routledg

Practical Socialism for Britain

First published in 1935, *Practical Socialism for Britain* presents an assessment of the Labour government's policy options and aggressively advocates for socialism as Britain's panacea. Citing apathy and panic-mongering as the greatest enemies of the Labour Party, the author asserts that the Labour Party can restore meaning and sincerity to politics by bringing about tangible development and eliminating the militarisation of politics. He also exhorts the Crown and the civil services to be politically neutral and to pledge allegiance to the Constitution. Strictly anti-fascist and anti-communist, this book will be of interest to students of history, political science, and government.

Practical Socialism for Britain

Hugh Dalton

First published in 1935
by George Routledge & Sons, Ltd

This edition first published in 2022 by Routledge
4 Park Square, Milton Park, Abingdon, Oxon, OX14 4RN
and by Routledge
605 Third Avenue, New York, NY 10017

Routledge is an imprint of the Taylor & Francis Group, an informa business

© Routledge, 1935

All rights reserved. No part of this book may be reprinted or reproduced or utilised in any form or by any electronic, mechanical, or other means, now known or hereafter invented, including photocopying and recording, or in any information storage or retrieval system, without permission in writing from the publishers.

Publisher's Note
The publisher has gone to great lengths to ensure the quality of this reprint but points out that some imperfections in the original copies may be apparent.

Disclaimer
The publisher has made every effort to trace copyright holders and welcomes correspondence from those they have been unable to contact.

A Library of Congress record exists under LCCN: 35013615

ISBN: 978-1-032-31090-9 (hbk)
ISBN: 978-1-003-30811-9 (ebk)
ISBN: 978-1-032-31111-1 (pbk)

Book DOI 10.4324/9781003308119

PRACTICAL SOCIALISM FOR BRITAIN

By
HUGH DALTON

LONDON
GEORGE ROUTLEDGE & SONS, LTD.
BROADWAY HOUSE: 68-74 CARTER LANE, E.C.
1935

Printed in Great Britain by Butler & Tanner Ltd., Frome and London

CONTENTS

CHAP.		PAGE
	PREFACE	vii

PART I. INTRODUCTORY

I	THE BACKGROUND OF BRITISH POLITICS .	3
II	RETROSPECT	16
III	THE AIMS OF SOCIALISM	26

PART II. DEMOCRACY

IV	WHAT IS DEMOCRACY?	31
V	THE HOUSE OF COMMONS	34
VI	REFORM OF PARLIAMENTARY PROCEDURE .	44
VII	EMERGENCY LEGISLATION	68
VIII	THE HOUSE OF LORDS	71
IX	SOME PROBLEMS OF GOVERNMENT . .	82

PART III. SOCIALISATION

X	FORMS OF SOCIALISATION	93
XI	BROADCASTING	102
XII	ELECTRICITY	105
XIII	TRANSPORT	117
XIV	COAL AND ITS PRODUCTS	129
XV	OTHER CASES	140
XVI	THE LAND AND AGRICULTURE . . .	149
XVII	WORKERS' CONTROL OF INDUSTRY . .	161
XVIII	TERMS OF TRANSFER.	167

CONTENTS

PART IV. FINANCE

CHAP.		PAGE
XIX	The Failure of the Financiers	181
XX	Monetary Policy	192
XXI	The Bank of England	202
XXII	Control of Long-Term Credit	210
XXIII	Control of Short-Term Credit	231

PART V. PLANNING

XXIV	The Nature and Objects of Economic Planning	243
XXV	Employment through Planned Development	252
XXVI	Geographical Planning	267
XXVII	National Parks and Forests and the National Trust	284
XXVIII	The Location of Industry	299
XXIX	External Trade	303
XXX	The Machinery of Planning	309

PART VI. EQUALITY

XXXI	Towards Social Equality	319
XXXII	Socialism and Private Property	329
XXXIII	Inherited Wealth	334

PART VII. PEACE

XXXIV	Cross Currents of Hope and Fear	347
XXXV	The Labour Party's Foreign Policy	365
	Index	387

PREFACE

THIS book has grown out of my work during the past three years as a member of the National Executive of the Labour Party.

The political events of 1931 have led the Labour Party, through electoral defeat and through a passing phase of discouragement and self-distrust, to a new and more vigorous life. In 1934 we have regained confidence in ourselves and, as the by-elections and the local elections show, we have regained the confidence of at least as large a number of the electors as in 1929, hitherto the high water mark of our advance.

Those who speculate on the results of the next general election are only divided as to whether we shall win a clear majority in the next House of Commons, or, falling a little short of this, shall constitute a powerful Parliamentary Opposition, needing, for that majority, only a relatively small access of further strength.

There is to-day a widespread interest in the Labour Party's policy, both domestic and foreign, and a growing desire, often in most unexpected quarters, for a Labour victory at the polls.

Since 1931 we have been engaged in thinking out our policy afresh, in greater detail than ever before, and in relation to the present needs, national and international, of these troubled days. As a member of the National Executive of the Party, and of its Policy Committee, I have had, together with many others, some share in this thinking and some personal responsibility for its results. Three years' work culminated in October, 1934, at Southport at the Annual Conference of the Party, which accepted the Executive's proposals *For Socialism and Peace*. This document, with others which it summarises, contains the marching orders which a Labour majority would take to Westminster, and Labour Ministers into their Departments. It represents the deliberate will of our Party, the basis of our next appeal to the country, the programme of our action if that appeal succeeds.

I claim for this book no official authority. It is an individual contribution and I have not hesitated to express my personal opinions and sometimes to emphasise them. But, on essentials, the programme which I advocate is that which the Labour Party, at its last three annual conferences, has approved. If any of my readers are curious to know how closely I stick to the official texts, they have only to read the latter for themselves.

Within the Labour Party during these three years there has been a healthy stir of ideas and some internal controversy. Much more, indeed, than in the Mac-Donald-Snowden era. This is as it should be. A political party without such stirrings is drowsy unto death. But a party which spends too long on introspection is out of health and shirking its duty, which is to go forth and conquer the greater world outside itself.

First we must persuade the electors to put faith in us, and then we must justify and strengthen that faith by effective action.

The balance of this book is not the same as the balance of importance of the questions treated. Some of the most important of these I am fully conscious of having treated very summarily. The limits of space and time, under which I have been working, have helped to make this inevitable. And, just because this book is an individual contribution, not an official programme, I have felt free to write at greater length where I thought I had something fresh to say, more shortly where the ground has already been well covered by others.

HUGH DALTON.

ALDBOURNE,
  WILTSHIRE.
    January, 1935.

PART I
INTRODUCTORY

CHAPTER I

THE BACKGROUND OF BRITISH POLITICS

"ENGLAND is different," a curiously remote island, cut off from Europe by a little ditch of sea water which, except mentally, has ceased to be a barrier, either in peace or war.

"For one who spent in Paris the greater part of the six months which succeeded the Armistice," wrote Mr. Keynes in 1919, "an occasional visit to London was a strange experience. England still stands outside Europe. Europe's voiceless tremors do not reach her. Europe is apart and England is not of her flesh and body." It is still true. And again: "an Englishman who took part in the Conference of Paris . . . was bound to become, for him a new experience, a European in his cares and outlook. There, at the nerve centre of the European system, his British preoccupations must largely fall away and he must be haunted by other and more dreadful spectres." [1] The spectres are there still, growing a little grimmer year by year. But too few Englishmen are haunted by them. If more saw them clearly, we might drive them off and save our island, and Europe, and the Outer Continents as well, from fear of dreadful dooms. But here I touch foreign policy.

The nature and conditions of British home politics are difficult for foreigners, and even, it seems, for some British circles to understand. From cloistered

[1] *Economic Consequences of the Peace*, pp. 2-3.

coteries visibility of the outside world is poor, whether from Carlton Club or Communist Cell or Highbrow Hall.

England is different. But how?

Pictures of national characteristics can only be painted with a broad brush, and I am concerned here only with qualities which bear on politics. Perhaps, if not thus limited, the picture would flatter us less. The British people, in the mass, differ from many others in their distrust of logic and distaste for doctrine; their cult of the practical and their gift for compromise; their sense of humour; their interest in sport; their sense of what they call " fair play," a term notoriously hard to translate into foreign languages; their capacity, gained through long practice, for all forms of self-government, including the art of running every sort of voluntary organisation; their dimness of class-consciousness, alongside their tendency to snobbishness. To talk or act, in politics, as though these qualities were not widespread among us, is to court rebuff.

Typical of us was the football match, played in a seaport town during the general strike in May, 1926, between the strikers and the police. It is related that a French journalist, sent across the Channel by his paper to report our bloody revolution, found that the only important item of local news that day was that the strikers had beaten the police by two goals to one. He took the next boat back to France, exclaiming in disgust, " You English are not a serious people ! "

Football, it might be held, is one of the clues to our national character. Those who play it, or watch it, or " follow " it from afar, are a large percentage of the British electorate, some part of which treats an election just like a football match, and backs its favourite team, and cheers it on, and wears its colours. Our taste for sport is a clue to our political pacifism.

We prefer throwing cricket balls to throwing bombs, and kicking footballs to kicking political opponents lying helpless on the ground. British political contests are generally strenuous, sometimes bitter while they last, often crude in their methods, often discouraging to those who love truth more than victory. But it is significant that one of our unwritten rules, which is seldom broken, is that rival candidates shake hands after the declaration of the poll, as after a sporting contest.

By contrast with some other countries, we have succeeded so far in keeping our politics free from deep personal hatreds, clean from the murder habit and from other extreme manifestations of bestiality and hysteria. I doubt whether in any other country a general strike could have lasted nine days, and a miners' lockout six months, without bloodshed. We have much to learn from many foreign countries, but less about the decencies of politics than about most other forms of human activity.

It is not surprising that neither Fascism nor Communism has struck easy root in our soil. Both preach violence or, by a quibble, proclaim it as inevitable. Thus both offend our instinct of political pacifism. Both are too weak to win even a single seat in Parliament,—the Fascists, hitherto, too weak even to have a try. Neither a Saklatvala nor a Mosley seems to find his spiritual home in British public life. Both speak like strangers in a foreign land.

Political murder gangs became social institutions after the War in Germany and Italy. Communists and Fascists murdered each other daily in the streets, and often murdered peaceful citizens as well, until between them they had murdered Liberty. In both these countries it was Communist violence which prepared the way, and made the atmosphere, for the triumph of Fascist counter-violence. And the failure of the constitutional parties of the Left to act boldly, or to attract the young, made this triumph easy. The Russian case was different. There Communism conquered chaos, in a land which had never known Liberty.

The only serious lapses in recent times from British political pacifism in home affairs have been, not in this island, but in Ireland. And the sequel is that Ireland, apart from its Northern province, is no longer part of our home affairs. But it was a growing sense in Britain of outraged political decency which stopped the exploits of Mr. Lloyd George's Black and Tans, and compelled the negotiation of the Anglo-Irish Treaty.

The earlier lapse was when, once more in Ireland, politics became militarised through the formation of rival private armies, Orange and Green. Sedition in Ulster, the miserable weakness of the Liberal Government, counter-sedition in the South of Ireland, Tory attempts to seduce the British Army. These were the successive scenes in the drama, which on the eve of the Great War was moving to its climax. Some think it loosed that war. They argue that the German Government plunged, calculating on our enforced neutrality in Europe, with civil war raging in Ireland and part of the Army refusing to obey orders. If this be so, Carson and his Tory friends bear a burden of moral responsibility beyond all human reckoning. With the outbreak of war, the curtain fell on our home drama. Once again England, and Ireland too, was different from foreign expectations.

No British Government should ever permit the militarisation of our politics. Private armies, if ever and by whomsoever formed, should be suppressed without hesitation, as recently in Sweden and in Denmark, in both cases by Socialist Governments, defending democracy and domestic peace. Arms and military drilling should be a monopoly of the Armed

Forces of the Crown. Private enterprise in this field is equally repugnant to civic Loyalty and to Socialism.

It is open to any political party to seek to persuade the British people to accept proposals for peaceful change, however far-reaching. The British Labour Party has put forward its proposals. My object in this book is to expound them.

Whatever may be true of other countries, I believe that here it is possible to make a peaceful, orderly and smooth transition to a better social order;[1] and that, with a working Labour majority in the House of Commons, five years of resolute Government could lay the foundations of that order. Thereafter, at the next election, the people would be free to choose whether or not the work of Socialist construction should continue.

The two great enemies of the Labour Party are apathy and panic-mongering. "You're all alike," says the tired woman in the mean street to the canvassing candidate, "you all make wonderful promises at election time, and then do nothing for us when you get to Parliament." Too often in the past she has been right.

[1] In support of this belief I can cite Karl Marx, wiser in this respect than some latter-day Marxists. He knew from personal experience that England was different. Driven from Germany as a political exile he found refuge here, lived, worked and wrote here, and lies buried at Highgate. He formed the opinion that though, in most countries, Socialism could only come by violent revolution, here it was otherwise. We must recognise, he insisted, that national characteristics were not uniform. Some countries—England, Holland and the United States of America among the number—had a tradition of political freedom and a Parliamentary climate, which made possible the achievement of Socialism, without violence, by democratic Parliamentary methods. His views on this point are well brought out in a pamphlet on *Marxism* by A. J. Williams, published by the National Council of Labour Colleges.

Politics, both in a democracy and under a modern dictatorship, is always in danger of degenerating into Ordeal by Oratory. And oratory, as Froude said, is the harlot of the arts. The divorce between words and deeds tends to discredit all political activity. It is easy to stand braying on a platform, drawing cheers by mouthing big phrases. But some who listen will have doubts. We of the Labour Party can help to restore meaning and sincerity to politics, if, when our next chance comes, we perform what we have promised, and if meanwhile we promise only what we honestly believe we can perform. Success in performance would kill apathy.

Panic-mongering is our other enemy. When first I stood for Parliament, I believed that the electors would vote on a rational comparison between party programmes. I was soon undeceived. Bogies were conjured up, to scare the credulous. In my second contest a leaflet was issued by my Conservative opponent suggesting to the electors that, if I was returned, all churches would be burned down, and all copies of the Bible destroyed.

Panic, running in subterranean streams, defeated our candidates in 1931. Millions of electors feared that, if we won, the pound would be worth less than a penny and that their small deposits in the Post Office Savings Bank would disappear. High authorities, including Messrs. MacDonald, Snowden and Runciman, shamelessly fed these fears. Likewise in 1924 panic defeated many of our candidates, because a Mr. Zinoviev was thought to have written to some obscure correspondent in this country a vaguely threatening letter. Panic-mongering will be tried again by our opponents. Terrible tales will be told of our intentions, which, therefore, we must make clear and well understood beforehand.

I pass now to consider briefly some important factors in our British situation, in their relation to the peaceful achievement of Socialism.

First, the Crown. " I have no fear of the Royal Family," writes George Lansbury. " They have shown their willingness to accept the nation's will too often to allow of any doubt on that score."[1] " I would never lift a finger," said the late John Wheatley, " to change this country from a capitalist monarchy into a capitalist republic." In this country, as in the British Dominions, we have acclimatised the Crown to the growth of democracy. The Scandinavians have done the same. So have the Belgians and the Dutch. Elsewhere there have been failures.

Many years ago, I heard a Liberal Cabinet Minister propose the Royal Toast in these words : " We are the descendants of the men who turned the Kings of England into constitutional monarchs, and therefore we are loyal to the Throne." Those words have stuck in my memory. The Labour Party, too, is in that line of descent.

The corridors of the Houses of Parliament are decorated with many scenes from our Civil War when Parliament first beat the King, and then beheaded him ; and with an earlier scene, King John coerced at Runnymede, sitting in the rain, his Crown awry. Members of Parliament, of all parties, show these pictures to visiting constituents. They frame the history of our political liberties.

But the Crown is no longer, as when John or Charles wore it, a Party emblem. There is to-day no Republican Party in this country, and nowhere any visible or audible hostility to the Throne.

This is a recent change. The earlier Georges commanded little respect. And the young Queen Victoria, just after her accession, was hissed at Ascot by a wealthy Tory crowd, because she had refused, in spite

[1] *My England*, p. 23.

of all the blandishments of Peel and Wellington, to give up her Whig Ladies of the Bedchamber, and to instal Tory ladies in their place.

Later it was only Gladstone's forbearance, in face of the Queen's undisguised aversion, that prevented the growth among Liberals of Republican sentiments. Even so, Joseph Chamberlain, after the French Revolution of 1870, said publicly that " a Republic must come soon in this country ", and his friend Dilke carried on frank Republican propaganda from within the Liberal Party. Again in 1910 there were murmurs among Liberals of a rising storm, when it was falsely reported that the King had refused to promise to create new peers sufficient to overbear the resistance of the Lords to the Parliament Bill. An election was threatened on the slogan, " the King and the Peers against the People ", and there was talk in the National Liberal Club of a Republican demonstration in Trafalgar Square. On the other hand, the Ulster gunmen and their Tory allies in this country rebuffed the efforts of the present King, on his accession, to find an Irish compromise. It was an Orange orator who threatened in a public speech to " kick King George's crown into the Boyne ", unless the Home Rule Bill were withdrawn ; and it was Joynson Hicks, later renamed Lord Brentford, who yelled at the Armed Forces of the Crown, " fire and be damned ! " This is a black chapter of Tory disloyalty.

The Labour Party has never adopted such attitudes towards the Throne. Yet for all democrats loyalty to the Crown is conditional on the Crown's loyalty to constitutional usage. If, contrary to all recent experience, this became doubtful, sentiment would soon change. The almost mystic halo, which now surrounds the Crown, would quickly fade. The cheers which now, even in the most depressed areas, greet any member of the Royal Family, would be mixed with other cries.

The most disloyal subjects of the Crown are those who seek to make it partisan, including those who run about behind the scenes pulling political wires that were best left untouched, trying from Royal backstairs to queer the pitch for Ministers or their policies. It was suspected in some quarters that such busybodies were at work in 1931 against the Labour Government. These rumours left a nasty taste behind.

If ever such intriguers should succeed in pushing the Crown into open partisanship, or even rouse serious suspicions of its political neutrality, they will shake its moral authority, and split British opinion down a new line of cleavage. A political party, which had the open support of the Crown against its opponents, might win the first round. But it could not count on winning the second, and it would have undermined, perhaps fatally, the Crown's stability.

To-day the Crown is honoured and safe, because it stands above the battle, respecting electoral verdicts, welcoming Ministers, whatever their policy, who are supported by the House of Commons, and acting constitutionally on their advice.

Like the Crown, the Civil Service should be politically neutral. It should be the loyal servant of the Government of the day, whatever its political colour. I believe that such loyalty can be counted on, by a Labour Government not less than by any other. My experience at the Foreign Office from 1929 to 1931 supports this view.

If, in particular cases, it should prove otherwise in future, there should be bumps and promotions. Some Socialists fear that, especially near the top of the service, class prejudice will show itself obstructive towards great changes. If so, the remedy is simple.

It is important to preserve the right relationship

between Ministers and officials. The Minister should tell the officials what his policy is. He should not, on large issues, ask the officials what to do. He should tell them what is to be done, and ask them to advise how best to do it, what difficulties stand in the way, and how these can most effectively be overcome. Otherwise civil servants are placed in a false position, that of civil masters.[1] At the Foreign Office, on Mr. Henderson's instructions, I circulated to all Heads of Departments, for their information and general guidance, copies of *Labour and the Nation*, the programme on which we had won the election. Thereafter there could be no doubt inside the Office regarding our principal objectives and, with the loyal and skilful help of the officials, we reached all those laid down in our election programme, except one, a general Treaty of Disarmament. On this we were focussing our preparatory efforts when the Government fell.

Just as civil servants should not be asked to settle policy, so they should not be asked to defend it in public. They should not, for example, be the spokesmen of the Government at international conferences. This is work for Ministers, or their political supporters.

Some minor weaknesses in our Civil Service there may be ; a tendency, which politicians should have checked, for a few high officials to take too much upon themselves ; a tendency sometimes to run in ruts, and to exaggerate difficulties ; some excess of Departmental self-consciousness ; some slowness in all inter-

[1] Mr. Lansbury (*My England*, pp. 142-3) gives a vivid account of the meetings of the Second Labour Government's Unemployment Committee, with Mr. Thomas in the chair, " in a sort of semi-dungeon high up in the Treasury Offices. We were surrounded by the reputed élite of the Civil Service. . . . There was always present one faithful watchdog of the Treasury, who . . . could always be counted on to find good and excellent reasons why nothing should be done."

Departmental mechanisms; occasional honest incapacity, especially among the older men, to change direction readily when policy changes; a tendency, much more marked in some Departments than in others, to damp down initiative in the junior ranks.

Such weaknesses as these may be largely remedied by active political chiefs. A Minister who takes pains to become acquainted with the personnel of his Department, not merely with a few senior officials, can redistribute duties and promote good men freely, not following seniority slavishly, but giving recognition to keenness and ability. Redistribution of duties is easier, the wider the range of effective mobility. We should seek to widen this range in all branches of the public service. The fusion of the Foreign Office and the Diplomatic Service since the War is wholly healthy. A further fusion, to include the Consular Service as well, would be better still. As Mr. Harold Nicolson puts it crudely, this would make " more jobs for the efficient, more pigeon-holes for fools ". More frequent interchange between the Colonial Office at home and the Colonial Service abroad, between the staffs of Departments such as the Ministries of Education, Health and Labour and of the Local Authorities which they control, and between the staffs of different Government Departments, would similarly be advantageous. It would quicken the circulation of ideas, extend individual experience, and dig men out of their ruts. With improved methods of recruitment for the staffs of Local Authorities, such as Sir Henry Hadow's Committee have recently recommended, and with the creation of a National Planning Authority and of an increasing number of Public Corporations and other public enterprises, such interchanges, given the will to make them, will become much easier.

There is a further point, especially important, in my judgment, for a Labour Government. Ministers should often take with them into their Departments, not only Junior Ministers whom they are prepared to trust and use,[1] but other persons, in whom they have confidence and who have special knowledge of the problems of the Department and of the Party's policy regarding them. Mr. Henderson did this, with excellent results, at the Foreign Office. And some of President Roosevelt's Ministers have done it, with great success, in Washington, though in America the lack of a permanent Civil Service comparable to ours alters the problem.

In this country the function of such outsiders would be to assist the Minister, and to co-operate with, rather than to replace, the permanent officials in preparing and carrying out policy, and in suggesting ideas. Such outsiders must possess tact, as well as knowledge and energy. But, given these qualities, they would be a healthy leaven in the bureaucratic lump. They need not, and often most conveniently would not, be Members of Parliament. Nor, of course, would they become permanent Civil Servants. They would come in with the Minister and go out with him.

How far and how fast a Labour Government could move, within the lifetime of a normal Parliament, would depend on the size of its Parliamentary majority, on the volume of support behind it in the country, and on the personal resources of the Party in courage, energy, knowledge and skill. There is, I believe, a tremendous and sustained support waiting, in nearly every section of the community, including the so-called " technicians " and the professional middle class, for a Government that will show fight against poverty and unemployment, and delay and muddle, that will act boldly, and get things done. The great majority

[1] Not, as sometimes happens, Junior Ministers who are planted on them against their will, and whom they treat as ciphers.

of the British people will judge policy, not by preconceptions, but by results.

We shall, of course, meet obstinate resistance from powerful and selfish vested interests and from clever tacticians among our opponents. But, if we hold a strong and steady popular support, and if our leaders decline to be either intimidated by High Finance or seduced by High Society, such resistance can be peacefully and constitutionally overcome. I discount heavily, in this common-sense and politically mature country, all panic talk, whether from Right or Left, of an "inevitable crisis," and all theatrical nightmares of violent head-on collisions, wrecking the train of democracy.

The Socialist idea has lately made great progress among us, and will make much more, on condition that it is propounded persuasively and in practical forms, and that it justifies itself in action.

> In the past the democratic system has won great triumphs in the political sphere. The Labour Party believes that the nation has the courage to seek the repetition of those triumphs in the sphere of economics. It sees no reason why a people who, first in the world, achieved through parliamentary institutions their political and religious freedom should not, by the same means, achieve their economic emancipation.[1]

---

[1] *For Socialism and Peace, the Labour Party's Programme of Action*, approved at the Annual Conference at Southport, 1934.

CHAPTER II

RETROSPECT

LIKE many other features in our political landscape, the British Labour Party is a tree native to this island. Planted in 1900 by a few Trade Unions and Socialist Societies in protest against the failures of both the Conservative and Liberal Parties, until the War its growth was slow. It was overshadowed by its taller rivals, who drew to themselves the moisture of the electoral soil and shared by turns the sunshine of political fortune. But the lightnings of the Great War struck and split the Liberal Party, and sent it crashing headlong. And from this moment the Labour Party, attracting to itself a mass of new adherents, particularly among the returning soldiers and the younger generation, grew in a few years to the stature of a National Party, challenging the Conservatives as an alternative Government, proclaiming Socialism at home and Peace abroad.

Its growth was greatly quickened by the opening of its membership to all individuals, " all workers by hand or brain ", whether members of Trade Unions or Socialist Societies, or not, who accepted its objects and were willing to be enrolled as members of Constituency Labour Parties. This widening of its constitution and its sources of support was due to the practical wisdom of its Secretary, Mr. Arthur Henderson, to whom, more than to any other one man, the Party owes its past rise and present strength.

Since 1918 anyone may join the Labour Party, and find work and welcome there, who shares its aspirations. There has been a large entry of men and women of all classes and occupations. But historically, and still to-day, the Party is solidly based on the Trade Unions. They have given, and still give, the Party its stability. They emphasise its practical outlook and its British common sense They have stood steadfast in their political faith, when others,—MacDonalds, Mosleys and suchlike Prima Donnas,—after a blaze of self-display, have gone their separate ways. The independent Socialist Societies, once a keen and healthy force, latterly have shrunk in numbers and influence, and one, once the most powerful of them all, has gone into impotent exile. To a Party, which now admits all Socialists to individual membership, such Societies have less to add than in the early days.

Socialist parties in most other countries have derived largely from Marx. With us, Marxian influence has been small. Here we derive, in so far as we derive at all from writers, chiefly from native sources, from Bentham and Owen, Morris and Ruskin, Blatchford, the Webbs and Shaw, Wells in some of his many moods, Tawney and Cole. But we derive less from the written than the spoken word, and less from systematised thought than from empirical action. The men who have stood out on the political side of the British Labour Movement have been men of simple and strong character, such as Keir Hardie, Arthur Henderson and George Lansbury or, less fortunately, masters of oratory, with an inclination to egoism, such as MacDonald and Snowden.

For those of us, who have been members of the Labour Party for more than a year or two, the past falls into clearly marked and well-remembered stages. Till 1923 we were a purely propagandist Party, preaching in Opposition a gospel of hope.

1923–4 marked our first short inconclusive essay in Minority Government, ending after nine months in a confused dissolution on a trivial issue, the now almost forgotten Campbell Case, and an electoral setback.

1924–9 were years of preparation, both in and outside Parliament, of sharp industrial struggle in 1926, of Tory reaction and of persistent unemployment at a figure, low by comparison with later years, but rightly thought intolerable then, of just over one million. Our policy was worked out afresh in greater detail. *Labour and the Nation* was compiled, and approved by the Annual Conference of the Party at Birmingham in 1928. Moreover, the Executive of the Parliamentary Party, on which I served from 1925 to 1929, privately prepared in the early months of 1929 a programme of action for the first session of a Minority Labour Government which then seemed a possible outcome of the next election. And so indeed it proved. The Second Labour Government flowered in the spring.

1929–31 were years beginning with high hopes, passing into a phase of growing Parliamentary frustration, ending in a crash of disillusion and defeat.

1931–4 have been years of recovery, in which we have re-examined our faith, restated our purposes, regained our drive.

And all the while we have been advancing steadily, though with fluctuating fortunes, to the increasing control of British Local Government. We control it now in London and in a number, growing from year to year, of cities, towns and counties. In this sphere the Party is doing to-day, often with great boldness and efficiency, the best work it has done so far.

The general election of 1929 gave us greater successes than most of our leaders had expected. None had expected a majority. But we came back only eighteen seats short of half the House of Commons. If there had been no University seats and no plural voting in respect of business premises, we should have been within some half a dozen votes of a bare majority. But we held 130 out of our 289 seats on a minority vote in three-cornered contests. As the next election showed, when Conservatives and Liberals combined against us, our hold was more precarious than it seemed.

When the Second Labour Government was formed, no voice, it is interesting to recall, was raised within our Party against accepting office under these conditions.

Looking back upon what followed, it is clear now that there were three possible courses open to the Party, for each of which a plausible case could have been put up. In the first place, we might have refused office, on the ground that we were a Socialist Party, but that there was no Socialist majority in Parliament. Could we have foreseen the coming of the trade depression, there would have been an even stronger case, than might otherwise be made, for such an attitude. But no one foresaw it then, not even the experts. In energetic opposition against an uneasy combination of Tories and Liberals, whether or not in formal coalition matters little, with every by-election victory eating into their slender majority, and with the unemployment figures rapidly rising after the first few months, discrediting the Government, we should have been very favourably placed to win a working majority at the next election, even if Tories and Liberals had then united against us in most of the constituencies. For both would then have been discredited by events. And, under these conditions, the next election must have come soon. Doubt only arises, when we wonder to what use our leaders of that day would have put such a majority, had they won it, and when, further, we reflect that it would have been won with the trade depression already deep, and deepening, so that only bold measures could have availed to pull us out of the mire.

In the second place, we might have accepted office and introduced at once bold Socialist measures, and been defeated on them. That this would have been our fate is certain, for Mr. Lloyd George warned us, in the first days of that Parliament, wagging a menacing forefinger, that, as soon as we attempted Socialism, out we should go. Defeated, we might either have obtained a dissolution and fought an election with a fair chance of winning, given the enthusiasm which boldness would have generated among our own supporters, and the still unexhausted impetus of our recent advance; or alternatively, without a dissolution, gone back into opposition, with a strategical advantage certainly no less than in the first situation considered above. The most serious practical argument against a quick dissolution would have been financial. We are a poor Party, and it would have been hard to find the money. But a mood of enthusiasm would have helped us to find it.

In the third place, we might have accepted office, and co-operated openly and frankly with the Liberals, aiming at accomplishing over a period of, say, four years, the maximum programme on which agreement could be reached. This course would have presented obvious difficulties and dangers, might have achieved very little in the end, and would have been distasteful, unless it quickly justified itself by results, to many of our supporters. But it would have been at least definite and intelligible.

In fact, we took none of these three courses. We took a fourth, which combined the disadvantages of them all, and none of the advantages of any. We accepted office, we brought in no bold measures,[1] and

[1] Our two boldest measures, Dr. Addison's Land Utilisation Bill and Mr. Morrison's London Passenger Transport Bill were only introduced when the Government was nearing its end. Neither of these Ministers was in the Cabinet in 1929.

we cold-shouldered and irritated the Liberals. This fatal combination was not, of course, a clear-cut decision. It gradually imposed itself, for lack of positive decisions to the contrary, and through the operation of personal timidities, vanities and jealousies. Mr. MacDonald and Mr. Lloyd George strongly disapproved of one another. And neither concealed it.

The first King's Speech omitted nearly everything which had been included in the programme drawn up, specifically with a view to this situation, by the Executive of the Parliamentary Party only a few months before. It was a mere travesty of *Labour and The Nation*, even if we exclude, as impracticable in the circumstances, all large measures of Socialisation. First contacts with "responsibility" and expert advisers chilled the Cabinet. From their first day in office some Ministers were in full retreat from their election pledges. The first King's Speech chilled the Parliamentary Labour Party.

The trade depression came, and unemployment mounted. Mr. Thomas was in special charge of this problem, with others to help him with bright ideas, which he consistently rejected, while Mr. Snowden refused him money, and even such credit as a revived Trade Facilities Act might have afforded. The Treasury argued that to revive this Act would damage the national credit and hinder their Conversion Operations. And under the Second Labour Government the Treasury were always on top.[1]

The achievements of this Government were, in some directions, very considerable. Most of all, by common consent, in Foreign Affairs, where the contrast between

[1] "How do you like your new Chief?" a Treasury official is reported to have been asked, soon after Mr. Snowden had succeeded Mr. Churchill. "We are delighted at the change," is the reported reply; "we feel that we have moved up from the pantry to the drawing-room."

Mr. Henderson's policy and methods and those of his predecessor was a remarkable tribute to his qualities and to the Labour Party, a contrast which becomes still more striking if we compare his performances with those of his successor. But also in a number of other Departments, notably, again by common consent, Agriculture and Transport.

Yet when all allowance is made, and the allowance should be large, both for the limitations imposed by Minority Government, and for the forces, outside British control, which intensified the trade depression, the Second Labour Government missed great opportunities on the home front. Looking back, it is easy to put most of the blame for what was done, or not done, on the three men who occupied key positions in the Cabinet in relation to home policy, and who crossed over when the crisis came. Certainly Mr. MacDonald, Mr. Snowden and Mr. Thomas,[1] each in his own way, was a political disaster. Certainly they exercised, individually and collectively, an undue influence in the Cabinet and in the Party. But all of us, I feel, must take some share of the responsibility, all members of the Parliamentary Party, all Junior Ministers outside the Cabinet, and other members of the Cabinet itself. We should have kicked up more row, been less loyal to leaders and more loyal to principles, not left the running to a handful of disgruntled critics, who criticised everything and everyone without discrimination.

[1] Mr. Thomas, speaking in the last days of the 1929 election campaign at Coventry, promised the electors that a Labour Government would at once attack unemployment by keeping young people longer at school and taking old people out of the labour market. When he became Minister for Unemployment, he was one of the most stubborn opponents of raising the school-leaving age, and he resisted even the modest scheme of retiring pensions for miners, to which the Party was definitely committed.

The Parliamentary Labour Party of 1929-31 was a magnificent army which was never led into battle. Had it been properly led, it would have followed anywhere, and gallantly. It was led instead through bogs and mists, by slow circuitous routes, to the very edge of a precipice. Here some of its leaders saved themselves by a most singular manœuvre, in which the Party, with negligible exceptions, refused to join. Peering over that edge, the Party was in mortal danger of losing its soul. But at the last it put principles before persons. It chose to take the plunge.

That only a dozen members out of a Party of nearly three hundred, in spite of tempting inducements which were offered to many, took the other course, that every Constituency Labour Party in the country refused it, and that seven million voters, in spite of all that followed, stood solid for Socialism, are amazing facts, and a wonderful tribute to the solidarity of the Labour Movement. The hope of many of us is that leadership in the Party in the future will be less individual, and more corporate, than in the past. We look now, not for one man, or for one or two, however gifted, but for a body of men and women who will faithfully interpret and speedily execute a Socialist mandate democratically given.

The full story of the crisis of 1931, and of the intrigues and preparations that led up to it, has not yet been told. Mr. Sidney Webb has written a narrative which helps to explain it.[1] But it still leaves much to be explained. Of the general election of 1931, and the tactics of panic-mongering and misrepresentation that were employed against Labour candidates, it is perhaps enough to say, at this distance of time, that they so far over-reached themselves as to set in motion a strong tide of revulsion, which is not yet

[1] *What Happened in* 1931; *a Record*, by Sidney Webb (published by the Fabian Society, price 2*d*.).

spent.[1] It will not be so easy next time, even with the aid of some new bogeys, to practise crude mass deception on so grand a scale.

The Prime Minister, as Mr. Webb puts it, " was at once the author, the producer and the principal actor " in the political drama of 1931. Few men did more to build up the Labour Party, and none has tried harder to destroy it. In this effort he has not succeeded. His career, in its final stages, illustrates the saying, hitherto more true of French than British politics : " le Socialisme mène à tout, à condition d'en sortir."

Like all who have travelled great distances, he has had his lucky days. At three of the most critical moments of his career he has been the victim of mistaken identity. The first was in 1900, when, as a comparatively unknown young man, he was elected the first Secretary of the Labour Party.[2] The second was in 1922 when, by a narrow majority over Mr. Clynes, he was elected Leader of the Party in Parliament, and thus became Leader of His Majesty's Opposition and prospective Prime Minister. On this occasion he owed his success to the votes of a number of Clydesiders,

---

[1] It may be worth recalling, as a characteristic incident, that not content with an overwhelming preponderance on the wireless and a practical monopoly of newspaper support, a prominent associate of the Prime Minister endeavoured to win over *The Daily Herald*, the one daily paper supporting the Labour Party, to the side of the National Government by threatening an advertisement boycott. The threat failed.

[2] The Labour Party, called at first the Labour Representation Committee, was formed at a Conference in the Memorial Hall, London, on February 27 and 28, 1900. Mr. Will Thorne, M.P., who was present, relates that " James R. Macdonald was chosen as the first Secretary. But many of the hundred and twenty delegates were under the impression that they were voting for James MacDonald, Secretary of the London Trades Council, who had played an important part in the preliminary stages " (*Daily Herald*, February 27, 1932).

newly arrived at Westminster, who desired to give their confidence to a robust Socialist of the Left. The third was on August 24, 1931, when he seems to have been mistaken by the King for a Party leader, whom a majority of his followers would still follow.

But evidence on this, as on many other important points, is scanty as yet. We must await the opening, in the fullness of time, of the archives and the diaries.

CHAPTER III

THE AIMS OF SOCIALISM

I TURN from retrospects to prospects. The lesson from the past is that the next Labour Government must be prompt and bold, confident in itself, in those who have voted it to power, and in its Socialist programme; prepared to be conciliatory in methods and on details, but firm on principles.

The aims of Socialism, which such a Government must strenuously pursue, are to release those creative forces which are to-day imprisoned and frustrated by the institutions of capitalism; to abolish poverty, social inequality and the fear of war; to make our society prosperous, classless and free.

Only as means towards these ends have the practical proposals, which I make and defend in this book, any value; and small value, even then, until translated into acts of change. " Power to do good," says Bacon, " is the true and lawful end of aspiring; for good thoughts are little better than good dreams, except they be put in act; and that cannot be without power, as the vantage and commanding ground." This is the only defence for his public way of life that any politician can offer.

The British Labour Party seeks to create a British Socialist Commonwealth, and to encourage, by its influence and example, the spread of Socialism in the rest of the world. But Socialism is a quantitative thing. It is a question, not of all or nothing, but of less or more. Doctrinaires on both sides of the controversy are apt to go wrong here. Broadly, we may measure the degree in which any particular community is Socialist by the relative extent of the " socialised sector ", and of the " private sector ", in its economic life. Within the socialised sector public ownership and control, in some form, are present, and private profit-making is absent. There is no civilised community which has no socialised sector in this sense, no nucleus of a planned public economy. All have a system of public finance and some public services,—including law, police, civil administration and some armed forces, as an irreducible minimum. In this country, at the present time, we have, in excess of this minimum, many public services—notably public education and public health—considerable public property and a number of other public enterprises, both within the range of national and of municipal government. But, relatively to many other countries, our socialised sector is narrow. Its rapid extension is one of the principal objects of the Labour Party.

But this is only one of our objects, which I shall discuss in turn under six headings : Democracy, Socialisation, Finance, Planning, Equality and Peace.

The programme of action which I outline in this book is an immediate programme, a series of next steps to be taken in the pursuit of our Socialist aims. I make no apology for not presenting an elaborate theoretical study of an ideal society. That is a stimulating but a different kind of exercise, which does not lack exponents. But, if our concern is with practical politics, we do better to decide the direction of advance than to debate the details of Utopia. We must see clearly the next stretch of the journey. But we need not spend time now in arguing whether, beyond the horizon, the road swerves right or left.

PART II
DEMOCRACY

CHAPTER IV

WHAT IS DEMOCRACY?

DEMOCRACY, like Socialism, is a quantitative thing; one may have much or little of it. It may take more than one form. Political democracy, working through elected Parliaments and subordinate elected bodies, based on geographical constituencies, is a form still widely followed, despite the recent ravages of "dictatorship" in Europe.[1]

In Britain, in the British Dominions, in the United States, in France and Belgium, in Scandinavia and Finland, in Holland and Switzerland, in Czechoslovakia, precariously in some other European countries, after a fashion in Latin America, the forms of Parliamentary democracy are still observed. Less completely, indeed, in Britain than in many of the rest, so long as our House of Lords is permitted to exercise even its limited powers under the Parliament Act.

But political democracy is not an end in itself. It is only a means to freedom and self-government and, in the hope of Socialists in these democratic lands, to Socialism.

Political democracy, moreover, in a régime of capitalism and great social inequality, is only half alive.

[1] Another possible form is based on occupational groupings, and I hope that in a Socialist Britain there will be a large element of this form of democracy, but supplementing, not replacing, Parliament and Local Authorities.

Political forms are twisted by economic forces. Citizens, legally equal, wield unequal power. Political democracy will only be fully alive when married to economic democracy, in a society of equals.

Yet to deny the reality of political democracy, even if only half alive, to deny, for instance, that an Englishman to-day breathes freer air than a German, is half-witted. And to deny that political democracy can, if enough men and women will it persistently, march towards Socialism, is defeatist and doctrinaire. There is, in blunt truth, no other passable road to Socialism in modern Britain. It is no easy road, and he who thinks it looks too steep or stony for his taste had best stay at home and cultivate his garden. He will find the contemplative detachment of that life much easier.

Loose talk in the last year or two has blurred in some minds the real distinctions between democracy and " dictatorship ". The essentials of democracy, in terms of political form, are two. First, periodical free elections and, second, between elections, a continuing right of free political speech, discussion and criticism, both inside Parliament and other elected bodies, and outside. But large powers of swift action constitutionally granted to the Executive are not undemocratic, such as the American Congress conferred on President Roosevelt, or as the British Parliament gave the National Government, when it desired, in 1931, to make quick reductions by Order in Council in many branches of public expenditure. A slow and lumbering Parliamentary procedure, checking all rapid action, is not of the essence of democracy. On the contrary, it is a weakness which, if not cured, gives their chance to criminals lying in wait to murder freedom.

The Labour Party, by tradition and conviction, is a democratic party. From the democratic approach

WHAT IS DEMOCRACY ?

to politics it has never swerved.[1] It seeks that British democracy shall become a living reality; that men and women shall have political freedom, and shall have it more abundantly ; and that they shall be persuaded so to use this precious gift that social freedom also shall be added unto it, anchored in prosperity, equality and peace.

Here, then, I pass from general considerations to a series of practical proposals, a programme of Socialist action, not for some imaginary community floating in the void of time, but for this country at this present day.

[1] Not all who claim to speak or write on its behalf have always succeeded in making its policy unmistakably clear. The National Executive of the Labour Party, therefore, found it necessary to issue on January 24, 1934, the following statement, which was reprinted in the Annual Report of the Executive to the Party Conference at Southport, by which it was unanimously approved in October, 1934. " The attitude of the Labour Party towards Dictatorship has recently been subject to grave misrepresentation by supporters of the National Government. The Labour Party, as has repeatedly been made plain in its official declarations, stands for Parliamentary Democracy. It is firmly opposed to Individual or Group Dictatorship, whether from the Right or from the Left. It holds that the best, and indeed the only tolerable, form of Government for this country is Democratic Government, with a free electoral system and an active and efficient Parliamentary machine for reaching effective decisions, after reasonable opportunities for discussion and criticism. The Labour Party bases its appeal to public opinion on the urgent need for far-reaching economic and social change as set out in its programme, to be brought about by constitutional and democratic means. In so far as any statements which are at variance with the declared policy of the Party on this question have been or may be made by individuals, these are hereby definitely repudiated by the National Executive."

CHAPTER V

THE HOUSE OF COMMONS

FIRST, as to our present political institutions. What changes are needed to make these more fully democratic, and more effective to translate into action the democratic will? Let us begin with the House of Commons.[1]

The British electoral system, based on the single member constituency and the relative majority at a single ballot, has very solid advantages. Not least of these is that our electorate is accustomed to it and accepts its results as doing rough justice to candidates and their supporters. It works best when there are only two strong parties; but this is precisely the characteristic position, towards which British politics tend always to return.[2] Displacements in the direction of a group, or multi-party, system have generally been short-lived.

The British system discourages freak candidates by its salutary provision for forfeiture of the election deposit by those polling less than one-eighth of the

[1] Mr. George Shepherd, National Agent of the Labour Party, has supplied much statistical and other information which has been very useful to me in writing this chapter.

[2] It is, moreover, the characteristic political position in all English-speaking communities which practise self-government, alike in the British Dominions and the United States of America. Third parties seldom live long, before they either destroy, or are absorbed by, one of the other two.

votes cast. It discourages small separate parties—
"splinter parties," as the Germans used to call them
—by making it difficult for these to secure representation in the House of Commons, even in proportion to their small total strength in the electorate. The electors, realising this, prefer to vote for candidates who, if returned, will act with parties which will count for something in the House. As between the two principal parties, the British system tends to emphasise in Parliament the strength of whichever is the stronger in the country. A majority, in terms of votes in the House of Commons, tends to be greater than the majority, in terms of relative total votes in the constituencies. Put in another way, a given turnover of votes in the country tends to produce a much more than proportionate turnover of seats.[1] This feature of the system is held by some to be a weakness. In my opinion it is, on the contrary, an advantage, since it makes coherent government possible and diminishes the chance of political deadlocks, and the excuse for feeble policies.

Foreign theorists, and a few home-grown ones, have urged the superiority of Proportional Representation. But there can be little doubt that this system, carried to an extreme of clumsy theoretical perfection, helped to destroy democratic government in Germany by

[1] It is, indeed, possible, under the British system, even if there are only two parties, that one of these, polling less than half the votes cast, should have a majority in the House. But this is an unlikely result. If there are more than two parties of considerable strength, and three or more candidates in many constituencies, the chance is greater that one party may command the House of Commons, though in a minority in the electorate. This, indeed, happened in 1924, when the Conservatives secured a large Parliamentary majority, though only polling 8,041,000 votes against 5,487,000 for Labour, 2,930,000 for Liberals and 183,000 for Communists and others. The practical remedy for such anomalies is a return to the two-party system.

creating an unending series of deadlocks and weak Coalition Governments, and thus discrediting Parliamentary institutions. There is to-day no active support for any form of Proportional Representation for Parliamentary elections in any important section of British political thought.[1]

The only modification of the British method of election which is worth considering is the adoption of the Alternative Vote, operating in the single-member constituency. This was included in the Labour Government's Electoral Reform Bill of 1931, in order, it appears, to please the Liberals. It certainly roused no enthusiasm in the Parliamentary Labour Party. I am not impressed by the arguments in its favour, except as the lesser of two evils, compared with Proportional Representation. There is less case for it than ever, now that we are rapidly returning to the two-party system.

[1] For this reason I do not labour the case against it. But I may remark in passing that it involves the substitution of unwieldy multi-member for single-member constituencies, thus destroying the possibility of any personal contact between the elected person and any appreciable number of his electors; it encourages the formation and indefinite survival of a multitude of small and sectionally minded parties; it makes a clear majority for any one party almost impossible; it leads, therefore, to Coalition Governments, either commanding a majority which must be based on compromise, or without a majority, impotent to act boldly, except by sending Parliament into indefinite adjournment. Add, among relatively minor, but still serious, objections, that it digs in every old leader of every party in a safe seat at the top of his party list, and makes it far harder even than with us to-day for young men to get a start in public life, and that it substitutes for the open rivalry of candidates of opposing parties, an underhand rivalry among candidates of the same party, angling for position against their colleagues. Every one of these comments might be illustrated from the political experience of post-War Germany and of other countries which have adopted this system.

THE HOUSE OF COMMONS

Our method of election, then, I would not change.[1] But our electoral law requires a number of amendments, before it can be claimed that even the formal framework of political democracy is furnished by the House of Commons. Our parliamentary elections are still fought under an electoral law which favours wealthy political parties and certain select groups in the electorate.

The simple rule of political democracy should be that every man and woman over twenty-one years of age, apart from peers,[2] criminals and lunatics, should have one vote and one only. The vote should be exercised in respect of the elector's place of residence. If he has more than one dwelling, he should be required to choose for which he would be registered. To-day plural voting still persists in University constituencies and in respect of business premises. Neither of these forms of the plural vote is defensible, and both should be abolished.

There is no justification for giving additional voting power to those who have a University degree. One must think very poorly of University graduates, if one supposes that they are such feeble citizens as to need this special prop on which to lean their citizenship. And one thinks much more highly of them in the mass than they deserve, if one supposes that they possess such exceptional political intelligence that they should have this special vent for its expression. It is sometimes argued that the existence of the University seats enables men and women of distinction to enter Parlia-

[1] Except in one particular, on which during the parliamentary debates of 1931 all parties were agreed. The double-barrelled constituencies in industrial towns, of which eleven still survive, should each be split into a pair of single-member constituencies.

[2] With the abolition of the House of Lords, peers should be entitled to vote, and to stand as candidates, for the House of Commons.

ment, who could not otherwise find their way to Westminster. The facts do not support this theory. The Members of Parliament for the Universities have been, with very few exceptions, party politicians who could as well have sat for any ordinary constituency.

The business premises franchise is not only undemocratic in principle, but inequitable in detail. A man who has an office in the constituency where he resides gets no second vote ; but if his office is in a neighbouring constituency, he becomes a plural voter. Moreover, an elector's wife, if her husband has a vote in respect of his office, has one also, though she may never have entered his office in her life. This is a fantastic absurdity.

Seven members sit in the House for the English Universities, three for the Scottish Universities, one for the University of Wales, and one for the University of Belfast. The number of University electors in England is 87,000, in Scotland 47,000, in Wales less than 6,000, in Belfast less than 4,000. Even if the principle of University representation were accepted —and it should not be—University electors are grotesquely over-represented, as compared with electors in ordinary constituencies, where there is, on an average, only one member for between 40,000 and 50,000 electors.

In England and Wales,[1] out of 26,431,000 parliamentary electors, 368,000 qualified through business premises and, of these, 140,000 women qualified through the business premises of their husbands.[2] In Scotland, out of a total electorate of 2,993,000, more than 54,000 qualified through business premises. The geographical distribution of these votes for business

[1] These are round figures, correct to the nearest thousand, taken from the Registrar General's Report of 1932 for England and Wales, and from the census figures of 1931 for Scotland.

[2] Or, in a small number of cases, husbands through the business premises of their wives.

premises is very unequal. They are concentrated in the central quarters of the largest cities ; in most middle-sized towns there are only a few hundred of them ; in the country districts hardly any.

The grossest case is the City of London, returning two members for an electorate of 43,000, of whom 36,000, or 83 per cent, are business voters. Manchester Exchange, in an electorate of 49,000, has 15,000 business votes, or 31 per cent ; Liverpool Exchange, in an electorate of 50,000, has 12,000, or 24 per cent ; Westminster Abbey, in an electorate of 48,000, has 14,000, or 29 per cent ; Holborn, in an electorate of 33,000, has 10,000, or 30 per cent ; Glasgow Central, in an electorate of 45,000, has 13,000, or 29 per cent.

All these, from a democratic point of view, are at present bogus, or largely bogus, constituencies. And there are a number of others not much better. A redistribution of seats, in view of the large differences which now exist in the number of electors in the various constituencies, should soon be made. The last redistribution took place in 1918 and there have been large migrations since then and very uneven rates of growth in different areas. But the abolition of the plural vote is an indispensable preliminary to any fair redistribution.

This raises the question of the number of members of the House of Commons. The present number, 615, is excessive and unwieldy. In my opinion, 500 is the maximum number which, on grounds of practical convenience, can reasonably be defended.

But there are obvious difficulties, largely personal, in making a reduction by as many as a hundred at one blow. I suggest that, with the abolition of plural voting, there might be an initial reduction to 600,[1]

[1] The abolition of the University seats, and the creation of one single member constituency in place of the City of London and Holborn, would reduce the present number to 601.

and a series of further reductions, say by twenty-five at a time, in each of the four succeeding Parliaments. Immediately after each general election a Commission should be set up to prepare a scheme of redistribution, to take effect at the next general election.[1]

Other changes should be made in election law. The present legal limits of election expenses, sixpence per elector in counties and fivepence in boroughs, are too high and should be reduced. Gifts and donations

---

[1] Such regular and periodic redistributions are provided for in the electoral law of several of the British Dominions and of a number of foreign countries. In order to minimise suspicions of gerrymandering, and likewise to minimise pressure by interested parties, a Redistribution Commission should work according to a set of simple rules. They might be instructed, for example, to operate only on the largest and smallest electorates, splitting up the former into pairs of separate constituencies, and splitting up the latter into geographically convenient fragments, which should be added to the adjoining constituencies within the same borough or county, or in some cases, merged in a group of counties, in such a way as to keep the electorates of the enlarged constituencies as nearly equal as possible. No changes in constituency boundaries should be made, except to carry out these two sets of operations. All constituencies with an electorate more than double the average for the country as a whole should first be cut in two, and all those with an electorate less than half the average should be joined, in appropriate fragments, to their neighbours. If the total number of constituencies was then greater than the required number, the constituencies with the next smallest electorates should be similarly dealt with. If, on the other hand, the total number was smaller than the required number, the constituencies with the next largest electorates should be cut in two. A gradual reduction in the number of constituencies will not enlarge the average electorate unduly, since, with the prospective decline in the total population, the total electorate will before long begin to diminish. It is a small additional argument for reducing the number of members, that this will mean a saving to the Treasury in respect of members' salaries and travelling expenses. Thus a reduction by a hundred would mean an annual saving of more than £40,000.

made by candidates or members to charitable or other institutions in their constituencies between one election and another should be included in their election expenses, particulars sent to the Returning Officer and published after polling day.

The present use of motor cars on polling day imposes a serious and unfair handicap on the less wealthy parties, and on the Labour Party in particular. Conservative and Liberal candidates can often command hundreds of cars, Labour candidates seldom a dozen. When voting strength is very evenly balanced, the larger number of cars turns the scale. The right solution is a threefold one : first, to increase the number of polling stations, especially in rural districts, so that no elector shall be more than a short distance from the poll ; second, to make it an electoral offence for anyone but the Returning Officer to give a free ride in a car on polling day ; third, to authorise the Returning Officer to hire and provide transport to and from the poll for any elector who can give reasonable evidence that he or she requires it.

A number of other minor changes in electoral law are needed, but I will not linger over these. There is, however, another question which seems to me to have an important bearing on the efficiency of British political democracy.

In my opinion there is a strong case for imposing an age limit on membership of the House of Commons. Even a retiring age of seventy would have some effect in reducing the present average age of the Chamber, and one of sixty-five would be still more effective. A convenient compromise, which would avoid any additional cause for by-elections, might be found in fixing sixty-five as the maximum age for any candidate at a Parliamentary election. The tendency for old men to continue in high political office, or in expectation of it, long after they have passed the zenith of their powers, is increasingly marked in recent British politics. This does not make for energy or decision in action, and it holds back the advance of new ideas. There is sardonic truth in the saying that, in politics, there are many promising young men of over fifty! When in all other branches of the public service the rule of a fixed retiring age is practically universal, while in many other professions and occupations it is rapidly gaining ground, it is difficult to defend the exemption of members of the House of Commons from this salutary provision. For the life of the politician is more strenuous and exhausting, both mentally and physically, than that of most public servants.

Such a reform, again for personal reasons, would not be easy to effect. It would be easier if there were a Second Chamber—especially if its members were paid the same salary as members of the House of Commons—in which elder statesmen might continue to serve, thus retaining a dignified platform from which they could still address the public.[1] An age limit on the holding of Ministerial office would be a natural corollary of such a change. Would it be too revolutionary to suggest seventy years of age for the Cabinet, and sixty for " Junior " Ministers ?[2]

A fixed retiring age in other branches of the public service, and in some outside professions, is accompanied by arrangements for pension. Without such an arrangement, compulsory retirement is a hardship, which it would be harsh to impose on men without private sources of income. I see no reason why pensions should not be provided for Members of Parlia-

[1] I return to this point at the end of Chapter VIII.

[2] It would be easy to name individual politicians, whose retirement at a fixed age, from the House of Commons or from Ministerial office, would be a loss to our public life. Such personal arguments can always be found against a compulsory retiring age in any profession. I believe that the general argument on the other side is stronger.

ment retired under the age limit, unless, as suggested above, they became members of a salaried Second Chamber. Such pensions should, I think, be based, as in other cases, on the number of years served in Parliament, and should in no case exceed some fixed proportion, say two-thirds, of the current Parliamentary salary. The total cost of such pensions would not be great, and would be more than offset by the economy which would be made if, as I have proposed, the number of members of the House of Commons were reduced.

CHAPTER VI

REFORM OF PARLIAMENTARY PROCEDURE [1]

THE present procedure of the House of Commons is amazingly unbusinesslike. It compares very badly with that of our Local Authorities, and is, in large measure, a relic of a vanished age, whose needs and purposes were very different from our own.

Those who sit for some years in the House are apt to become acclimatised to its time-wasting procedures and to lose their first natural glow of impatient indignation. The atmosphere, both physical and mental, is enervating. Those who want to get things done, wilt; those who want to get things said, luxuriate; those who want neither, are not uncomfortable. Legislative output is severely limited by antiquated parliamentary methods, and its cost, in terms of strain and time, is high.

It is easy to call witnesses outside the ranks of the Labour Party to support this view. Thus the late Lord Buckmaster has said that it would be a good thing, if on the mantelpiece of every Parliament there were placed a row of fossils of extinct forms of life, underneath which should be written in bold letters, " we perished because we could not change ". The procedure and rules of Parliament, he went on to say, were quite out of date. He thought there should be

[1] I thank the Editors of the *Political Quarterly* for permission to make use of an article of mine on this subject in their issue of September, 1934.

some limitation of speech, otherwise we should become suffocated. There were issues too vital and too grave to permit of time being wantonly wasted by unprofitable debate.[1]

My present object is to show that the parliamentary machine can be modernised and rationalised, so as to enable it to yield a greater legislative output, while democratic principles are fully maintained, and Parliament is better enabled to discharge its functions.

It is of the essence of democracy that there should be reasonable and adequate, but not excessive, facilities for Parliamentary discussion. A minority must be able to attack, to criticise and to suggest, but not to prolong such proceedings unduly, nor finally to obstruct the will of the majority. On the other hand, a majority should be prepared for give and take in small details, though standing firm on big principles. For a dissatisfied minority, the ultimate remedy is to transform itself, by due electoral process, into a majority.

It is not permissible, under the rules of order, to accuse a member of "obstruction", but a large part of the activities of every Parliamentary Opposition is nothing else. In the two Parliaments of which I have been a member, I saw this problem from both sides, first as a member of the Opposition, and then as a junior member of the Government.[2] Speeches

---

[1] Reported in *The Times* of December 14, 1933. And Sir Robert Horne (reported in *The Times* of January 30, 1934) said that some method of expediting business in the House of Commons must be achieved. The reason why representative government was regarded in many countries to-day as a failure was because its methods were too slow for the purpose of dealing with present day emergencies.

[2] I took my share, according to the present "rules of the game", in obstructing the Conservative Government from 1924 to 1929, and was once suspended during an all-night sitting, in good company, including George Lansbury and the

on most debated issues are too many and too long.[1] Members are often " put up to talk " by the Whips— this is the phrase in current use—simply in order to eat time. Other current phrases are to " keep it going " and to " prevent the debate from breaking down ", that is to say from coming to an earlier end than the Whips expected. To avoid such a misfortune, which would often enable progress to be made with the next Order on the Paper, the Whips, on both sides, scour the libraries, the smoking rooms, the dining rooms, even the bar, in search of reluctant, and often quite unprepared, orators. These conventional practices cannot reasonably be defended. The critic's contemptuous description of Parliament as a " talking shop " is not unmerited.

There is a rule which gives power to the Chair to check repetition, but it has fallen, as the lawyers say, into desuetude. Members are seldom pulled up by the Chair for repeating one another's arguments, or even their own. Often they speak without having been in the House when earlier speeches were being

late John Wheatley, for stretching these rules to breaking point. But between 1929 and 1931 we Labour Members learned, both from Conservatives and Liberals, that we had been a very tame Opposition, mere children in the art of wasting time.

[1] Lord Eustace Percy (*Government in Transition*, pp. 108-9) attributes " the failure of the House of Commons to focus public attention on important issues " and " its hopeless inefficiency as a publicity agent " to the fact that " while journalistic technique has been steadily tending in the direction of picturesque compression, parliamentary debates have been no less steadily tending in the direction of disjointed discursiveness. A House, whose members so often begin their speeches with the words ' I do not propose to follow the honourable member into the fields he has traversed ', cannot expect to produce any sort of impression on the mind of the public." The regular broadcasting, under present conditions, of a series of average parliamentary speeches would be a disaster for democracy !

made, and repeat the more obvious points inadvertently. It would be well if the rule against repetition could be better enforced.

It is, I think, an open question whether a time limit should be imposed on individual speeches. More fundamental proposals for the better allocation of parliamentary time are made below. And, if the total time available on any subject is limited, those who take too large a share of this limited ration will incur a wholesome unpopularity with their fellows.

There might also be a general recommendation to the Chair, in calling upon members, to prefer those who had spoken least, and not allow the more prolific talkers to catch his eye. A record could always be within the Chairman's reach, showing the number of columns of Hansard spoken by various members up to date.

Our parliamentary procedure has had no systematic overhaul, since the Liberal Government in 1906, fresh from its victory in the constituencies, made a number of changes in the Standing Orders of the House of Commons.[1] The Standing Orders of the House are

[1] A series of debates on various proposals to amend the Standing Orders took place between February 28, 1906, and April 16, 1907. It is interesting to re-read them to-day. The " dinner hour " interval from 7.30 to 9 p.m., was abolished, in spite of a protest by Balfour ; the unstarred Parliamentary Question was invented ; the Standing Committees were increased from two to four, one of which was to deal only with Scottish Bills, and it was provided that all Bills, except those dealing primarily with finance or confirming Provisional Orders, should go upstairs, unless the House otherwise directed by a motion put without debate ; closure procedure was also extended to Standing Committees. Other reforms were discussed, but not adopted. Keir Hardie advocated a time limit for speeches and was supported by a number of Conservatives, including Acland-Hood, the Conservative Chief Whip.

The Government had contemplated the possibility of setting

entirely within its own control. No question of interference by the House of Lords arises. The proposals which follow are far from being a complete and exhaustive scheme for the reform of parliamentary procedure. They indicate only some of the more urgent, important and practicable changes.[1]

The two principal reforms needed are a more businesslike use of parliamentary time, and a more up-to-date form of legislation. I will take these two points in order.[2]

There is to-day no systematic plan for the allocation of parliamentary time. Various forms of closure and guillotine are used sporadically. Sometimes a big Bill has a detailed time-table made for it, but only if serious obstruction is expected, or has already begun. This time-table procedure is so far from being universal that it is common form for the Opposition to denounce it,—often " on principle "—and further time is spent in debating, and in trying to amend, the time-table on the floor of the House. A large part of Government business slops along without any time-table whatever, and often slops over beyond 11 p.m., and sometimes into all-night sittings, which exhaust the minds, bodies and tempers of the participants and

up machinery for the allocation of time between different classes of business, and Mr. Austen Chamberlain (as he then was), objecting to the procedure of " closure by compartments ", proposed that time should be allocated by " an impartial Committee of the House ". The Prime Minister, Campbell-Bannerman, said that he had long been in favour of a Committee to allocate the time of the House. But on this most fundamental question nothing was done.

[1] The proposals of Dr. W. Ivor Jennings in his interesting book on *Parliamentary Reform* (Gollancz, 1934) go in some directions farther, in others less far.

[2] These and other important matters are dealt with in a Memorandum on *Parliamentary Problems and Procedure*, on pp. 120–2, of the National Executive's Report for 1934, which was adopted at the Southport Conference.

help to bring Parliament into ridicule and disrepute. Physical fitness and mental freshness, both in Ministers and in the general body of M.P.'s, are necessary conditions, seldom now fulfilled, of efficient democracy.

Frequently it is obstructive talk by a single member, or by a small handful, which keeps hundreds of others hanging about the Chamber and its purlieus, waiting for a vote on some relatively unimportant issue. In the 1929 Parliament one or two Tories made themselves conspicuous by their habit of obstructing until the last trains and buses had gone, so as to make it impossible for Labour Members, without cars of their own and living at a distance from Westminster, to get home till morning. A rationalised procedure should stop such monkey tricks.

The Labour Party proposes, therefore, that at the beginning of each session a small Committee of the House should be set up, and should continue in being throughout the session, to deal with the allocation of time on all Government Bills, and perhaps also on other items of business. This might be called the Committee on the Allocation of Parliamentary Time, or, more shortly, the Committee on Time.

This Committee would be chosen in proportion to the strength of parties, and the Chief Whip would be the natural leader for the Government, though other Ministers might sometimes attend. It should be the primary duty of the Committee to make a detailed time-table for every Government Bill which had been read a first time, covering all its future stages: so long for Second Reading, so long for Committee, for Report, if any, and for Third Reading. Time could be allotted to particular stages in units less than complete parliamentary days, e.g. in half-days, or even in hours. And special allocations could be made, for the Committee stage, to clauses or groups of clauses, as is now done in guillotine resolutions. It would probably be convenient not to allocate time for Report and Third Reading until the conclusion of the Committee Stage.

Every Government Bill would be automatically referred to this Committee, whose recommendations would be reported to the House from time to time. But there should be no power to debate, or to move amendments to, them on the floor of the House. There should, however, be power to challenge a division on any block of recommendations as a whole. If accepted by the House, such recommendations would go into effect, and it would be the duty of the Chair to enforce them at each subsequent stage. Time-tabling on all Government Bills would thus become universal and would be done upstairs, not wasting time and exciting passion on the floor. Private talks between the Whips could still go on and, if they resulted in agreement, this could be regularised by the Committee, but the Government Whip would be in a stronger position than now to check unreasonable claims for time by the Opposition, and the Opposition could state their case publicly on the Committee.

This is a minimum proposal, simple and obvious. But, even if we went no farther, we should, I believe, work a practical revolution in parliamentary procedure.[1] We should be able, when necessary, greatly

[1] This proposal is not new. It has hovered in the background of discussion for some time. But the Labour Party in 1934 first put it into precise shape and made it part of their official programme. I have noted above that in the debates of 1906–7 both Campbell Bannerman and Sir Austen Chamberlain expressed approval of such an innovation. The Select Committee on Procedure, which reported in 1932, stated that " the view of the Prime Minister [Mr. Ramsay MacDonald] was that a guillotine resolution should become a normal procedure, but that the framing of it should only be settled after consultation with a panel or Consultative Committee ". The Select Committee recommended that " if the guillotine is to

to speed up the rate of legislative output and, except in very exceptional circumstances, to avoid late sittings after eleven at night. We should rationalise debate and rob obstruction both of its main incentive and of its effectiveness. Such a Committee is an essentially democratic device and, since the proceedings of Committees are less fully reported by the Press and are witnessed by fewer spectators than the proceedings of

become normal procedure, the time available for discussion of the different clauses and stages of a Bill should be allocated by a small expert Committee, to whom the Bill should be referred by a vote taken without debate after the Motion ' that the Bill be committed to a Committee of the whole House ' has been carried. It is understood that the timetable should be drawn up after consultation with the Government, the Opposition and other Members specially interested in the Bill ". These are conditional and half-hearted recommendations, which contain no proposal to time-table proceedings in Standing Committee. But they point haltingly in the right direction. Lord Eustace Percy (*Government in Transition*, pp. 116-17) is more emphatic. " The definite planning of parliamentary time is the key to any real reform of parliamentary procedure. . . . Mere proposals of this kind for a detailed allocation of parliamentary time may appear to the public a very inadequate method of dealing with the inefficiency of the House of Commons. In fact, however, such proposals are probably more effective than any more ambitious schemes for giving a new complexion to the House of Commons." I agree with this judgment. He adds that " without definite planning of the time of the session as a whole, any attempt to plan the time to be allocated to particular measures will arouse resentment and suspicion ". I refer to this point below. It is also interesting to note that dissatisfaction with the working of the Government's timetable on the Unemployment Bill of 1934 led to a motion being placed on the Order Paper by a group of members drawn from all parties, declaring that " it is desirable that an impartial and representative Committee of the House should be set up with authority to determine ", in all cases where a time-table is proposed, " the number of days to be allotted to each stage of the Bill and the precise allocation of time during those days to the various parts of the Bill ".

the House itself, there would probably be less playing to the gallery, and fewer scenes and less heat in getting decisions in the Committee than in getting them on the floor of the House.

It is for consideration whether this Committee should not also allocate time for items of Parliamentary business, other than Government Bills, e.g. certain classes of Government motions (including, in particular, supplementary estimates), official Opposition motions, and private members' Bills which had secured a high place in the ballot.

The Government would retain the power of determining what business should be taken each week and each day, i.e. the power of determining the *order* of business. But for each particular item of business there would be a maximum quota of time determined by the Committee. If less than this maximum were consumed on any item, business would be correspondingly accelerated.

The proceedings in the Committee stage of Bills, as in all other stages after First Reading, would be governed by the time-table. This would greatly simplify the task of the Chairmen of Standing Committees, who at present have very inadequate powers to check obstruction. Within the limits of the time-table the Chair should always have power to select the more important amendments for discussion.[1] With few exceptions, of which the Finance Bill should probably be one, all Bills should go upstairs, after Second Reading, to a Standing Committee.

The Standing Committees should be increased in number, and reduced in size. At present there are only five, including one dealing only with Scottish Bills, and the membership of each is between fifty and

[1] This power to select amendments was in November, 1934, conferred on Chairmen of Standing Committees, but without the guidance of a time-table.

sixty. This is much too large for businesslike discussion. We should, I think, contemplate an increase in the number of Committees to seven at least, including the Scottish Committee, and a reduction of the membership of each to not more than thirty.

It has been suggested by some reformers that Standing Committees should be made " functional ", that is to say that all Bills dealing with a particular subject should be sent to a Committee with a practically unchanging membership, so that members would be enabled to specialise in their Committee work on a subject on which they were already expert, or on which they were ambitious to become expert. Thus there might be one Standing Committee on Social Services, another on Trade and Industry, etc. This idea could not, I think, be applied with any logical exactitude, for the subject matter of legislation is too varied. But it might become one of the guiding ideas in the composition of Committees and the distribution of Bills and of members among them. There is, however, a practical danger to be avoided. The number of Committees, even if increased, will still be smaller than the number of Government Departments liable to introduce legislation. A " functional " Committee, therefore, would often cover the functions of two or more Departments. And this might impose a troublesome limitation on the Government's freedom to select the most urgently necessary legislative programme. If, to take only one example, both Health and Education were part of the field of a " functional " Committee on Social Services, it would be impossible to take simultaneously the Committee stages of a Bill on Housing and a Bill on Education.

This consideration is specially important, since a most valuable step in expediting the process of legislation would be to devote certain Parliamentary days, apart from the hour set apart for Questions, entirely to Committee work.[1] The Committees could meet, as now, at eleven in the morning and sit till one. The House would assemble at a quarter to three, and adjourn at a quarter to four, at the end of Questions. The Committees could then meet again in the afternoon, say at half-past four or five o'clock, and sit till ten or eleven in the evening, with, say, an hour's break for an evening meal. Some such time-table as this would enable much more continuous and effective study to be given to a Bill than is now possible when, as a rule, the Committee sits only for two hours in the mornings, disjointedly from day to day.

When the parliamentary session is in full swing and a number of Bills have passed their Second Reading, there seems no reason why at least two days a week should not be thus devoted to Committee work. A number of important measures could then advance abreast through their Committee stage.

The Report stage of Bills kept on the floor of the House might reasonably be limited, as a general rule, to Government amendments and a maximum of one day, and of Bills sent upstairs to a maximum of, say, one day for Government amendments, and another half-day for other amendments. Often less than these maxima would be sufficient. Standing instructions, somewhat on these lines, might be given by the House to the Committee on Time. Some such regulation is essential, for repetition of debate is at its worst on the Report stage.

Financial procedure in the House of Commons is exceptionally time-wasting. It involves a series of repetitive debates, required by Standing Orders dating from the year 1707.[2]

---

[1] This is permissible under the present Standing Orders, though the power has seldom, if ever, been used.

[2] It has been calculated that financial business now occupies more than one-third of the total of Parliamentary time (Jennings, *op. cit.*, p. 166).

If the main object of a Bill is either to raise public revenue, or to authorise public expenditure, there must, before the ordinary First Reading stage is reached, be two preliminary stages. A financial resolution must be proposed and passed, first through Committee of the whole House, and then through Report stage. Even in the case of a Bill which does not deal primarily with finance, if " the creation of a public charge " is a subsidiary feature of it, i.e. if it necessitates any incidental public expenditure, however small, a similar procedure is imposed. The Bill can pass its First and Second Readings, but, before it can enter on its Committee stage, a financial resolution authorising the public charge must be passed first through Committee of the whole House, and then through the Report stage.

The historical purpose of this repetitive procedure was to prevent financial legislation being rushed through the House before members realised what was happening. It dates from a time when Parliament was on the watch against constitutional encroachments by the Crown. It is wholly unnecessary to-day, both because the Crown has become constitutional, and because the modern practice of printing and circulating Order Papers in advance gives members notice of all coming business. It has degenerated into a tedious and stupid anachronism, illustrated, for example, by the annual debates on the Tea Duty. This is debated now four times every year, on the Committee Stage and on the Report Stage of the Budget Resolutions, and on the Committee Stage and on the Report Stage of the Finance Bill. In addition, like any other item in the Finance Bill, this duty may be referred to by speakers on the Second Reading, and again on the Third Reading of the Bill. And the arguments on either side are few and painfully familiar.

The remedy is simple.[1] Financial resolutions should be abolished. The Finance Bill, and likewise any Bill imposing a public charge, should be treated like any other Bill, and pass through the ordinary stages only ; First and Second Reading, Committee, Report (if any) and Third Reading. The Committee on Time would, as on every other Government Bill, make a time-table for it. An explanatory memorandum, in simple and untechnical language, should be circulated with the text of every Bill before the Second Reading debate, and should draw attention to any public charge involved.

This common-sense change would mean one small, and purely formal, alteration in the existing procedure. The Budget Speech is now delivered as a preliminary to the Committee Stage of the Budget Resolutions. Under the proposed procedure it would conveniently be made on a motion for the First Reading of the Finance Bill. The law which gives new taxes, or taxes annually renewable, validity from the moment when the Budget Resolutions are passed, would need amendment, so as to give validity to such taxes when the Finance Bill passed First Reading.[2]

Alternatively, and pending this simple change in the law, the Budget resolutions might be retained, though all other financial resolutions were abolished, but they should be required to pass through both their Committee and Report stages, the latter without debate, on the day of the Budget speech.

---

[1] But, like many other simple remedies, it has eluded many inquirers. I first heard it suggested by my colleague Mr. Lees Smith.

[2] This is, I think, the only exception to the statement made above that changes in the Standing Orders of the House of Commons can be made by that House alone without the need for legislation. But this is not a statutory change in which the concurrence of the House of Lords is necessary, for the required amending Bill would be a Money Bill within the meaning of the Parliament Act.

On the Second Reading of the Finance Bill a general debate could take place on the Government's proposals both for raising and expending the public revenue, or, in other words, on the financial aspects of the Government's Economic Plan. Precedents for such an extension may be found in more than one of the Budget speeches of Mr. Churchill. And it is always the habit of the Chair to allow a very wide range of debate on this occasion, some ex-Chancellors of the Exchequer, in particular, tending to roam discursively and at great length over vast areas of platitude and precept.

It should be added that the abolition of financial resolutions would not affect the rule, whereby only a Minister of the Crown may propose the imposition of a public charge. This very wholesome limitation, which favourably distinguishes British public finance from that of some foreign countries, would remain in full force.

The complaint is often made that Parliament has lost all effective control over finance, and many proposals are made which are intended to " re-establish " this control. None of these proposals seems to me to have much utility. I agree with Lord Eustace Percy that " the legend that in some Golden Age in the past Parliament exercised strict control over the Government's expenditure is an almost pure fiction ".[1] It is the Treasury which, in fact, exercises control, far more efficiently, and often far more obstructively, than any body of private members could possibly do. " Control ", in this context, nearly always means control by way of restriction. It needs a strong and constructively minded Chancellor of the Exchequer to prevent his officials from forcing a perpetual succession of false economies upon other Departments.

From planning the time-table for a particular Bill we pass logically to the problem of planning the time-

[1] *Government in Transition*, p. 107.

table for the parliamentary session as a whole. Here the Government must be the prime mover, though the Committee on Time will be its indispensable agent. At present much time and energy are wasted on carrying a number of Bills, including private members' Bills, through some of their stages and then abandoning them. Hence the parliamentary phrase " the slaughter of the innocents ". Unforeseen circumstances, of course, may require the introduction of a Bill when the session is well advanced, but it should be the general aim of the Government to make up its mind as to its programme before the session begins, to introduce all its Bills early and, having introduced them, to pass them through all their stages, unless discussion in the House and in the country causes the Government so far to change its mind as to withdraw the Bill. The Committee on Time will not, indeed, be able to do its work to the best advantage, unless it has before it a reasonably complete picture of the sessional programme. As regards private members' Bills it would be better if fewer got a Second Reading, but if most which got a Second Reading passed, amended where necessary, into law.

If, however, the Government is to begin each session with a coherent plan, it follows that sessions must not be too long, and that Ministers must have sufficient time, when Parliament is not sitting, to put their plan into shape, as well as to concentrate upon their major Departmental problems. When Parliament is sitting, particularly if the Government has only a small or uncertain majority, really effective concentration is, to put it mildly, very difficult.

I pass to the second principal reform. The form of legislation should, in many cases, be more general and less detailed than has been the practice hitherto. Bills with a hundred clauses and a dozen schedules are a legislative monstrosity, and should be discontinued. The drafting of such Bills involves long delays, due to the need for protracted technical consultations. It has been estimated that not less than three months is at present required for drafting a so-called " big Bill ". Successive drafts travel to and fro between the Department, or Departments, concerned and the office of the Parliamentary Counsel to the Treasury. Ten to fifteen drafts have sometimes been made before a Bill is ready for printing.

This is an intolerably slow process. It might, indeed, be somewhat speeded up, if the staff of the Parliamentary Draftsmen's office were enlarged, which probably should be done in any case, and if Ministers could make up their minds more quickly on points of detail. But the real remedy is much more fundamental. Detail should be applied in Ministerial Orders, authorised to be made within the limits laid down by a comparatively short and simple Statute.

The National Government has travelled far along this road—in the multitude of economies enforced by Orders in Council in 1931, in the recommendations of its Import Duties Advisory Committee, in its Agricultural Marketing Schemes [1] and in other measures.

---

[1] In a leading article in *The Times* of July 29, 1933, it is claimed that " the Milk Marketing Scheme ", which the House of Commons had just approved, " possesses a constitutional interest which deserves closer analysis. The new procedure which has been invented under the pressure of an overcrowded legislative programme bids fair to meet all that is sound in the criticism . . . that the House of Commons cannot be expected to legislate for industries with the necessary knowledge and speed . . . and to meet it within the existing Parliamentary framework ". It is then explained that an agricultural group either submits a scheme, or asks the Minister to prepare one. A public inquiry is then held into this first draft. " This step in procedure is closely analogous to the procedure upon a private Bill which is examined by a Select Committee. The report of this inquiry is submitted to the Minister, together with a confidential report from the Chair-

It is no chance that this Government's first three essays in speed were in enforcing economy—mostly in the social services, as a stepping-stone to lower income-tax—in setting up tariffs, and in helping the farmer and the agricultural landlord. These are the three aims on which most of its supporters are keenest. Their enthusiasms are narrow and concentrated, and hence effective. Here, perhaps, is a moral for the supporters of the next Labour Government, to concentrate on essentials and not diffuse their energies.

The substance of many of the particular Orders thus made by the National Government is open to strong criticism. But the principle underlying these procedures, as distinct from their detailed application, is sound. It is in line with the needs of the times, and with the Labour Party's own proposals.

Mr. Hore Belisha has put the case admirably.[1]

man. He makes what amendments, if any, seem good to him in the light of these reports, and a final draft of the scheme is submitted for the approval of the House of Commons by affirmative resolution. This stage corresponds to the third reading of an ordinary Bill, and does not really impose upon members any unusual handicap. It is true that they have not discussed as a House of Commons the principle of the scheme or the amendments made in previous stages. But all the evidence taken at the inquiry is open to them, and they have already pronounced in favour of the principle of such schemes by passing the Agricultural Marketing Act. . . . This new procedure . . . contains so much promise of being able to combine the liberation of Parliament from excessive detail with the preservation of an effective measure of Parliamentary control that . . . it might be found suitable to deal with other industries. . . . The strictures passed upon it by Mr. Maxton . . . can only be explained by supposing that the apostle of revolution does not recognise revolution when he sees it. For the present House of Commons is revolutionary in the sense that it prefers action to formality."

[1] In a speech to the Barnsley Chamber of Commerce, reported in *The Times* and quoted in *The New Statesman*, March 3, 1934.

The scientific regulation of our imports and exports has required that the Executive should have far more pliable powers than it possessed under the old working of the Parliamentary system. In this, too, a revolution has been achieved. We are showing how the Parliamentary system can be reconciled with swift action. The precedent of the Import Duties Advisory Committee is capable of extension, and Parliament, instead of being overwhelmed with detail, shows a tendency to become the grand assize of the nation in which general verdicts are given.

Parliament should settle general principles ; Ministers should settle their detailed application, by way of orders and regulations. This is sound modern democratic doctrine. Sir Arthur Salter has expressed this point of view very forcibly.

If Ministers in office usually become increasingly incapable of consecutive thinking, the explanation is to be found only partly in the greater range and complexity of the problems now presented to them. It is equally due to the Parliamentary environment in which they work. Throughout the greater part of the year they are exposed to daily questioning, and frequent debates, on the details of their administrative action ; their bills are subject not only to criticism in main principle but to amendment in every detail ; the drain on time and energy involved is doubled by the personal representations and pressures which are added to these public proceedings. This system worked well enough when the issues were mainly political and relatively simple. It does not work now. It is indeed visibly breaking down throughout a great part of the world. If Parliaments are to retain their essential powers, and to discharge their responsibility to the public, on which free government depends, it looks as if they must voluntarily surrender the powers and rights which are less essential and which they are least competent to exercise. Suppose, for example, that Parliaments met for only two or three months in the year. In that time they could approve in main principle the legislation to be enacted for the ensuing year, leaving its detail to be worked out and applied by Order in Council ; they could review the action of the Executive during the preceding year and either, by approving it, give it a future lease of life, or, by censuring it, secure a change and the appointment of a new Cabinet. Ministers would then have three-quarters of the year to work out, in conjunction with those best qualified to advise them, the general policy for which they had received a mandate.[1]

This statement shows sympathetic insight into the sorrows of Ministers. But it goes too far. Two or three months a year is too short a period for a parliamentary session, though, for the reasons given by Sir Arthur Salter, our present length of session, often running to eight and sometimes nine months,[2] is too long for maximum efficiency. It is interesting to notice that in Sweden, that model democracy of Northern Europe, Parliament sits every year for only five months, from mid-January to mid-June.[3] This period would, I think, be the minimum suitable to British conditions, and would indeed almost certainly require to be extended if, even with the aid of a rationalised procedure, a large volume of legislation is to be passed.

Sir Arthur Salter, moreover, contemplates that Orders in Council would not be subject to any review by Parliament, except in general terms and often after an interval of many months. This gives too much

[1] *The Framework of an Ordered Society*, pp. 41–2.

[2] Thus in the 1929–30 session Parliament sat for 38 weeks and one day, in 1930–1 for 37 weeks and two days, in 1931–2 for 31 weeks and two days, in 1932–3 for 29 weeks and one day.

[3] Lord Eustace Percy suggests that the session should run for six months, from February 1 to July 31, with two breaks of ten days each at Easter and Whitsun, and with power to the Government to summon special additional sessions when necessary (*Government in Transition*, p. 112).

REFORM OF PARLIAMENTARY PROCEDURE 63

power to Ministers, and too little to the House of Commons. We need a reasonable compromise between these too drastic proposals and our present practice.

The use of Orders in Council, and other forms of Ministerial Order, is already well established in this country. The arguments in favour of this practice are overwhelming. They are set out in the *Report of the Committee on Ministers' Powers*, commonly called the Donoughmore Committee, issued in 1932,[1] and in the *Memorandum on Parliamentary Problems and Procedure*, adopted by the Labour Party Conference at Southport in 1934. They may be summarised as follows : the present pressure on Parliamentary time ; the technical nature of the subject matter of much modern legislation ; the need, from an administrative point of view, of time to work out technical detail ; the difficulty of foreseeing, before the passage of a Bill, all the contingencies and local conditions for which provision will have to be made ; the desirability of continuous adaptation to changing conditions, without the need to introduce amending legislation ; the value of making new experiments and of applying their lessons ; the need in urgent cases, e.g. a sudden outbreak of foot and mouth disease, for swift administrative action.

The Donoughmore Committee, containing, like all other Committees appointed while Mr. MacDonald was Labour Prime Minister, only a minority of political supporters of the Labour Party, established an unanswerable case, as against the objections of Lord Hewart and other old-fashioned lawyers, in favour of the wide use of delegated legislation. It proceeded to recommend that all Orders in Council and other Ministerial Orders should be submitted to a special Standing Committee of each House of Parliament. Either of these Standing Committees would have power

[1] Cmd. 4060 of 1932.

to withhold its approval from any such Order not, indeed, ostensibly on the merits of the Order, but on the ground that it was improperly made under the enabling Statute. Any Order so disapproved would then be subject to debate, and to possible rejection, in either House.

This proposal goes much too far. By comparison with present practice, it is reactionary. It would create delay and uncertainty, particularly as regards Orders requiring to be made when Parliament was not sitting. It would impose a heavy additional burden on busy Ministers, who would be continually required to appear before these Committees and argue at length on behalf of the validity of their Orders. And it gives undue influence, and new opportunities for obstruction, to the House of Lords.

The Labour Party, therefore, in the Memorandum quoted above, does not accept this proposal. But it recognises that the Standing Committees of the House of Commons may, not in all cases, but in suitable cases, the range of which could be determined by experience, perform the duties suggested by the Donoughmore Committee. In other cases, the present opportunities for Parliamentary criticism are quite sufficient. In other cases, again, it may be provided by Statute that powers conferred on Ministers may be exercised without further reference to Parliament,[1] although, of course, it would remain open for members of the House of Commons to put questions to a Minister on his use of such powers, or to move to reduce his estimates, the equivalent of a vote of censure, or, on other appropriate occasions, to criticise his policy.

To this I would add a further suggestion. It should be provided, I suggest, that any Ministerial Order, requiring Parliamentary approval, should be deemed

[1] Power, for example, to acquire land compulsorily for public purposes. See Chapter XVI.

REFORM OF PARLIAMENTARY PROCEDURE 65

to be approved, unless both Houses of Parliament rejected it within a given period. This would impose a proper limitation on the powers of the House of Lords, and equally on that of any other Second Chamber which might take its place.

I now turn to two other problems of Parliamentary procedure, that of the use of private members' time and that of private bill legislation promoted by Local Authorities.

Out of the five working days in a Parliamentary week, in the first part of the Session, two are normally given to private members' business: Wednesdays to private members' motions, two such motions being taken during the day, and Fridays to private members' Bills. Government business, therefore, is limited to three days a week. About half-way through the session the Government generally takes away all private members' time. These arrangements work badly. Some private members' motions, though by no means all, serve a useful public purpose by ventilating important questions and drawing a declaration of Government policy. But they are purely academic. They issue in no action.

Of private members' Bills, introduced on Fridays, a very small proportion reach the statute book.[1] Frequently they are "talked out", without even a vote on the motion for second reading. Long and numerous obstructive speeches are often made on one Bill, in order to spin out time and prevent the Bill standing next on the Order Paper from being reached. Even if a private member's Bill passes its Second Reading, it is often blocked in Standing Committee and has no chance of becoming law unless the Government will "take it up".

[1] In the period 1924–9 the number of such Bills passed was 29 out of 119 introduced. Of all private members' Bills during this period 60 were passed out of 430 introduced.

I suggest that a Government, intent on putting through a big legislative programme of its own, should take all private members' time, not half way through, but at the beginning of the session, and should relinquish time to private members, when the Government programme was well under way. But two days a week is an excessive ration, and I would suggest that half a day a week for private members' motions, or a full day once a fortnight, would be adequate. Likewise, for private members' Bills one day a fortnight would be sufficient. But this day should be more effectively used. A Bill which gets a Second Reading should be assured a reasonable chance of passing into law, and the Committee on Time should make hypothetical time-tables for Bills, whose authors were lucky in the ballot, before such Bills were presented for Second Reading. Normally, half a Parliamentary day, and even half a Friday, which is a short day, should be sufficient for a Second Reading debate on a private member's Bill. Two such Bills, therefore, might receive a Second Reading on a Friday and pass on, under the time-table, to Standing Committees.

The farcical procedure, whereby a long list of private members' Bills, having reached various stages, stand on the Order Paper, day by day, and are called over by the Clerk at the end of a sitting, a single member, by calling out " object ", having the power to block them, should be ended. If a Bill is worth a Second Reading, it is worth further systematic discussion.

Private Bill legislation, when promoted by Local Authorities, is very costly, time-wasting and inconveniently concentrated in London. This paraphernalia should be swept away.

In general a Local Authority, I suggest, should apply to the appropriate Minister for Orders, which he should have power to grant, after an expeditious local inquiry and the hearing of objections. But these should usually be stated by laymen in plain language, and not by highly paid lawyers in elaborate jargon. Under the procedure outlined above, the House of Commons might have power to challenge any such Ministerial Orders.

There is also another approach to this question, namely by the passage of a Local Authorities Enabling Bill, extending the range of functions which Local Authorities may legally undertake without seeking the specific approval of Parliament. The Labour Party has often advocated such a measure, which should find a place in a five years legislative programme.

In this chapter I have sketched a series of reforms, practical rather than theoretical, designed to increase the efficiency of Parliament. By such means, I believe, we can vindicate Democracy and, when the electors demand it, accomplish Socialism, and make the old Mother of Parliaments young again, and healthier by far than some of her ailing offspring on the Continent of Europe.

CHAPTER VII

EMERGENCY LEGISLATION

EMERGENCY Legislation is a well-recognised variety of British law. Special emergencies, according to the judgment of the Government of the day, call for special measures to surmount them. This is explicitly stated in the Report of the Donoughmore Committee,[1] a body on the whole very Conservative in its outlook. The Committee give as examples the Defence of the Realm Act, the Emergency Powers Act of 1920, and the financial legislation of the National Government in 1931. The latter, it will be recalled, included, not only wholesale economies, but strong powers of control over the export of capital. The Committee proposes no limit on emergency legislation except that " it is the essence of constitutional government that the normal control of Parliament should not be suspended either to a greater degree, or for a longer time, than the emergency demands ". The Labour Party's Memorandum, mentioned in the last chapter, is in close agreement on this point with the Donoughmore Committee.

I quote in full the relevant passage from this Memorandum.

> In the event of the victory of the Labour Party at a General Election being accompanied or followed by an emergency situation for which the normal powers of government are not now adequate, the Labour Govern-

[1] *Report*, pp. 52–3.

ment, formed as a consequence of that victory, would seek for the necessary emergency powers from Parliament to deal with the position. This method follows the course adopted by Governments in 1914, 1926 and 1931. The Labour Government would ask for such powers, and such powers only, as the nature of the emergency required. Their use would be for the period of the emergency only, and for the problems which it raised, while the Orders and Regulations issued under the Emergency Act would be subject to discussion in, and approval by, the Houses of Parliament. In the event of the situation requiring such a measure, it would, of course, be introduced as soon as the Labour Government met the House of Commons, and be passed through Parliament forthwith. Resistance to such a measure by the House of Lords would involve the use of all necessary powers in accordance with Constitutional precedent; and the Party would interpret its mandate from the electorate as conferring upon it full authority to proceed in this way. The powers taken would have a definite and clear relationship to the character of the emergency created, and they would be operated with a view to the most rapid return possible to the processes of normal government.[1]

Two points in this passage need emphasis. First it deals with a hypothetical situation. There is no reason to assume, or even to regard as probable, any " emergency situation ", in the event of a victory of the Labour Party, however sweeping, at the polls. The programme of the Party has been plainly stated. It is a programme of Socialism and Peace, of Reconstruction, Planning and Employment, and of Social Equality. But it is not a programme of violence or confiscation or inequity. It is to be achieved by democratic and constitutional means. It is the British habit to respect electoral verdicts and the Governments they bring in

[1] *Annual Report of the National Executive of the Labour Party*, 1934, p. 122.

their train, most of all at the outset of their period of office, when their moral authority is fresh and unquestionable. We are entitled to expect that this habit would be maintained, and that even vehement opponents of the Labour Party would, if defeated at the polls, behave with propriety and public spirit.

If, however, this expectation is disappointed, and attempts are made by unpatriotic persons in any section of the community, either by their own acts or by acts to which they urge others, to dislocate the economic or financial life of the country, or in any other way to create or exploit " an emergency situation ", it will be the duty of the new Government, both to those who supported them at the election, and to the country as a whole, to govern resolutely, and to take whatever steps are necessary to safeguard the national interests. If it is clearly understood beforehand that this will be done, it is less likely that it will need to be done.

In the second place, the passage which I have quoted makes reference to the House of Lords. The House of Lords, unlike the House of Commons, derives no moral authority from a general election. I shall have more to say about this body in the next chapter. Here I merely emphasise that, if a newly elected House of Commons, and a new Government in which that House has confidence, judges that an emergency exists, and that certain legislation is required to deal with it, the House of Lords has no moral authority to dissent. If it does so, it must take the full constitutional consequences. In an emergency there will be no time for lengthy argument, only for brisk action.

CHAPTER VIII

THE HOUSE OF LORDS

QUITE apart from any hypothetical part which it might play in a hypothetical emergency, the House of Lords is a blot on British democracy. No such collection of personages, hereditary nobles, though subject to a continuous dilution by the manufacture of new noblemen, is, or would be, tolerated as a Legislative Chamber in any British Dominion or in any foreign state which claims to be self-governing.

In the words of Mr. Ramsay MacDonald,

> purchased peerages can carry no social respect and no political authority, and therefore the House of Lords as it exists whilst this is being written is doomed. . . . To form people who have inherited or bought peerages into a constituency has obviously no justification in reason.[1]

The House of Lords has a long black record, both in its hostility to measures of social improvement and in its supine acceptance of reactionary measures.[2] The single instance in its recent history when it accepted a motion for the closure of debate was when a Labour peer, Lord Arnold, was attempting in 1926 to state a case against the extension of the legal hours of work in coal mines. The Lords on this occasion were less anxious to listen than to scramble through their work

[1] *Socialism, Critical and Constructive*, pp. 283-4 (Pocket Library Edition, January, 1929).
[2] Mr. A. L. Rowse gives a good summary of this record in his pamphlet on *The Question of the House of Lords* (Hogarth Press, 1934).

and go home to dinner. From 1906 to 1909 they so abused their powers by the rejection and mutilation of what seem, at this distance of time, a most mild series of reforms introduced by the Liberal Government of those days, culminating in the rejection in 1909, contrary to all constitutional precedent, of the Finance Bill of that year, that it was found necessary to pass the Parliament Act of 1911, and to inform their Lordships in advance that, if this measure were rejected, the Crown, on the advice of Ministers, would add sufficient new peers to their number to make a Ministerial majority.

The Parliament Act deprives the Lords of all power over Money Bills, certified as such by the Speaker of the House of Commons, and limits their power to hold up any other Bill [1] to a period of two years, if in this period the House of Commons has passed the Bill in three successive sessions, whether of the same Parliament or not. But, even so, the Lords retain vast powers of obstruction and delay. These could be used to make hay of the whole legislative programme, other than the Budget, of a Labour Government. The Labour Party, therefore, is committed, as a democratic party, to the abolition of the House of Lords.[2]

And what manner of legislative chamber, we may ask in passing, is this House of Lords ? Viewed by a spectator on a normal day, it is a droning, drowsy place. One sympathises with the late Duke of Devonshire, who once declared that he fell asleep and dreamed that he was addressing the House of Lords, and woke and found that it was true. The attendance of the peers is derisory. Habitually the great majority neglect their legislative duties.

[1] Except a Bill to extend the duration of a Parliament beyond five years.
[2] This is no new attitude. Labour members spoke and voted for the abolition of the Lords during the debates on the Parliament Bill nearly a generation ago.

THE HOUSE OF LORDS 73

The House of Lords counted, at the beginning of 1932, 729 members (excluding thirty minors who had not taken their seats). The average number taking part in a Division, over the period 1919–31, was 83. The House divided during this period on 439 occasions. Only 119 of the peers voted in as many as one hundred of these Divisions, only thirteen in as many as two hundred. The peers who never voted in a single Division number 111. 371 of the peers, or more than half, never spoke in any debate during this period, and those who in these thirteen years spoke at least ten times number only 98.[1] In their capacity as legis-

[1] I take these figures from an article by J. Crighton and H. J. Laski published in *The New Statesman* of March 4, 1933. The authors add an interesting table showing the occupations, as published, of the peers. 246 owned land. Directorships were held, in Insurance Companies by 112 peers, in Finance and Investment Houses by 74, in Banks by 67, in Railway Companies by 64, in Engineering and Shipbuilding by 49, in Mining other than Coal by 29, in Coal, Iron and Steel by 27, in Shipping by 26, etc. In these figures there is, of course, much over-lapping of individuals. How many peers showed any genuine activity in their Directorships is not disclosed. A considerable number, it may be surmised, acted as part of the window dressing only, to attract innocent funds and custom. E. T. Hooley, one of the outstanding financial crooks of the pre-War period, boasted that he was the pioneer in the use of noble " guinea-pig " directors as baits for the investing public. " When I bought the Dunlop business in 1896 ", he says, " I thought it would be a good idea to have some well-known people on the board, and so I got hold of an Earl, now deceased, and said to him, ' I'll give you £10,000 for a Duke and £5,000 a piece for a couple of ordinary peers. I don't mind who they are, so long as they are fairly well-known.' ' Right you are, my boy,' he replied breezily, ' it won't take me long to find them.' Nor did it. He brought the Duke of Somerset along and another noble Earl. That was good enough for me. The new company duly came out with its titled directors and was a roaring success." Quoted by Thomas Johnston, *The Financiers and the Nation* (Methuen, 1934), pp. 37–8. Has the race of titled guinea-pigs died out? I think not.

lators, at any rate, the peers have thoroughly earned the title of " the idle rich ".

Yet, when it is desired to mutilate or destroy a measure passed by the House of Commons, a sufficient handful of Tory partisans can always be scraped together for this purpose.

A study of authoritative text-books, such as Anson's *Law and Custom of the Constitution*, suggests that there may be a good historical and legal case for the view that the Crown, on the advice of Ministers, may issue writs of summons to Parliament, not to all peers indiscriminately as now, but to selected peers only. A reasonable basis for such selective summons might be found in the record of individual peers, in attendance, votes and contributions to debate in the previous Parliament. Those who had fallen below a minimum standard of performance in these respects, and had thus failed to respond loyally to the Royal summons to assist in legislation and deliberation on great public issues, might properly have their names struck off the list. The number of effective members of the House of Lords would thus be much reduced and, if there were further serious exhibitions of partisanship and failure to co-operate with the majority in the Commons, a comparatively small creation of new peers, supporters of the Government of the day, would be sufficient to overcome recalcitrant obstruction by the Second Chamber. This method of handling the problem is, I suggest to constitutional experts, at least worthy of careful consideration.

Yet, in their prim seclusion from the outer world, the Lords cherish some strange illusions. A notable feature of their attitude towards themselves is their " collective self-approval ", as was remarked by Lord Snell on May 7, 1934.

In those spring days of 1934 an old man's fancy had turned to thoughts of " House of Lords Reform ".

Lord Salisbury's Bill, to strengthen the powers of the Lords to thwart the Commons, and to deprive the Crown of its prerogative to create, on the advice of Ministers, sufficient peers to make the Commons' will prevail, led to a long and interesting debate.

One Noble Lord observed that "if the Crown assented " to the abolition of the House of Lords, " the allegiance of a great number of people would be lost ". Another Noble Lord declared that to attack the House of Lords was to attack the foundations of Christianity. Loyalty to the Throne and a true understanding of the Christian religion wear strange disguises in their Lordships' circle. And yet these men are legislators, removable, as the Constitution stands at present, by no election short of death !

The Labour Party proposes to modify the Constitution, so as to provide them with an earlier exit. A Labour Government's mandate must include authority, to quote words spoken by Mr. Winston Churchill long ago, in support of the Parliament Bill, " to clear the road which leads from the representatives of the people to the steps of the Throne."

The Labour Party's intentions have been plainly declared. It will seek a mandate at the next election to entitle a Labour Government, by due constitutional process, to treat the House of Lords as an antiquated traffic obstruction on the democratic highway, and to remove it. I quote again, for the sake of clarity and precision, from the *Memorandum* approved by the Labour Party Conference of 1934 :

> A Labour Government meeting with sabotage from the House of Lords would take immediate steps to overcome it ; and it will, in any event, take steps during its term of office to pass legislation abolishing the House of Lords as a legislative Chamber. If the Party obtained a mandate from the people in support of its policy, the Labour Government would regard it as a duty to carry

that policy through by the necessary legislation and administrative action. The Party will, therefore, at the next General Election, make it clear to the country that in placing its policy before the people, it is also asking for a mandate to deal forthwith with any attempt by the House of Lords to defeat the will of the people by rejecting, mutilating or delaying measures which formed an essential part of the programme approved by the electorate.

Precisely how, and in what sequence, relatively to other items in its programme, the Labour Party's intentions regarding the House of Lords should be carried out, must depend on circumstances. And one of the circumstances must be the conduct of the Lords themselves towards a Labour Government and its proposals. It would be possible to pass a Bill abolishing the House of Lords under the procedure of the Parliament Act. It might be necessary to seek, in accordance with constitutional precedent, a speedier settlement of accounts. The primary purpose of a Labour Government would be to carry through its programme of economic and social change. Mere constitutional change, though important, would at the outset be secondary. But it might quickly become primary, if the Lords chose to make it so. And British public opinion, slow to anger on what might seem an abstract question, might soon boil over on a practical issue and demand an early remedy for gross obstruction of a newly elected House of Commons.

On the question whether there should be any Second Chamber and, if so, of what kind and with what powers, there is a variety of opinion in the Labour Party. In what follows I state only my personal opinion.

There is an undoubted attraction in the view that no Second Chamber is necessary. Government would then be vested in Crown, Cabinet and Commons, the Commons expressing, through the Cabinet and to the

Constitutional Crown, the will of the people. Such a constitution would be fully democratic in form, and strong in its simplicity. It might be further strengthened against exaggerated discontinuities by substituting, for the present method of Parliamentary general elections, the method of partial renewal practised in most of our Local Government elections, a fraction of the members of the House of Commons, say one-fifth, retiring by rotation every year.

To such a constitution we may come in time. But, as an immediate solution, it might lack stability. A Labour Government might impose it, and a succeeding Government, of another political colour, reverse it and reintroduce a Second Chamber, distasteful in its composition to Socialists and other democrats, and armed with excessive powers. Cromwell set up a Single Chamber, but it did not last long. The House of Lords sailed back on a reactionary tide. To constitutional prudes Single Chamber Government looks too naked to be decent. Fearful of nameless dangers, they call for another layer of clothing.[1]

There is, therefore, much to be said for examining the possibilities of a Second Chamber which shall be free from the overwhelming objections rightly urged against the House of Lords. Many suggestions have

[1] The argument that a Labour Government should not so act as to provoke a reaction by a succeeding Government, must be given its due weight by common-sense judgment in particular cases. But not more than its due weight. Because dogs bark, the caravan must not be halted. There is, of course, a risk of the reversal of all measures of socialisation. But I do not much fear this, if the new institutions have got into good working order, and justified themselves in action. The wholesale repealing by one Government of its predecessor's measures is a harder and less attractive business than it sounds, and is not, in fact, the British political method. But some particular measures, more than others, may invite repeal, and in my view the creation of a Single Chamber would be one of these.

been made as to the powers and composition of such a Chamber. I take for granted that, whatever its composition, its powers should not be greater than those of the Lords under the Parliament Act. Certainly, indeed, they should be less, for the possibility, which now exists, of a two years delay in the enactment of all measures other than Money Bills, is preposterous.

But composition matters more than powers. The Second Chamber must be so composed as not to have the *will* to thwart the Commons. Except under a Tory, or worse than Tory, Government, such as the present, when they sleep soundly, the Lords, run by a gang of Tory partisans, have by their past conduct discredited any idea of helpful relationship between the Commons, rightly dominant in policy, and a subordinate, but co-operatively-minded, Second Chamber. But such a relationship is not impossible.

The simplest way to create it is to provide that members of the Second Chamber shall be chosen by the House of Commons itself. This method was first adopted in Norway, and has been copied in other modern democratic constitutions. It is ably defended by Mr. H. B. Lees Smith in his book on *Second Chambers in Theory and Practice*, and is supported, in conjunction with other changes, with which we are not here concerned, by Mr. and Mrs. Webb in their book on *A Constitution for the Socialist Commonwealth of Great Britain*. They call it a Committee of Revision. It was also recommended by the Conference of members of all Parties, presided over by Lord Bryce in 1918, as the method of selecting three-quarters of the members of a reformed Second Chamber.

This method has advantages over various alternatives which have been proposed, e.g. nomination by the Crown on the advice of Ministers, direct election by popular constituencies, and indirect election through the Local Authorities. It is the best available form of indirect election.

There is no need to adopt the rigid Norwegian rule, whereby the choice of the popular Chamber is limited to its own members. It is better to allow the widest range of choice. I have suggested, for example, in a previous chapter, that Elder Statesmen, too old to continue as members of the House of Commons, might suitably be elected to such a Second Chamber. A member of the House of Commons chosen by his fellows to sit in the Second Chamber should, of course, resign his seat.

Minority Parties in the House of Commons should have their fair share in selecting members of the Second Chamber. To ensure this, some method of proportional representation should be adopted. Most unsuitable, as I have argued above, as a method of choosing members of the House of Commons by direct election, this method has advantages in certain cases of indirect election. A very simple form of it would be, if, for example, a House of Commons of six hundred members had to select one hundred members of the Second Chamber, to allow any six members of the former to unite in choosing one person to serve in the latter.

Of the members chosen by the House of Commons, all might be chosen at the beginning of each Parliament and might sit in the Second Chamber for the duration of that Parliament, subject, of course, to the possibility of being chosen again in the next. Or, if a greater continuity of membership were desired, they might be chosen to sit for the duration of two Parliaments. At any given time, under this plan, half would have been chosen by the sitting Parliament, and half by its predecessor. There is something to be said for both these methods. I suggest that the maximum power which the Second Chamber should be entitled to exercise should be to delay a Bill, other than a Money Bill, for one Parliamentary session and, with a co-operative spirit prevailing between the two Chambers, even this power would very seldom be exercised.

The true function of the Second Chamber should be to examine Bills passed by the House of Commons and to suggest amendments not destructive of their main principles, to modify legislation, but not to defeat it. Improvements in drafting, to remove ambiguities and narrow the scope for subsequent litigation, and the avoidance of unintended inconsistency with existing legislation, would be two of the chief duties which such a Revising Chamber might usefully perform.

Bills dealing with comparatively non-controversial subjects might sometimes be conveniently first introduced in the Second Chamber, and put into good shape before being submitted to the House of Commons. There are many such Bills commanding a large measure of popular support, but for which there is, under the present high pressure on Parliamentary time, no opportunity of sufficient consideration. Their chances of passing into law would be thus increased, since the time required to be spent on them in the House of Commons would be diminished.

A Second Chamber, small in numbers and constituted on these lines, would, in my judgment, be a useful element in the Constitution, not undemocratic in its basis of selection, neither able, nor likely to aspire, to challenge the supremacy of the House of Commons, and furnishing, one may reasonably hope, a settlement, moderately stable, of a long constitutional controversy. Its name is not a matter of the first importance. But to give it dignity and follow the nomenclature adopted in several of the Dominions and in a number of foreign countries, I should not grudge it the title of a Senate.

The House of Lords, through the Law Lords, is now the supreme Court of Appeal. This legal function has no logical connection with its legislative powers. It could continue to be exercised, by judges appointed as at present, when the Lords as a legislative Chamber had been abolished.

CHAPTER IX

SOME PROBLEMS OF GOVERNMENT

IN 1933 the National Executive of the Labour Party issued a Report on *Labour and Government*, which was submitted to, and approved by, the Annual Conference of the Party at Hastings in that year.[1]

This Report must be read in relation to some of the events of 1929-31, on which it represents a retrospective judgment by the Party and an intention to prevent their repetition. The Report deals with some of the problems which would confront the Party, when in office or on the threshold of office. The general intention is to emphasise by appropriate means the Party's democratic character; to check tendencies towards a " dictatorship " within it, either by the Prime Minister or, in a lesser degree, by the Chancellor of the Exchequer; and to provide for closer contact and more effective consultation between the various sections of the Party during any future period of Labour Government.

The principal recommendations in the Report are as follows:

(1) The final decision as to whether, after a general election, the Party should take office or not, must rest with those members of the Party who have been elected to Parliament. This is a fundamental requirement of Parliamentary democracy. But the Parliamentary

[1] *Report of the Thirty-Third Annual Conference of the Labour Party*, 1933, pp. 8-11.

SOME PROBLEMS OF GOVERNMENT 83

Labour Party, before taking its decision, should have before it the views of the National Council of Labour and its three constituent bodies, the National Executive of the Labour Party, elected by the delegates to the Party's Annual Conference, the Executive of the Parliamentary Labour Party, elected by the Labour Members of Parliament, and the General Council, elected by the delegates to the Annual Trade Union Congress.

Further, if the possibility of a Minority Government again arises, the National Executive would immediately summon a special Conference, on the same basis of representation as an Annual Party Conference, at which also the members of the National Council of Labour would attend. The view of this Conference would, likewise, be before the Parliamentary Labour Party, when it decided whether or not the Labour Party should agree to form a Government.

(2) In the event of a Labour Government being formed, the final responsibility for the appointment of Ministers must continue to rest with the Prime Minister, who would, of course, be the elected leader of the Parliamentary Party. But the Parliamentary Party should choose three of its members who, together with the Secretary of the Labour Party, should advise and consult with the Prime Minister concerning such appointments.

(3) The Prime Minister should be subject to majority decisions of the Cabinet, and should only recommend the Crown to dissolve a Parliament, which had not run its normal course, on the decision of the Cabinet, confirmed by a decision of the Parliamentary Labour Party.[1]

(4) Public expenditure, and finance generally, should,

[1] Mr. MacDonald recommended the dissolution of 1924 without any proper consultation with his Cabinet colleagues, much less with the Parliamentary Party. In the formation of the National Government in 1931 he acted in complete disregard of any responsibility, either to the Cabinet as a whole, or to the Parliamentary Party.

like any other important question, be a matter of Cabinet decision in relation to the Government's policy as a whole. It is recommended that " the excessive authority in this field which has in the past been exercised by the Chancellor of the Exchequer " should be diminished.[1]

(5) There should be closer contacts, in many directions, than under the last Labour Government: between Ministers themselves, both members of the Cabinet and others; between Ministers and members of the Parliamentary Party; between Parliamentarians, whether Ministers or M.P.'s, and the Labour Movement outside Parliament.

It is recommended, in particular, that three Members of the Cabinet should devote themselves to *liaison* duties. One of these should specialise in keeping contacts between the Prime Minister and his colleagues on the one hand and the Parliamentary Party on the other. With the Chief Whip he should attend regularly, and other Ministers might attend occasionally, the meetings of the Consultative Committee of the Parliamentary Party.[2]

[1] The officials of the Treasury, always inclined towards the aggrandisement of their Department, found in Mr. Snowden, as I have already remarked, a chief after their own hearts. A member of the Second Labour Cabinet told me that he once wished to place a certain question on the Cabinet Agenda. He was informed by an official of the Cabinet Secretariat that this was against the rules. This particular question, like almost every other, " involved finance ", and the Minister was referred to a Cabinet Minute of 1924, which laid it down that no Minister could raise in the Cabinet any question involving finance, unless he had first secured the approval of the Chancellor of the Exchequer. This remarkable Minute was obtained by eager Treasury officials from the Cabinet through the willing agency of Mr. Snowden during his first term of office as Chancellor.

[2] This Committee is elected by the Parliamentary Party from those of its members who are not Ministers. It takes the place, when the Party is in office, of the Executive of the Parliamentary Party.

It is further recommended that "the fullest opportunity should be given for Ministers to make statements to members of the Parliamentary Party regarding their Departmental work" and that, "in order to make fuller use of the services of private members, Ministers should keep in touch with groups of members interested in, and having special knowledge of, particular problems dealt with in their Departments".[1] Further, with regard to proposed industrial legislation, with which it is directly concerned, the General Council of the Trade Union Congress should be fully consulted.

The intention of all these *liaison* provisions is excellent. The need for something of this kind was felt by many of us, with increasing and finally with overwhelming force, during the second Labour Government.

But these provisions are formidably complex. I believe that they would be workable and salutary, provided there is goodwill and energy and common sense in plenty, and reasonable forbearance in pressing personal points of view. Otherwise the whole machine will choke.

It is terribly easy—anyone can do it—to make a paper plan providing, in theory, for a "suitable" network of Committees, of "adequate facilities for consultation" and of "appropriate co-ordinating machinery". But, in practice, a network "suitable"

[1] This idea, of unofficial Committees of Ministerialists, helpfully working in conjunction with particular Ministers, is practical. One or two Ministers in the Second Labour Government adopted it, and the National Government encouraged the setting up of "Economy Committees", composed entirely of Conservative members, in 1931 and 1932. This is a useful precedent. A rival idea, that of creating official Departmental Parliamentary Committees, on which all parties would be represented, has only theoretical attractions, and would delay rather than accelerate business, give new opportunities of obstruction to the Opposition, and impose new burdens on Ministers.

for what ? For trapping time, for delaying decision, for consulting till the hot iron has grown cold, for co-ordinating all activity to a standstill. This is the danger, and it is very real. We have a fondness for committees in the Labour Party, and we must watch ourselves, lest we become victims of this habit-forming drug.

However excellently they are prepared, however exhaustively they are pursued, at some point these consultations must end. At some point one man, or a few men, must be given power to act, to go ahead, to put a stop to more talk and to the circulation of more memoranda.

But one conclusion emerges very clearly. The requirements of effective *liaison* conflict fatally with the idea of a small Cabinet, five or six or seven, of so-called " Super-Ministers ". This idea has never been accepted by the Labour Party, but it has been a good deal talked and written about by individuals. The arguments used in its favour seem to me to be theoretical, and to break down when brought into contact with practice.

It has been suggested that a few Super-Ministers— for " Industry ", for " Social Services ", etc.—should be placed over groups of Ministers, responsible for separate Departments, most of which are now separately represented in the Cabinet. But what would be the gain of this ? These would not be " Ministers without Portfolio " ; they would be Ministers with too many Portfolios. Someone must be finally responsible, in Parliament and elsewhere, for each Department. That someone, when any critical issue arises, must be the Super-Minister. Otherwise, what is the meaning of his title and his function ? He would, therefore, have to keep in touch with all important and many unimportant issues, in each of his group of Departments, and to do this with an improvised, scratch staff. He would inevitably become overworked and ineffective. The small Cabinet of Super-Ministers seems to be based on the idea that running a single Department efficiently is only a second-class job. This is a false approach.

Nor would a small Cabinet, in practice, be likely to be quicker and more decisive in action than a large one, provided the work of the latter were properly organised. Members of a small Cabinet would probably have to spend much more time and effort in consultation with Ministers outside the Cabinet than would be saved by limiting the numbers present at Cabinet discussions. Members of the second Labour Cabinet, it is reported, did not, with one notable exception, waste time in Cabinet by excessive talk. Indecision, indeed, there was, but the Great Master of Indecision was in the Chair.

Two other arguments weigh heavily against a small Cabinet. This would tend to be composed of older leaders of the Party. The younger generation would have less chance than ever of influencing policy.

The other argument is psychological. The Labour Party is less tolerant than it was, in the days of Mr. MacDonald and Mr. Snowden, of the idea of a few superior people who will settle what can be done and what cannot. The Party, I fancy, will prefer, as a safeguard against excess of individual leadership, that corporate leadership shall be shared by more, rather than fewer, leaders.

What is required is to have in the Cabinet several Ministers with leisure to think, to watch the changing political and parliamentary situation, to take stock, from time to time, of achievements and failures up to date, and of the progress of the Government's programme, to initiate new ideas and new problems of policy to be studied, to keep their heads above the waters of detail, which are apt to drown Departmental chiefs. These Ministers must be free from, or only very lightly burdened with, Departmental duties. They could be used for three other sets of duties, which would conveniently fit in with one another. First, the duties just indicated ; second, the *liaison* duties mentioned above ; third, as a nucleus of Cabinet Committees.

If new Departments are needed, and probably some will be, they should be created, and properly staffed, with a view to permanence. At some stage in the life of the next Labour Government, for example, it may well be desirable to create a new Ministry of Finance, separate from the Treasury, to supervise new socialised and semi-socialised financial institutions.[1]

But we should not repeat the disastrous experiment of 1929 and make some Minister, nominally non-Departmental, responsible for Supra-Departmental duties, as when the office of Lord Privy Seal was used to give Mr. Thomas, without any proper staff, an opportunity " to deal with unemployment ".

If, however, we reject the idea of the small Cabinet, we must reorganise the working of the Cabinet of some twenty members, which we shall still retain.[2]

Less business, particularly small detail, should be brought before the Cabinet. Individual Ministers should be encouraged, rather than hindered, in going

[1] This, however, would require new legislation, as would a number of other highly desirable redistributions of duties between different Departments. We should not take up much time with legislation of this kind, until we have completed our most urgent tasks.

[2] Certain mergers of offices might be made, without legislation, simply by appointing one man to hold two or more offices. Thus there is a strong case for one Minister of Defence, to combine the duties of the Ministers for War and Air and the First Lord of the Admiralty. Also for merging the Dominions Office with the India Office, or with the Colonial Office, as of old, or possibly with the Foreign Office.

ahead with their Departmental policies, once these have received the general approval of their colleagues. More responsibility, also, should be devolved on Cabinet Committees, with power to act, without reference back, within broad lines laid down by the Cabinet as a whole. It is not useful to make a precise plan at this stage for these Committees. Much must depend, when the time comes, on personal factors and on what problems press hardest. But I shall have something more to say on this subject, from another angle, in Chapter XXX on the Machinery of Planning.

PART III
SOCIALISATION

CHAPTER X

FORMS OF SOCIALISATION

SOCIALISTS hold that public ownership and control should replace private ownership and control over a steadily increasing part of the economic field. The Labour Party proposes that, within the normal lifetime of a Parliament in which it has a majority, an important group of industries and services, central in the life of the nation, shall be added to the socialised sector.

There are many possible forms of socialisation. As Mr. Tawney has put it:

The constitution of the industry may be "unitary", as is (for example) that of the Post Office, or it may be "federal", as was that designed by Mr. Justice Sankey for the coal industry. Administration may be centralised or decentralised. The authorities to whom it is entrusted may be composed of representatives of the consumers, or of representatives of professional associations, or of State officials, or of all three in several different proportions. Executive work may be placed in the hands of civil servants, trained, recruited and promoted as in the existing State Departments, or a new service may be created with a procedure and standards of its own. The industry may be subject to Treasury control, or it may be financially autonomous. The problem is, in fact, of a familiar, though difficult, order. It is one of constitution making.[1]

Since this passage was written, in 1921, a new type

[1] *The Acquisitive Society*, pp. 141–2.

of constitution has gained ground, that of the Public Board, or Public Corporation.

It was, I think, the late William Graham who first popularised this latter title. It conveniently describes a certain type of economic organisation, Socialist in its essential character, but allowing for great variety in detail.[1]

We must avoid the temptation to construct a doctrinaire and cast-iron pattern, and seek to make all socialised industries and services conform to it. There is no one best way of organising all socialised enterprises. Still less is there one permanent best model, to be created in one act and to remain unchanged throughout the future. We must experiment, adapt, learn from experience, and encourage variety of form to fit variety of conditions.

Direct administration by a Minister through a Government Department is apt to be regarded nowadays as an old-fashioned form of Socialism, not a suitable model for new socialised undertakings. The Post Office is the classical British example. But even here a process of adaptation is taking place. Excessive centralisation of administration in the hands of a few high officials has been broken down. A new "functional Board" has been created, to advise the Postmaster-General on policy. Publicity has been improved, and a Public Relations Officer appointed. As regards finance, Treasury control, previously very rigid, has been somewhat relaxed. The contribution of the Post Office to the national exchequer has been stabilised for a term of years, and any additional surplus will be at the disposal of the Post Office for development and experiment, reduction of charges and improvement of the conditions of its staff.

[1] Not to be confused, of course, either with the institutions of the so-called "Corporative State", or with the private "corporation" of America.

These changes illustrate the power of public criticism to modify the constitution and methods of a public enterprise.[1] They are evidence of the vitality of Socialist institutions and their responsiveness to public opinion.

None the less, modern thought and experience tend to favour for new socialised enterprises a less close and direct dependence on the Government and on Parliament than that of the Post Office. Hence the increasing support for the idea of the Public Corporation.

The essential features of this form of economic constitution are the following:

(1) the socialised industry or service must be unified, within the national area, under a single control, though there may be in suitable cases a large measure of local devolution in administration;

(2) this control is to be exercised primarily by a Directorate, or Board, of public servants, remunerated by fixed salaries, and not by any share in the profits of the undertaking;

(3) there must be no element of private profit, in the sense of the participation by private investors in any surplus realised by the undertaking;

(4) payments to private investors, in respect of assets taken over when the corporation is formed or of loans raised afterwards, must carry no control over the socialised undertaking by the recipients of such payments, not even the nominal control exercised by shareholders in a joint stock company;

(5) each public corporation must work according to a plan, whose aim is efficient public service, but the plans of different corporations must be continuously co-ordinated in a larger national plan;

(6) the ultimate power of control over the corpora-

[1] On all this see an interesting article on *Post Office Progress*, by W. A. Robson in *The New Statesman* of June 16, 1934.

tion must rest with Parliament, acting through a responsible Minister.

This, of course, is not an imaginary type of organisation. Many examples of it exist, both in this country and elsewhere, and some of these will be discussed below. But, before passing to particular cases, there are some general questions to be answered.

By whom, and on what qualifications, should the public servants be appointed, who are to compose the Board of Management ? Normally by that Minister who is responsible to Parliament for the general conduct of the public undertaking. But the appointments may be made after appropriate consultations.

The number of members of the Board should not be so large as to delay, by overmuch discussion, the taking of decisions, or to encourage the appointment of merely ornamental members. But it should be large enough to allow of some specialisation by members on different aspects of the Board's work.

The Chairman at least, and probably some other members, should be full-timers. But it will generally be convenient that some members should hold part-time appointments only. No rigid rule seems necessary here. On the other hand, there should be a rigid age-limit on all appointments.

The members should be appointed for a fixed term of years, and be eligible, subject to age limit, for re-appointment, but the terms of appointment of the different members should not all expire at the same time.

The qualifications of the members should be ability and willingness to perform the duties imposed upon them. Not all should be "experts" in any narrow sense, though experience of the industry or service in question, of labour conditions, of finance or of marketing are important qualifications to be taken into account. But all should have energy and a faith in the future possibilities of the enterprise. No hidebound partisans of the old order are fitted to direct the new. Willingness to serve loyally, under the new conditions, is an obvious and essential qualification.[1]

As regards finance, the element of private profit, as distinct from fixed payments to private investors, should from the outset be eliminated. Any claim, based on private property rights, to share in any financial surplus realised by the corporation, is inconsistent with the fundamental idea of socialisation. Such a surplus, in a socialised enterprise, has other destinations.

In general, the ideal arrangement is that, as regards extensions and improvements, a public corporation should be self-financing ; that its surplus should be sufficient, not only to pay for all its own developments, but also to make a contribution to the national revenue, and that its budget should be burdened with no interest payments to private individuals. The British Broadcasting Corporation has already achieved this ideal. Open though it may be to criticism on other grounds, it is, on its financial side, a Socialist model.

Other public corporations will not reach this goal immediately. In their early years they will usually have to meet certain charges arising out of compensa-

[1] This does not mean, in spite of misrepresentations to the contrary by some of our opponents, that membership of the Labour Party would be an essential qualification. Certainly it would not be a disqualification. But only an embittered anti-Socialist, or an ignorant doctrinaire, imagines that no men of ability outside the official ranks of the Labour Party would be willing to do their best, if holding a position of responsibility in a socialised enterprise, to make it a success. Any such idea has already been disproved by experience.

It is interesting in this connection to observe that President Roosevelt, when setting up the Tennessee Valley Authority, required its members to make a declaration of their " belief in the feasibility and wisdom of the Act " establishing the Authority.

tion arrangements, and also out of new loans for capital development after socialisation. But generally it should be the aim of the corporation's financial policy to clear its budget of all such charges within a reasonable term of years, and in this task the State, as argued in later Chapters,[1] may properly co-operate.

The corporation may sometimes pay interest to the State for loans of public money. But in this there is nothing repugnant to Socialist ideas. In special cases the corporation may receive a grant-in-aid from the Treasury. But this should be neither a permanent nor a frequent arrangement.

Neither payments for interest and sinking fund, nor for wages and salaries at a proper level, are to be regarded as " first charges "—either in preference to the other—on the corporation's revenue. Both sets of payments are necessary charges, which the corporation must meet out of the sale of its goods or services. If it fails to balance its Budget, it must look for assistance to the State. But the State, if such a situation arose, would be entitled to make a searching examination into the affairs of the corporation, and to prescribe remedies for any inefficiency which might be disclosed.

This leads on to a consideration of the standards of efficiency, by which the performance of public corporations, and of other forms of socialised enterprise, should be judged.

The aim should be to combine good, and rising, standards of service to consumers and users, with good, and rising, conditions of employment, including the elimination, so far as possible, of short-term fluctuations in the numbers employed. When an industry or service is socialised, competition within it, in the old sense, disappears. But competition, in a new and more scientific sense, should take its place. The

[1] See Chapters XVIII and XXXI.

enterprise, in all its branches, should "work within glass walls", and be subject, in Mr. and Mrs. Webb's phrase, to "measurement and publicity". "The deliberate intensification", they write, "of the searchlight of published knowledge we regard as the cornerstone of successful Democracy."[1] Full statistical and other relevant information should be continuously collected and widely published, so that the enterprise may be judged by the acid test of results, and "common consent be reached by the agency of accurately ascertained and authoritatively reported facts".

In particular, in all public establishments there should be a system of comparative costings, as in munition factories during the War. This is specially important when control of production is decentralised, as would probably be the case in a socialised coal industry.

The State Planning Department, referred to in a later chapter, should collect and co-ordinate all statistical information from the various socialised enterprises, and suggest conclusions regarding future policy.

Socialism, therefore, will not abolish competition, but will institute planned public competition, in place of unplanned private competition, and will plan to avoid the waste and misdirection of resources which, under capitalism, are a chronic disease.

Research is a prime factor in efficiency. We should spend freely on this. A Labour Government should give greatly increased scope to scientists, working both in the direct employment of socialised enterprises, and in Universities and other scientific institutes.

The prices charged by a socialised enterprise cannot be left to its own determination. They must be a

[1] *Constitution for the Socialist Commonwealth of Great Britain*, p. 196. In this remarkable book, which every student of Socialism should read, the authors develop this idea at considerable length.

matter for discussion with representatives of consumers and users and, in the last resort, for determination by some suitable tribunal, acting within the framework of National Planning sketched in a later chapter. They are also a proper subject for Parliamentary comment.[1]

The ultimate control over socialised enterprises must rest with Parliament. This is an elementary principle of democratic Socialism. But such control should operate through periodical discussion of the general policy of the enterprise, and of the actual results achieved, not through day-to-day intervention by politicians in the details of administration. Few members of Parliament are competent, nor have they time, in the course of their busy lives, to make themselves competent, to judge such details. The wider the field over which socialisation extends, the greater the number, and the more complex the inter-relations, of socialised enterprises, the less the competence of politicians becomes. The function of Parliament, increasingly as socialisation extends, is to confine itself to general principles of action, and general judgments on results.

Socialism, as it is progressively achieved, will bring a great change in the social atmosphere. With the disappearance of private profit will go the power, often harsh and arbitrary, exercised by its recipients or their agents over their employees. The fear of victimisation, for political or Trade Union activities, will vanish. Trade Unions, and other professional associations, will be firmly established, and will assume

[1] I have in mind here, primarily, domestic prices. A socialised enterprise, in coal, or iron and steel, for example, which exports part of its product, must be furnished with its own foreign selling agency, or Export Board. Its export prices will be determined by the conditions of demand in its export markets, but these, in turn, will be affected by trade treaties and other international agreements.

new positive functions.[1] The workers will acquire a new status, both individually and collectively, no longer mere " hands ", but honourable partners in a true social activity, working no longer for capitalists, but for the community, to produce, not profits, but plenty.

[1] See, for a fuller discussion, Chapter XVII on " Workers' Control of Industry ".

CHAPTER XI

BROADCASTING

THE British Broadcasting Corporation was founded in December, 1926, on the expiration of the licence granted in 1922 to the British Broadcasting Company—a private combine of five or six concerns which manufactured wireless equipment, and operated wireless stations. The Marconi Company, for instance, operated the London station, 2LO.

The Corporation is controlled by a Board of five Governors appointed by the Postmaster-General for five years.[1] Subject to the ultimate control of Parliament, the Governors are responsible for policy, as " trustees for the national interest ", but the Corporation's Charter empowers the Postmaster-General to order the B.B.C. to refrain from broadcasting any matter of which he disapproves, while on the other hand the Corporation must " send any matter which any Department of His Majesty's Government may require to be broadcast ".[2]

On its financial side the Corporation, as remarked

[1] It is a pity that there is no age limit on these appointments. At present two out of the five Governors are over sixty-five.

[2] This last is a most important power, as a Labour Government, with most of the Press blaring against it, might sometimes find. Before the coming of the cheap popular press it used to be said by politicians of the Left that " the platform will always beat the press ". To-day the wireless can beat the press.

above, is a Socialist model. It pays no interest or profit to any person, except for small and temporary bank overdrafts. It has never financed its developments by loans. It pays its way out of its licence fees, and has paid for extensions and improvements out of revenue. It has, moreover, made a steady and increasing contribution, from its growing surplus, to the Treasury.

The number of licences issued rose from 2,178,000 in 1926 to 5,974,000 at the end of 1933, and 6,300,000 in the middle of 1934. The revenue, at ten shillings per licence per year, amounted in 1933 to £2,968,000.

Out of this sum £1,283,000 was paid over to the Treasury under the terms of the Corporation's Licence, together with a further £225,000 as an "emergency contribution". An additional £121,000 was paid in Income Tax. The Treasury, therefore, drew from the Corporation £1,629,000 in 1933. The Corporation's assets, chiefly freehold land, buildings and fixed plant, are valued at over £2 millions and its payment of interest on bank overdraft was less than £900 in 1933.[1]

The Corporation is always being publicly criticised, and the fact that this is possible, and that much of the criticism takes effect, is a strong argument in favour of its present constitution. We demand higher standards from public than from private enterprise, and we get them.

No one can buy time on the air in this country. Broadcasting here is for use—including information, education and amusement—and not for profit. The results of competitive profit-seeking by foreign Broadcasting Companies, and the hideous din of commercial advertisers, do not encourage us to imitate such foreign models. On the other hand, in countries without political freedom, the State-controlled wireless becomes

[1] These particulars are taken from the B.B.C.'s Seventh Annual Report for 1933.

a mere instrument of boring and tendencious Government propaganda.

We have chosen a good middle path and, for the first complete model of a public corporation in Britain, a naturally expanding service with a bright future.

It is worth considering whether there should not now be established as a subsidiary to the B.B.C. a public monopoly of the manufacture of wireless equipment.

Such a subsidiary would, of course, be directed by a separate Board, whose members would need to be chosen on different " grounds of ability " from those of the B.B.C. itself.

CHAPTER XII

ELECTRICITY

LIKE broadcasting, but on a vastly larger scale, the supply of electric current is an expanding service with a bright future. In Britain we have already travelled more than half-way towards its socialisation. It should be one of the first tasks of a Labour Government to complete the journey.

The history of British electrical supply does not help the defenders of capitalism. In large part, it is a story of wasteful inefficiency, of lack of enterprise, and of high profits based on high charges drawn from lazy local monopolies.

During the War the demand for electrical energy, especially for making munitions, rose sharply, revealing, more visibly than before, the grave inadequacy of existing arrangements both for generation and distribution.[1] Several ponderous Committees, appointed by the Government, sat on the problem, and issued reports, reciting discreditable facts, advising sensible, though moderate, reforms. It was pointed out, for example, that in London alone there were in 1918 some seventy generating stations, representing between them some

[1] In what follows I have drawn, among other sources, on the pamphlet on the *Reorganisation of the Electricity Supply Industry*, published by the Labour Party, price 2d. This pamphlet contains an historical survey, followed by a study of present problems, leading up to practical proposals for reorganisation, which were accepted by the Labour Party Conference at Leicester in 1932.

fifty different systems of supply, twenty-four different voltages and ten different frequencies. This ridiculous and costly chaos was reproduced with local variations throughout the country. As was stated by the Electricity Commissioners in 1921, " it is now recognised that this lack of co-ordination has resulted in unnecessary expenditure of capital, wasteful consumption of coal, and higher charges for electricity than would have been the case had there been larger areas of supply, a greater concentration of generating plant in larger units, and more economically situated power stations. Owing in many cases to the small size and relatively high running costs of public stations, manufacturers have been compelled to adopt the unsatisfactory course of installing their own generating plant, thus extending the wasteful systems of generation on a small scale in a multiplicity of small stations. Moreover, the adoption of many different systems of supply, frequencies and pressures has involved the manufacture of corresponding types of electrical plant and apparatus, and thus deprived those concerned of the advantages that would have accrued both in home and foreign markets from concentration on the production of a few standard types." This is a good statement of the case for the national planning of this industry.

The Electricity Commissioners had been set up by the Electricity Supply Act of 1919. But they were born lame. The Bill in its original form had in it some thing of that spirit of bold reconstruction, which dwelt for a little while in many hearts after the Great War ended. A central body of Electricity Commissioners was to be set up, regional areas of control established, a system of large generating stations and interconnection created, and the requisite compulsory powers conferred on the Commissioners and the regional boards. But in the heavy air of the House of Lords the spirit of reconstruction fainted sooner than outside. Practically all the compulsory powers were removed from the Bill.[1] The Commission's functions were reduced to little more than giving technical advice on request. Progress under this Act, by way of voluntary cooperation, was almost negligible. The vested interests stood stiffly on their dignity and on their small monopolies. Hardly one budged. The House of Lords had given its blessing to stagnant privilege. Not for the first time.

In 1925 the Weir Committee reported that " we are neither generating, transmitting nor distributing electrical energy as cheaply as we might, nor are we consuming electrical energy to anything like the same extent as other highly civilised industrial countries ". The Committee estimated British consumption of electricity, per head of the population, at only 110 units a year, as compared with 145 in the City of Shanghai, 500 in Sweden, Norway and the United States, 550 in Tasmania, 700 in Switzerland, 900 in Canada and 1,200 in the State of California ! All these figures referred to supply from " authorised undertakers " only. If supply from private generation were added, the British figure would have been raised to about 200, and the figures for the other areas by varying, but generally smaller, proportions. In Germany at this date the consumption from all sources was probably between 300 and 400, and the spectacular electrification of the Soviet Union had scarcely begun.

British backwardness in electrification was thus revealed both as a menace to our industrial future and a disgrace to our national intelligence.

The Weir Committee recommended that more than 400 existing generating stations should be closed ; that generation should be concentrated in 58 large

[1] " The Bill emerged from the House of Lords shorn of everything calculated to effect the necessary reforms," said the British Electrical and Allied Manufacturers' Association.

selected stations, including 15 new ones ; that a high-tension main transmission system—the " Grid "—should be built, connecting the selected stations with one another and with the existing regional transmission systems ; and that to carry out this work a Central Electricity Board should·be created.

And thus in 1926 even the Conservative Government felt itself compelled to take action, and to introduce a Bill containing large elements both of Socialism and of planning. Lord Hailsham, then Sir Douglas Hogg, piloted this Bill through the House of Commons and, with his customary forensic skill, though speaking on this occasion from an easy and persuasive brief, routed those Tory unteachables, who still supported unplanned private enterprise. The House of Lords, moreover, accepted on this occasion from a Conservative Government a stronger measure than that which they had refused from a Coalition Government five years earlier.

The Electricity Supply Act of 1926 followed, in the main, the recommendations of the Weir Committee. It established the Central Electricity Board, whose members were to be appointed by the Minister of Transport, as a Public Corporation to construct and own, on behalf of the nation, the National Grid ; to be an executive body to carry out schemes of development prepared by the Electricity Commissioners ; to close redundant generating stations ; to control the operation of, though not to own, the selected stations ; to buy the entire output of these stations ; to pass it, where necessary, through the Grid, and sell it in bulk to " authorised distributors ". The Board has power to borrow up to a limit fixed at present at £60 millions, and the amount of the Board's Stock now outstanding is just under £50 millions, repayable by cumulative sinking funds within periods varying up to sixty years from the date of issue. The stockholders are pure rentiers, having no power of control and no right of foreclosure. The Treasury may guarantee the principal and interest of the Board's loans, but has not done so hitherto.[1]

This Act has already brought about a striking transformation. In spite of its limited powers, the Board has already accomplished great things.[2] By the aid of the Grid and by closing down a large number of small stations, it has greatly improved the load factor in the selected stations, that is to say secured a more even distribution of demand over the twenty-four hours. By this means, and by the construction of a small number of new stations of high generating power, it has substantially lowered the average cost of generation. It has standardised frequency throughout the country, and planned supply in nine out of the ten areas into which England, Wales and Scotland have been divided. Only the North Scotland area, containing a population of less than a million scattered over an area of more than 20,000 square miles, remains without a plan.

The construction of the Grid was completed before the end of 1933, at a cost of just over £26½ millions, a sum less than the estimated saving during the next ten years in capital expenditure on generating stations and plant, which the Grid will render unnecessary. In 1930–1 over 45 per cent of the total plant installed in public generating stations was held in reserve. With the Grid in full operation, it is estimated that this proportion can be safely reduced to 15 per cent.

Almost alone among British industries, electrical energy has increased uninterruptedly throughout the

[1] With the result that the Board has to pay slightly more for its money than most Local Authorities.
[2] See the *Annual Reports of the Central Electricity Board*, especially the Fifth Report for 1932 and the Sixth Report for 1933, from which I have taken some of the particulars which follow.

trade depression. Since the Central Electricity Board came into existence, the figures have been as follows, in millions of units, excluding current privately generated :

1927	8,234	1931 11,431
1928	9,073	1932 12,241
1929	10,294	1933 13,554
1930	10,914	

Thus in six difficult years the annual consumption of electricity increased by more than 60 per cent. Between 1929 and 1933, since the onset of the depression, the British output increased by nearly 30 per cent, while that of the world as a whole increased by less than 5 per cent and in many countries seriously diminished. The rate of increase, moreover, in British output is still rising, the consumption for the first nine months of 1934 showing an increase of more than 16 per cent over the same period in 1933. This is good evidence of the practical utility of planning, even in an incomplete form in a single industry.[1]

The success of this instalment of socialisation is a strong argument for going farther along the same road.

The chief defects of the present position are the following. The Board, though it owns the Grid, does not own the generating stations. It controls the selected stations, which are owned, some by private companies, others by local authorities. Many of the

[1] While visiting the Soviet Union in 1932, I mentioned, in the course of a conversation, this steady increase in the British output, even during years of deep depression. The Russian Communist, with whom I was talking, was completely incredulous. " Your Government may say that," he answered, " for propaganda purposes. But we know better." He had been taught that British capitalism was on its deathbed and that there could be no recovery, not even in electrical output. The Marxian Seminaries oversimplify reality. They can't see the trees for the wood, and even the wood is half hidden in a doctrinal early morning mist.

latter have been handicapped in extending business and reducing costs by being limited to their municipal areas.

In addition to the selected stations there were still in 1932 nearly 4,000 privately operated generating stations used by industrialists, many very small and uneconomic, which still account for nearly a third of the total electric energy generated in Great Britain. They are outside the control of the Board and the Commission. Their substitution by selected stations is proceeding, but only slowly. The total number of stations closed, as redundant, between 1927 and 1933 was 146.

The distribution and sales organisation remains in the hands of more than 600 authorised distributors, again outside the control of the Board and the Commission. Many of these are inefficient and unenterprising.

The prices charged by different distributors vary inordinately from less than $3d.$ to more than $9d.$ a unit for lighting and domestic supplies, and from less than $1d.$ to more than $6d.$ for industrial supplies. The Board, through the Grid, is reducing, and will continue to reduce, generating costs. But these account for only half the price to the consumer. The rest is due to distribution costs which are hardly falling at all, and cannot fall greatly unless distribution, like generation, is brought under unified national control, and small and uneconomic units are eliminated. Barely a third of the population is at present using electricity for domestic purposes, even for lighting alone. There is here a vast unsatisfied potential demand, which, if it were tapped, would give a greatly improved load factor, and so help to reduce cost. The large number of distributors seriously hinders the standardisation and cheapening of apparatus.

The Labour Party, therefore, proposes that a

National Electricity Board should be established, to be appointed, as the Central Electricity Board now is, by the Minister of Transport, and to take over the duties both of this Board and of the Electricity Commission. The National Electricity Board should own, not only the National Grid, but also all selected generating stations, and should have power to acquire all or any privately owned generating plant. And it should take over, and become responsible for, the whole business of the authorised distributors. The Minister of Transport would be responsible for the broad lines of policy, the Board for the effective direction and management of the service. The House of Commons would receive full reports of the Board's work, and could discuss these, and also the general policy behind them, on appropriate occasions.

The Minister of Transport should also appoint a National Consultative Committee, consisting of representatives of various interested parties, such as Local Authorities and industrial and domestic consumers. This Committee would meet at regular intervals, and would afford opportunity for full and frank discussion with the Board. Complaints could be ventilated and proposals made and examined.

The Board would, no doubt, find it convenient to set up regional administrative machinery, especially for distribution, though generation would tend to become more and more concentrated.

It should be a primary duty of the Board to promote the increasing use of electricity, both in urban and in rural areas, both for industrial and agricultural power, for lighting, public and private, and for an ever widening variety of domestic purposes. The development of an effective sales and service organisation, far ahead of anything now existing, is essential.

The policy of charging uniform prices throughout the country for electric power, as for postal services, or at least of adopting a uniform schedule of prices, varying with consumption, is simple, intelligible and fair. It averages costs of supply over all purchasers and all districts.

As a factor determining the location of industry and population, the cost of power and light would then be eliminated. Other factors would then determine it, including the steady pressure of geographical planning.[1]

A unified and socialised service could at once begin to move towards a uniformity of prices, starting with heavy cuts in areas where prices were highest. In many of these areas, hitherto starved of electricity, there would be an immediate and cumulative response in increased demand.

As with broadcasting, so with electricity, there is a strong case for socialising also the manufacture of equipment and appliances. But, compared with socialising electrical supply itself, this is not urgent.

Socialised electricity is one of the keys to planned prosperity. The service of electrical supply must first itself be planned. But this is only the beginning. The Electrical Plan must dovetail into, and facilitate, the National Plan as a whole.

This little island, with its short distances and its great coal supplies, is ideally suited for intensive electrification. Cheap electric power is one of the surest roads to a permanent lowering of the costs of production throughout British industry.

Cheap electrical energy will be one of the motive forces that will break up our overgrown cities and industrial towns, scatter our population and our industries in smaller and healthier communities, sweep the skies clear of smoke, restore the sunlight that the smoke has blocked, save needless toil and dirt not only in the factory and on the farm but, even more important in terms of human values, in the home. We should

[1] See Chapter XXVI.

apply a substantial part of the financial resources devoted to the National Plan to the rapid extension of electrical supply.

Here we can learn a lesson from Soviet Russia. Lenin's formula, Electrification plus Soviet Power equals Socialism, has become classical. He taught the Russians to plan electrification on a gigantic scale. This has been a central feature both of the First and of the Second Five-Year Plans, and it has been one of the outstanding successes of these programmes. Starting from a very low level, the output of electrical energy in the Soviet Union reached 7,000 million units in 1930, 11,000 millions in 1931 and 17,000 millions in 1932. It is planned to reach 100,000 millions in 1937. Allowing for current privately generated in Great Britain, the total output at the end of 1932 was about equal in the two countries, with the Russian increasing considerably faster. The annual consumption per head of the population over the whole Soviet Union, including the vast undeveloped Asiatic areas, was about 100 units in 1931, as compared with 375 in Great Britain. Whether the tremendous increase contemplated in the Second Five-Year Plan will be accomplished, remains to be seen. But in the judgment of a British electrical expert [1] who has studied the Russian achievements on the spot, " the First Five-Year Plan of electrification has undoubtedly been fully, or more than fully, achieved ". Included in the Second Five-Year Plan is the electrification of 12,000 miles of railway track, equal to nearly half the total track mileage of the British railways.

These are the ripening fruits of one man's bold conception of a Socialist future. The late Arthur Cook once described himself as " a humble disciple of Lenin ".

[1] Mr. T. G. N. Haldane, from whose interesting essay on *Power and Industrial Developments*, in *Twelve Studies in Soviet Russia* (Gollancz), I have taken the figures quoted above.

He met with jeers. If, indeed, justification is not by faith, but by works, Lord Hailsham, the sponsor of the Conservative Bill of 1926, has claims, of which he may be unconscious, to the same title.

Nor is the Soviet Union the only country from whose electrifying energy we have something to learn. In the United States, out of the great variety of policies pursued by the Roosevelt Administration, one of the most striking is the programme for new publicly owned hydro-electric power stations. This is taking shape first in the river valleys of the Tennessee and the Columbia. Other similar schemes are to follow. Each is designed to be a focus of economic and social planning in the surrounding area. "I want to make the American people dam-minded," said the President in a speech in the summer of 1934.

Or let us turn our eyes to Canada. The Ontario Hydro-Electric Power Commission has had a longer run than either Lenin's or Roosevelt's projects. This is a wonderful advertisement for Socialism in action. Canadian public enterprise on the northern shore of Niagara has far outdistanced American private enterprise on the southern. The Province of Ontario, both in its urban and its rural areas, is now intensively and very cheaply electrified. The Commission, a Public Corporation appointed by the Provincial Government, was set up in 1910. At first it supplied current to twelve municipalities, in 1928 to 550. In 1910 it generated a thousand horse-power, in 1928 a million. To-day it owns and operates ten large power stations based on the waters of Niagara. It has financed itself by loans issued by the municipalities it serves. A large part of these loans has been paid off out of the Commission's series of budget surpluses. And the prices charged have steadily fallen, as demand has grown.

British electric energy must be predominantly based on British coal. Compared with countries more mountainous or possessing more rapidly falling rivers, our water-power resources are slight, though both in Scotland and North Wales they make a contribution now, capable of some increase. Tidal water power is a resource for the future. The Severn Barrage scheme, after long expert inquiry, has been declared practicable, and likely to be a cheaper generating agent than coal.[1] But the time for mobilising this reserve is not yet. The cost of bringing it into play would be large. And we must add to this, in framing a true social balance sheet, the cost of further wastage in the South Wales coalfield, whose product would be largely displaced. In a later phase of British Socialist planning, when these devastations of unplanned capitalism have been repaired, it may have an important place. But to-day and to-morrow coal will make our power.

[1] See Report of the Severn Barrage Committee, 1933. The Committee estimated that a net annual output of 2,207 million units could be generated from a tidal power station at the barrage and that the cost of such power would be only two-thirds of that generated at a coal-fired station of equal capacity.

CHAPTER XIII

TRANSPORT

FROM power to transport is an easy transition. These are the twin key industries in an organised modern society, the two levers which move the complex mechanisms of our material civilisation.

In Britain the future prospects of transport as a whole are still bright. But some sections are in the shadows. This is due not only to the likelihood of further technical progress, which may put them out of date, but to a deeper cause, the lack, in our present arrangements, of conscious co-ordination based on any plan.

There has been much talk and writing in recent years on British transport problems, a number of inquiries, including a Royal Commission which sat for three years, from 1928 to 1931, and a little legislation. But the solution of these problems tarries. The Labour Party has indicated its view of this solution in a pamphlet on *The National Planning of Transport, the Case for the Unification and Co-ordination of British Transport*.[1]

Nor should any serious student of the subject miss Mr. Herbert Morrison's book on *Socialisation and Transport* (Constable, 1933). Mr. Morrison has in his mind a clear and realistic picture of Socialism in action, and he succeeds remarkably in conveying this

[1] Published by the Labour Party, 1932, price 2*d*. I have drawn freely on this pamphlet in the course of this chapter.

picture to the minds of his readers. It is not necessary to agree with every detail of the argument, nor with every emphasis, to appreciate this contribution highly.

There are five principal transport agencies to be considered, the railways, road transport of goods and passengers, coastwise shipping, canals and other inland waterways, and air transport. The fourth of these is in decline, incapable of much rejuvenation, the fifth still in its infancy, but growing fast.

The old idea, that free competition between private rivals is socially advantageous, is increasingly discredited in the world of transport.[1] Co-ordinated planning is essential to the public interest.

The history of British railway development does not flatter private enterprise. Especially in the second quarter of the nineteenth century there was a flood of company promotions " good, bad and indifferent ", to quote the report of the recent Royal Commission on Transport. " Extremely high prices were paid for land to buy off the opposition of influential landowners and meet claims for compensation in respect of depreciation, real or fancied, to estates and the destruction of amenities." Abnormally heavy Parliamentary costs were incurred, as the result of the cumbrous Parliamentary procedure and the extortionate charges of the lawyers. All this was paid for with money subscribed by investors. Most of the companies, therefore, were badly over-capitalised from the start. Some of the more prosperous watered their capital later, hoping thereby to conceal the extent of their profits. Nominal capital was often increased, without fresh borrowing or increase of real assets. £100 of

[1] Mr. Morrison in Chapters IV and V of *Socialisation and Transport* develops a most powerful argument, on grounds of efficiency of service, against free competition and in favour of consolidation. This argument is illustrated from the history of London transport, but is of more general application.

stock, getting a dividend of 8 or 9 per cent, was transformed by a mere stroke of the pen into £200, getting a dividend of 4 or 4½ per cent. The shareholders' income was the same as before. But the new and lower rates of dividend looked more modest and respectable, and could be quoted to justify resistance to claims for lower fares or charges, or for higher wages and better conditions of employment.

Pre-war conditions of employment on the railways are now generally admitted to have been a disgrace to the Companies, which in those days refused all recognition of Trade Unions, on the ground that " discipline " would thereby be undermined, and the physical safety of the travelling public imperilled. It needed a strike, in 1911, to shift the Companies from this primitive standpoint. The Railway Trade Unions are responsible, not only for great improvements in the working conditions of their members, but also for stimulating the Companies to greater enterprise. When trade is bad, the line of least resistance in the minds of capitalist employers is to cut wages. If Trade Unions resist, employers are led to explore other roads to lower costs or to increased demand.

The Railways Act of 1921 merged more than 120 separate undertakings, many extremely backward and inefficient, into four large Companies, the Southern, Great Western, London, Midland and Scottish, and London and North Eastern. But why stop at four? Why not have merged those four into one? Not because the problems of unified administration and management would have been more intractable: many would have been simpler and easier. Rather because the authors of this Act deluded themselves into the belief that competition between the Companies was, within limits, healthy and would, within these healthy limits, continue. Further, because they shied at the thought of a single private monopoly, even under public regulation, and shied still more violently at the thought of a public monopoly of railway transport. The much bolder conception, advocated to-day by the Labour Party, of a public monopoly, uniting under a single direction many forms of transport, of which the railways would be only one, did not, one may be sure, occur to their minds as a practical possibility. The rapid growth of road traffic since 1921 has put many new ideas into circulation. But the Railway Companies have had less than their fair share of these. Their directorates are costly and top-heavy. Between them the four Companies have close on a hundred directors, drawing fees of close on £100,000 a year, an average of £1,000 a year each.[1] Nearly all are pluralists, holding a number of other directorships simultaneously.[2] Most, it may be suspected, are mere passengers on the railway Boards, and few can claim any practical knowledge of transport questions. Each of the four Boards has its contingent of well-known Conservative politicians, able to speak as " representing the Railway Companies "—this is a familiar and well-accepted Parliamentary phrase—when their Bills

[1] Thus in 1931 the Southern Railway had 17 directors, the Great Western 25, the L.M.S. 23 and the L.N.E.R. 26, a total of 91. The directors' fees paid out during the year were, for the Southern £18,000, for the Great Western £24,100, for the L.M.S. £26,200, for the L.N.E.R. £21,000, a total of £89,000. In 1930 the total number of directors was 93, and the total of directors' fees £104,000. Thus it would be untrue to say that the directors had contributed nothing to economies in railway costs.

[2] To take a few outstanding examples, Sir George Courthope, M.P., a director of the Southern, held 18 other directorships, Sir Robert Horne, M.P., a director of the Great Western, held 13 others, Sir John Beale and Sir Thomas Royden, directors of the L.M.S., held 25 and 13 others respectively, and Sir C. C. Barrie, M.P., a director of the L.N.E.R., held 34 others. What minute fraction of their time and mental energies, one wonders, are these gentlemen able to devote to railway problems ?

come before either House of Parliament. These political representatives lack candour, or a sense of humour, when they object to Socialism on the ground that it involves control of business by politicians, or to Trade Union representatives in politics on the ground that they speak for a sectional interest.

Whenever I return from abroad, I feel a sense of patriotic shame at the spectacle of the average British railway station. Our stations, especially in the large towns, are a national disgrace—dark, dirty, dingy, draughty, inconvenient and ugly ; cold antiquated waiting-rooms, with prehistoric furniture ; bad buffets and unsatisfactory and expensive restaurants, where no one would eat unless compelled by circumstances. The United States, Switzerland, Sweden, Germany, to mention only a few foreign examples seen with my own eyes, leave us far behind. No wonder the British railways have lost traffic to the roads! " Why are so many of their stations the picture of misery ? " asks Mr. Morrison. The railways must be put in a position, he argues,

> to brighten themselves up, to electrify, and to convert that large number of dreary unattractive-looking buildings called railway stations into that centre of cheerfulness, brightness and social life—the transport station of the future, meeting the requirements of road and rail.[1]

The electrification of the railways has been delayed, partly by lack of enterprise in the railway managements, partly by difficulties in the way of raising new capital, owing to the poor state of railway finances, partly by fear of the effects of competition by road transport.

The Southern Railway, which has steadily electrified a growing mileage on its suburban and semi-suburban lines, is an honourable exception. And it has found

[1] *Socialisation and Transport*, pp. 83 and 102.

that electrification has paid handsomely. Electrification of the railways may be defended on three main grounds. First, it would lower operation costs and enable a faster and more frequent service, both for passengers and goods, to be provided. Second, by abolishing smoke from steam trains, it would promote cleanliness and comfort, both on the railways themselves, particularly in tunnels, and in the neighbourhood of railway lines. Third, it would cheapen electric energy, both to the railways themselves and to all other users of electricity.

The first argument is very strong as regards suburban and other short distance traffic of high density. British experience, though limited, is already conclusive on this point. As regards main line and long distance traffic, of lower density, the Weir Committee on Main Line Electrification reported in 1931 in favour of a scheme of complete electrification, to be accomplished in a period of fifteen to twenty years. They recommended that the railways should be supplied directly from the Grid by the Central Electricity Board. They put the capital cost of electrification to the railways at £261 millions, and to the Central Electricity Board at £80 millions. They estimated that, without assuming any increase in traffic, the railways would secure a return of about 7 per cent on the capital cost which they would incur. This return would be higher if traffic increased. The financial advantages of electrification would be cumulative, as we approached the completion on a national scale of the substitution of steam haulage by electricity.

With the rate of interest standing, as it did in 1931, at 5 per cent, a minimum rate of return of 7 per cent on electrification would give a minimum surplus of 2 per cent. Since the Committee reported, the rate of interest has fallen to about 3 per cent. This raises the minimum surplus to 4 per cent, and greatly strengthens the financial basis of their argument. They estimated that the expenditure of £261 millions by the railways and £80 millions by the Central Electricity Board, if spread over twenty years, would find employment for 60,000 men a year throughout this period in the electrical and allied industries, and in the iron and steel, the structural and building and other industries. As against this there would be a gradual reduction in the railways' locomotive staff. But this should come about, not by dismissals, or down grading, but by limitation of new recruitment and proper arrangements for superannuation. There would also be some reduction in the demand for coal, in so far as a smaller quantity would be required for electrical than for steam haulage of a given traffic. But, as against this, more coal would be required for the electrical haulage of a larger traffic, for the carrying out of the electrification programme itself, and through the general increase in economic activity which railway electrification would directly and indirectly stimulate. A total expenditure of £341 millions is large. But it is less than the £500 millions which was spent on roads in the ten years 1921–31.

Railway electrification is an outstanding example of a great public work of national development, which should be put in the forefront of a Labour Government's Development and Employment Programme. But the improvement which it would bring to the financial position of the railways must not accrue to the advantage of the private shareholders. For under private ownership the railways, except to a trifling extent, have neglected electrification. It is, therefore, a necessary condition of its adoption that the railways should at the outset pass into public ownership and into a co-ordinated system of national transport.

The second argument for electrification, the abolition of dirt from smoke, is obvious. The benefit will accrue not only to all who use and work the railways, but to all who live and work in close proximity to railway lines.

The third argument, that the cost of electrical energy will thereby be cheapened, both for the railways and for all other users of electricity, depends on attaching the railways to the Grid. This would much improve the load factor in the national generation of electricity, of which the railways might be expected, according to the Weir Committee, to use as much as twenty per cent. This improved load factor would cheapen the cost to all consumers, especially in rural areas, where the transmission lines to railway sub-stations could be cheaply tapped. The increased demand due to the railways would, moreover, necessitate the construction of new generating stations, which could produce electric power more cheaply than even the best selected stations can do now.

This third argument has great weight as against the rival claims of the Diesel electric locomotive, which has lately received much publicity. These may well be better than steam locomotives for work on branch lines with low density. But it is significant that the railway companies have not brought Diesel locomotives into use, as they could easily have done, in place of steam locomotives. This fact suggests that it is "improbable that the large savings claimed by the manufacturers of Diesel engines would, in fact, be realised." [1]

The railway companies own a number of subsidiary properties, which contribute to their profits,—docks and harbours, steamboats, hotels and road transport. Their road transport interests, acquired since 1928 when power was obtained from Parliament to "get on the roads", consist partly of road transport services

[1] *Socialisation of the Electrical Supply Industry*, by G. H., p. 102 (Gollancz, 1934), an admirable short study.

operated by the companies themselves, partly of holdings in road passenger transport concerns. This brings me to the second principal transport agency, road transport.

The increase in the number of motor vehicles, both for passenger and goods transport, has been and still is very rapid. Legislative regulation, beginning with the Labour Government's Road Traffic Act of 1930, is being developed, but is still far from being fully effective, either as regards service to the public or conditions of employment, particularly for transport of goods. Hours and wages on the roads should be brought up to the standards of the railways. Otherwise no proper comparison of costs and efficiency can be made. At present road transport is in a state of uneconomic competition, both within itself and with other forms of transport, leading among other consequences to unnecessarily heavy costs of road maintenance, much avoidable congestion, and a great number of accidents. But the Transport and General Workers Union, under the bold and energetic direction of Mr. Ernest Bevin, is rendering great services, not only to road transport workers, through the improvement and standardisation of their conditions, but also to the efficiency of road transport organisation.

Canals and inland waterways in this country will have only a limited sphere in the future. Coastwise shipping is a more important factor. Often it is the cheapest form of transport. But co-ordination with other forms of transport is essential, if money is to be spent on reconditioning some of our ports and harbours.

Air transport is now supervised by the Air Ministry. As will be argued in a later chapter, civil aviation should be internationalised. But, pending this development, there should be close national co-ordination, under the joint control of the Ministry of Transport and the Air Ministry.

The Labour Party proposes to set up a National Transport Board, to be appointed by the Minister of Transport and to be responsible, subject to the general policy laid down by the Minister and approved by Parliament, for the efficient management and direction of British transport as a whole.

The Statute setting up the Board should provide that the latter should take over forthwith the railways, including all their subsidiary properties, and certain sections of road transport, and should give powers to take over later any other transport agencies, which it was administratively practicable and convenient to bring into national ownership. The Board would be directly responsible for all nationally owned transport. It would also be empowered to exercise indirect control, by licensing and other modes of regulation, over privately owned transport. Local forms of transport owned and operated either by Local Authorities, or by private persons within their areas, would continue in most cases undisturbed. Local Authorities might, indeed, often increase their purely local transport services. But they would consult with the National Transport Board, and there would be some measure of national regulation. I add, to avoid all misunderstanding, that private motor cars would not be nationalised.

The Board would have to find solutions for many difficult problems of co-ordination, management and development. The detailed nature of these solutions cannot, with any practical advantage, be debated now. But certain general principles can be laid down.

The primary aim of a public transport monopoly would be, not profitmaking, but efficient public service. As Mr. Morrison puts it, we

> must think more and more in terms of transport as a whole, and less and less in terms of railways, road transport, canals, coastwise shipping and airways; and we

must handle our transport organisation with directness and decision, instead of assuming that by accident and good luck the provision of transport by competitive scramble will somehow work out for the best. Once we have done that, we can pursue the sensible course of enabling each form of transport to serve in the field where it is best fitted to serve. There are transport needs for which the railway is not the best medium; for example, light traffics, branch routes connecting sparsely populated areas or rural areas with the great towns; door to door deliveries for moderate distances; and so on. There is a field within which road transport is unquestionably superior to the railway, just as there is a field within which the railway is superior to road transport; so with the canals; so with coastwise shipping. A unified, comprehensive transport system would concern itself primarily, not with capturing traffic for this or that form of transport, but with determining the most economical and efficient method of meeting this or that public requirement.[1]

The Labour Party proposes that, as in the case of electricity, there should be set up a National Consultative Committee, consisting of representatives of various classes of transport users, of Local Authorities and other special interests, to confer with the Board from time to time, and ventilate complaints and suggestions. Also that full reports of the work of the Board should be published and presented to Parliament, where they would be subject to discussion and criticism on appropriate occasions, as would the Minister of Transport's general policy, of which the Board would be the executive agent.

Possibly some form of quasi-judicial tribunal should be set up to deal with appeals concerning charges and facilities. But this raises wider issues concerning national planning.

National control of transport charges, as of elec-

[1] *Socialisation and Transport*, pp. 88–9.

tricity charges, will be an important factor in national, and especially in geographical, planning. From the point of view of agriculture in particular, the present charges, especially on the railways, frequently discriminate against home produce in favour of imports. This is an objectionable form of inverted protection which should disappear.

The London Passenger Transport Board illustrates planning within a comparatively small but densely populated area. The Board owns and operates all underground railways, trams and omnibuses in the London Traffic area, and co-ordinates these with the main line railways in the area. Its members are appointed, not by the Minister of Transport, as Mr. Morrison's Bill of 1931 originally provided, but, under an amendment made by the National Government, by five Appointing Trustees.[1] This is a bad arrangement, which makes it difficult for public criticism to play effectively either on the Board or on the Trustees who choose its members. There are other points for criticism in the present London Transport scheme, but it is an important step along the right road.

[1] The Chairman of the London County Council, a representative of the London and Home Counties Traffic Advisory Committee, the Chairman of the London Clearing Bankers, the President of the Institute of Chartered Accountants and the President of the Law Society—a motley and inappropriate crew !

CHAPTER XIV

COAL AND ITS PRODUCTS

IF power and transport are the twin keys to modern civilisation on its material side, neither can turn, in this country, without coal. Compared with coal, imported oil is still a minor factor. As the symbol of our national wealth, the Woolsack, like much else in the House of Lords, is more than a century out of date. For the last hundred and fifty years at least the Lord Chancellor should have sat upon a Coalsack.

The history of the British coal industry has a quality of its own, epic and grim ; tyranny and toil ; capitalist exploitation—of man, mineral and natural beauty—at its most ruthless and its ugliest ; class cleavage at its sharpest.

No one who has known British miners, and has had the good fortune to form friendships among them, can think of any other section of the community quite as he thinks of them. There is a sturdiness in them, a directness, a courage, a mass comradeship, that makes them stand out from the rest. In the hell of war there were no braver soldiers than the miners. And still, in the purgatory of peace, except when unemployment brings him unwanted safety, the miner is always in the trenches, risking life and limb day by day in the darkness below ground. And both in political and industrial battles, fighting for better conditions, the miners and their gallant women folk have, for more than a generation, been the shock troops of the Labour Movement.

The pitman, like the landworker, lives mostly in small remote communities, far from the noisy self-concern of cities, closer to nature. As an unemployed Durham miner told a journalist from London:—" you can go to the end of any street here, and see the country and, you know, it has a cleaning effect." [1]

The Labour Party has long been pledged to socialise the mining industry. There will be some stiff initial problems. This industry is chronically depressed, and carries a mass of unemployment, of which neither electricity nor transport has any equivalent. Its future prosperity, and its contribution to the national prosperity, is even more conditional than theirs on unification within a Socialist framework, and planned co-ordination with related industries. Even so, any great expansion, in terms of numbers employed, in coal mining in the narrower sense, as distinct from coal treatment, is not likely. Rather the reverse. But, as the late Arthur Cook was one of the first to foresee, we may build a higher standard of life within the old industry for a smaller number, and create new outlets, especially in the new industries of coal utilisation, for men displaced and for the rising generation.[2]

[1] From an article in *The Times*, March 21, 1934.
[2] Particularly urgent in the mining areas, in view of the heavy weight of immobile unemployment, is the raising of the school-leaving age and the provision of retiring pensions for elderly miners. I have heard it suggested that boys leaving school at sixteen would be less willing than at fourteen to follow their fathers down the pit, if there are alternative employments open. If so, in the years to come we may reverse, in favour of the miner, the present harsh operation of the law of supply and demand, and consolidate a higher standard of life on the basis of a reduced and reluctant labour supply; men may have to be tempted down the pits by wages high enough and hours short enough to compensate them for the greater risk and toil and dirt of hewing coal than of working above ground. And this would be plain social justice.

COAL AND ITS PRODUCTS 131

By common consent of all except the coal owners, the mining industry is one of the least planned and least efficient products of modern British capitalism. A succession of Commissions and Committees have looked into it, in whole or in part, and with varying degrees of emphasis have condemned its present practices. Notably the Sankey Commission of 1919 and the Samuel Commission of 1925. More recently the Coalmines Reorganisation Commission, which was appointed under the Coal Mines Act of 1930, but has hitherto, owing to the resistance of the coal owners and its own hesitations, done very little reorganisation, has passed the following judgment.[1]

> The picture presented by the greater part of the industry is one of haphazard development of each coalfield by a large number of unco-ordinated units brought into existence on no rational plan, nearly all working below capacity, competing suicidally, whether in capital expenditure or in prices or both, for a market that cannot absorb the product of all.

They add that, even if these defects were removed by appropriate structural changes, " the present system of mineral ownership would stand in the way of effective and lasting reorganisation " ; and express the pious hope that " Parliament will presumably remove sooner or later—whether by nationalisation or by some less sweeping reform—this impediment ", of private rights to royalties and wayleaves, carrying rights of veto over all proposed developments.[2]

[1] In a Report published on December 20, 1933.
[2] The National Government has passed an Act to socialise all oil and natural gas which may hereafter be found beneath the surface of this island. Lord Londonderry, whose family for generations has waxed fat on coal royalties, defending the Bill in the House of Lords on April 19, 1934, spoke as follows: " I need hardly tell your lordships that, with the very strong views I hold in connection with the rights of

Let us give an illustration from South-West Durham. Here a whole chain of pits have been closed and abandoned through the failure of a number of colliery companies to co-operate in installing a central pumping plant for this area. The need for this and its practicability were recognised by all the companies, but no agreement could be reached for sharing the cost. So nothing was done. Soon afterwards a pit near the head of the water closed down. The next pit thereupon got more water than it could deal with. It also closed. The next followed; and the next; until a series of six or seven pits, several of which still contained large quantities of workable coal, were all drowned out. If they are not properly pumped, the water will endanger a number of other pits farther to the east, which are still working. Already it has increased their working costs.[1]

The Reorganisation Commission's condemnation of haphazard development applies no less to coal treatment and by-product works than to coal getting.

The Labour Party's policy regarding coal must deal, therefore, both with the coal industry in the narrower sense, and with coal treatment. As regards the former, the industry must be socialised, all coal becoming the property of the State, and all the assets of the colliery

private property, I have been very exercised in my mind over this measure. But I have come to the very definite conclusion that, in this connection, these rights, which may be said to exist over royalties, must give way to the interests of the country in ensuring the exploitation of a commodity on which so much of our national well-being depends, from the commercial standpoint as well as from the point of view of national defence." " So much ! " How much ? Infinitely less than on coal.

[1] This example of private " enterprise " is common talk in this part of County Durham. It is graphically described by Mr. Thomas Sharp in his striking picture of *A Derelict Area : A Study of the South-West Durham Coalfield* (Hogarth Press, 1935).

companies, as such, likewise passing into public ownership. I say " as such ", because a number of private concerns now combine the ownership and management of collieries with other industrial activities, e.g. in the iron and steel trade. This may make for capitalist convenience, but under socialisation would make for muddle. The iron and steel industry should be separately reorganised, and the collieries separated from the present mixed undertakings. Colliery companies' by-product plants, on the other hand, should be appropriately organised in connection with coal treatment as a whole.

The constitution of the socialised coal industry should probably provide for a decentralised administration, separate coalfields having a large measure of autonomy, subject to central control, and Pit Committees being established at each pit with appropriate functions, especially as regards safety.[1] Each new mining disaster, with its tale of death and heroism, shocks public opinion for an instant and draws charitable subscriptions for the dependants of the victims. But most, if not all, of these disasters could by proper precautions be prevented.

In each department of this new industrial constitution, at the pit, in the district and at the centre, the mining community should, through appropriate arrangements, exercise its proper share of authority and take its proper share of responsibilities. And there must be central planning of the industry as a whole.

It is, I believe, a great mistake [says Mr. Peter Lee]

---

[1] During the present year, 1934–5, the National Executive of the Labour Party and the General Council of the Trade Union Congress are re-examining the details of such a constitution at the request of, and in consultation with, the Miners' Federation. The scheme submitted in 1925 by the Labour Party to the Samuel Commission was published under the title, *Coal and Commonsense*.

to close down any mine before all workable coal has been extracted. So long as our national needs can be met by the coalfields already operating, no new coalfields ought to be opened out. But as the old ones become worked out, it would then be time to commence new ones, and the miners who had become unemployed could be transferred to the new pits.[1]

There is great force in this argument. Unified public ownership of all coal, and the adoption of central pumping and other co-operative devices, will make a great difference to the practical definition of " workable coal ". On a long view, it is not in the national interest, either that workable coal should be abandoned, or that we should use up our coal resources recklessly and wastefully.

The opening of the Kent coalfield, for example, has probably been premature. Certainly its development should not be pushed forward to the neglect of coal measures which are still workable in the older fields.

Mr. Lee's words have another lesson. To-day large mining populations hang miserably around closed pits, in the hope that these will one day re-open. Often they do re-open for a while, then close again. In recent years I have seen pits in County Durham open and shut, and open and shut, like the jaws of a tired man yawning. The present position is, from the community's, and still more from the miners', point of view, intolerable. There is no one to-day who can make an authoritative declaration that such and such a pit will never work again. Under a unified public ownership, such a declaration must, where necessary, be made promptly, and proper provision made for the workers affected.

Coal distribution, both wholesale and retail, must be reorganised. Local Authorities should, as recommen-

[1] General Secretary's *Quarterly Report to the Durham Miners' Association*, May, 1934.

ded both by the Sankey and the Samuel Commissions, be given power to deal in coal within their areas, though in many cases, where the Co-operative Societies are able to act as efficient distributors, such powers should not be exercised. This is a matter for friendly adjustment, in the light of varying local conditions, between the Societies and the Authorities. A unified selling agency, or Export Board, should be set up to handle coal exports.

I turn to coal treatment, hitherto shamefully neglected and its small beginnings even more haphazard and unco-ordinated than coal getting. "There is blood on the coal," as Robert Smillie used to say. But there is a wonderful store of wealth inside it. Burnt raw, in our bad, dirty, un-neighbourly old British way, most of this wealth is worse than wasted.[1]

I have argued elsewhere in this book for the establishment in the mining areas of a number of large-scale publicly-owned plants for the extraction of oil from coal. Several strong lines of argument converge in support of such a programme. Those who now occupy the highest posts of responsibility in the Miners' Federation, men like Mr. Joseph Jones, the present President, and Mr. Ebby Edwards, the present Secretary, are wide awake to these possibilities. The Executive of the Miners' Federation stated in their report to their Annual Conference at Edinburgh in July, 1934,

> the petrol industry is already an enormous one. But we look forward to the day when the vast majority of the workers will have motor-cars, and when a consider-

---

[1] We have made little or no progress, in spite of much talk, since about 1920 in smoke abatement. The London area, in particular, is stagnant. The number of domestic fires burning raw coal has been allowed to increase. See the gloomy official reports of the Investigation of Atmospheric Pollution, issued by the Department of Scientific and Industrial Research.

able proportion of the population will fly their own aeroplanes. What a stimulus would be given to the coal industry if the major portion of our future petrol requirements was obtained from British coal.

Within the framework of a national plan for coal utilisation, the various processes of treatment now in use, and others which scientists may add to them, should not be regarded as rivals, so much as complements. Each process yields different products.

Even with a very rapid increase in electrification, the gas industry should still have a big future. But its old method of high temperature carbonisation, yielding only gas and coke, is of less social value than low temperature carbonisation, yielding smokeless fuel that will burn freely in an open grate, as well as gas and tar, which in turn yields oil of good enough quality to secure contracts from such fastidious buyers as the Admiralty and the Air Force.

But smokeless fuel is the principal product of this process and we must seek to cheapen its cost of production and make a large and steady market for it, especially in substitution for the raw coal of domestic fires.

The hydrogenation process can probably be expanded even more rapidly. Its principal products are petrol and fuel oils, for which the future market, if properly organised, should be practically unlimited. The cost of producing motor spirit by this process has been reduced from 2s. 6d. to 8d. a gallon in the last seven years, and should be susceptible of further reduction. The National Government has conferred a practical monopoly in this sphere on Imperial Chemicals, which holds all the relevant patents, and has been guaranteed protection, through the present duty on imported oil, for a term of years. This stimulus is on much too small a scale, and goes to swell the profits of a private concern. A Labour Government should extend it to the new publicly owned oil-from-coal plants proposed above.[1]

We should spend freely on research and experiment in the uses of coal. The valuable activities of the Fuel Research Board should be greatly extended. The possible utilisation of small coal, having little value for burning raw, should be fully explored. And so should other processes, including pulverisation, on which some experts build high hopes.

There is a further wide range of coal products, which should be systematically exploited under a national plan : pitch for road making and briquetting, with large possibilities of export ; tar acids, yielding drugs and dyes and bakelite, which is already used increasingly for wireless and electric fittings, telephone receivers, etc. Here we have the basis for several important industries, which could conveniently be established, close to the pitheads and the coal utilisation plants, in the depressed mining areas.

To organise coal treatment and its many component industries within a national plan, is a great constructive task for the next Labour Government. Maybe some of these projects would need, in the early years at any rate, some form of subsidy, direct or indirect. Subsidies to-day are in fashion. Farmers and landlords, shipbuilders and shipowners, and the miscellaneous crowd of manufacturers and others, who are the beneficiaries of tariffs, quotas, derating, income tax remissions and the like, receive them from the National Government. Objection to subsidies, in principle, is a relic of individualism. But subsidies should carry

[1] As regards patents, the Patents and Designs Act of 1907 provides that " any Government Department may at any time use the invention for the service of the Crown on such terms as may be agreed on with the approval of the Treasury between the Department and the patentee, or, in default of agreement, as may be settled by the Treasury, after hearing all the parties interested."

with them public control and should fit into a plan which serves the public interest.

A well devised scheme of encouragement to coal treatment would not only lay the foundations of new production and prosperity, but would save money to the Treasury, the Unemployment Fund and the Local Authorities in mining areas. Encouragement could, perhaps, best be given by increasing the present import duties on petrol and other oils, while leaving home products untaxed.[1] But there are many other alternative methods.

The unified planning of coal extraction and treatment, as a single public enterprise, though with many parts, will facilitate many adjustments now impossible. The charging, for instance, of lower prices, in towns at any rate, for smokeless than for smoky fuels. We should aim at driving smoky fuel right out of use in all large centres of population.[2] A national coal authority could not only play on demand through this instrument of discriminating prices, but could conduct a vigorous campaign of anti-smoke propaganda, advertising the practical virtues of smokeless fuel and facilitating its supply.[3]

[1] Other considerations favour such a step. A slight increase in the price of petrol would help to check the disproportionate increase, now tending to take place, in road transport. Again, the British motor industry is to-day handicapped in its export trade, which might grow very rapidly, by taxation based on horse power. Such taxation, it is argued with great force, discourages the production of many types of car suitable for export. Hence a change over, partial or complete, from horse power to petrol, as the basis of taxation, could be so arranged as both to bring in more revenue and stimulate this promising branch of export trade.

[2] But this will take time, and we must avoid action that will raise the cost of fuel to those who have no practical alternative to raw coal. There is much to be said for subsidising, at any rate until new habits become established, a low price for smokeless fuel.

[3] All Government and Local Government offices might set an example in burning smokeless fuel.

Unified planning would also allow of another form of price adjustment, to which the miners rightly attach great importance. This relates to the prices paid for raw coal by the various branches of the coal treatment industry. These in the past, like the " transfer prices " charged inside mixed undertakings, e.g. for coal transferred from the collieries of such an undertaking to its own iron and steel plant, have often been too low. Thus wages at the colliery have been kept artificially low and losses have been alleged by the employers in respect of this branch of their business in order to create artificially high profits in other branches. A unified system must transmit prosperity from coal treatment to coal getting. Of the fruits of planning and public enterprise the coal hewer must have his fair share.

CHAPTER XV

OTHER CASES

ELECTRICITY, transport, coal and its products; these, according to current opinion in the Labour Party, would stand early in the list of enterprises to be socialised by the next Labour Government. They are all ripe for this change. But there are many other cases, either equally ripe, or nearly so, or even now ripening before our eyes. The land I discuss in the next chapter, financial institutions in the next Part, of this book. Others I shall mention in this chapter. But only an unrealistic pedant would set down in print, in advance of the occasion, any precise list of priorities. Even private and unpublished conclusions on priorities must remain provisional, until the opportunity for action comes.

We must not pitch our programme low, or prepare ourselves to be content with slowly crawling forward. The next Labour Government must start off with a well-planned rush. "My advice to you is, 'be audacious'," said Mr. Lloyd George to the Labour Party nearly twenty years ago. That was good advice, and it is time we took it.

On the other hand, as I have said already, we need not waste time now debating the details of Utopia, or the problems of a completely Socialist society. We shall have our hands, and minds, full of preliminary work for some while yet.

Opinion, fortified by experience, is setting strongly

OTHER CASES 141

in our direction. The case for Socialism is to-day becoming a commonplace in ever-widening circles.

> In the last few years [says Sir Arthur Salter] we have seen broadcasting, London Passenger Transport and (though less completely) electricity made public services. There are vast spheres of enterprise ripe for a similar treatment; other forms of insurance, transport, the sale of munitions, the distribution of the main necessities of life, and others. . . . We should certainly, I think, be able to bring more than half the country's economic life under public ownership and management, and throughout the whole of this sphere we could, by familiar methods, secure a progressive equalisation of incomes, stabilisation of employment, the lowest prices which large-scale organisation without the toll of large private profits could make possible, and at the same time give to the majority of the nation the satisfaction of feeling that they are working for a public service from which private profits had been eliminated.[1]

This is good enough to be going on with!

Practical Socialists often make a division of industries and services into three broad classes: those already ripe for socialisation; those not yet fully ripe, because less important or less unified, but requiring some measure of reorganisation and public regulation; and those, of comparatively minor importance, which may at present be left under completely private enterprise.[2]

[1] In a broadcast talk, published in *The Listener* of December 12, 1934, under the title, " Planned Socialisation and World Trade ". He continues: " I believe that, even in the sphere in which private enterprise remains, the State . . . must plan, control and in broad outline determine the direction of the development which takes place. . . . I contemplate a rapid increase of socialisation, both in the extension of the public services and in the purposive direction of public control of all those activities which are left to private enterprise."

[2] See, for example, a *Report on the Public Control and Regulation of Industry and Trade*, submitted to the Trade Union Congress in 1932. Also *For Socialism and Peace*, pp. 9-10.

How fast we shall be able to move, in dealing with cases in the first two classes, will depend, as I have argued earlier, both on our own qualities and on the political and economic situation in which we find ourselves. But the speed both of socialisation, and of reorganisation under public control, is likely, I think, to accelerate after the resistances of the initial period have been overcome. The earlier cases handled will serve, in large measure, as precedents for the later. The friction of political opposition may be expected to diminish, and many honest doubts to disappear, as the novelty of the process wears off and an increasing number of working models become established ; provided always that they show good results in practice, better service for their consumers and users, better conditions and status for their workers. With plain men, only inefficiency can discredit Socialism in action.

New socialised enterprises must become accepted and accustomed elements in the social environment and, once they reach this stage, they will be reasonably secure of continuance. Not even the typical Tory, nor the reactionary National Government, proposes to-day to denationalise the Post Office,[1] or the Royal Dockyards, or to disestablish the Central Electricity Board or the London Passenger Transport Board, or the B.B.C., or to narrow the present legal range of municipal activities. All these are now accepted things.

I do not, therefore, fear, subject to this essential condition of Socialist efficiency, any general reversal

[1] Quite the contrary. "The Post Office is a prosperous institution, and the public, no less than its own staff, appreciate and benefit by the efficiency of its administration. Itself a trading concern, it has given a fillip to commercial enterprise, and by improvement of its services is contributing to the commercial efficiency of the country." (*The Times*, leading article on December 14, 1934, in praise of Sir Kingsley Wood, Tory Postmaster-General and ornament of the Anti-Socialist Union.)

of further acts of socialisation, if, some years after their performance, a Labour Government were succeeded, temporarily at least, by a Government of the Right. The progress of Socialism, in terms of concrete achievement, will tend to move the centre of gravity of political thought farther to the Left. At each succeeding stage the Right will want to stand still, the Left to continue the Leftward journey.

In some cases we can proceed in one step to a fully socialised constitution. In others, socialisation must come by stages, and be preceded by reorganisation with a measure of public stimulus and control. Here, as regards procedure, there is no need for uniformity. But the initial step might often be the appointment of a small body of Commissioners, with power to make orders for reorganisation, including the amalgamation of many small units into a few large ones. Such Commissioners could be set up without legislation and their draft schemes or orders submitted to the appropriate Minister, and by him, amended if necessary, to Parliament. It is worth consideration whether some body of Commissioners, in the form of a permanent Industrial Reorganisation Commission, to act in appropriate Sub-Commissions, if necessary with co-opted members, should not be established as a section of the National Planning Authority proposed in a later chapter.

As a general rule, when the total scale of any private industry or service becomes considerable, the continuance within it of a large number of small independent units becomes either impracticable or undesirable. Either there is a drive within the industry itself towards some form of combination into larger units, or there is wasteful competition between small units at a low level of efficiency. Either, therefore, the industry takes steps to consolidate its own structure, or public authority is forced to intervene for the same purpose. But in either event consolidation brings an increasing element of monopoly, an increasing private power to control output, or price, with a view to higher profits. This situation calls for counter-control in the public interest.

Moreover, self-consolidation by capitalist interests, even if it results in greater efficiency, is apt to be open to grave objection. Recent developments in the iron and steel industry illustrate this. The interests of the workers in the industry have been subordinated to those of the shareholders.

> There have been certain crude attempts at what has been termed " rationalisation ", but without any . . . proper conception of the objective to be attained. There have been amalgamations of financial interests without, in most cases, the necessary financial adjustments. Labour has been rationalised, but not financial commitments.[1]

Further,

> the " rationalising " methods of private enterprise . . . disregard social obligations in respect of the effect upon local communities by the closing of works without any pre-considered arrangements as to the disposal of the labour displaced.

The most shocking, and now notorious, example of this disregard is the town of Jarrow, ruined by rationalisation in the shipbuilding industry.

It follows that, in any industry of importance, the process of consolidation, once begun, must be subject to deliberate planning, both of the industry as a

---

[1] *What is Wrong with the British Iron and Steel Industry?* (issued by the Iron and Steel Trades Confederation, 1931, price 2*d*.), p. 13. This criticism regarding finance, it is interesting to observe, is also made in an article by a Special Correspondent in *The Times*, August 16, 1933, on " Iron and Steel, the Waste of Duplication ".

whole, including its skilled labour force, and of its place in a larger national plan, which shall have regard, among other considerations, to the most desirable location of industry. Consolidation, if successful, will strengthen and simplify the structure of an industry, and will accelerate its transition to a socialised constitution.

But often the public hand must give the initial push towards consolidation. The iron and steel trade has needed some pushing, and even a threat by the Government to withdraw the tariff protection recently given to it, unless it took quicker steps to put its house in better order. " Owing to the excessive individualism still cherished by many of our industrialists, the industry has found it extraordinarily difficult to adapt itself to post-war conditions." [1]

In iron and steel unification has now gone some distance. A practical scheme for its transformation into a Public Corporation was submitted to, and approved by, the Trade Union Congress in 1934. This Corporation, it is contemplated, would work through a series of Sectional Boards for each of the large divisions of the industry.[2]

Armament firms, included in this industry, stand in a special position. The Labour Party, on grounds of international policy to be discussed later, is committed to the abolition of the private manufacture of arms. The delimitation of arms manufacture, which, when socialised, should probably be organised separ-

[1] *The Times* leading article, August 16, 1933.

[2] The Report suggests " ten or a dozen " separate Boards, e.g. for pig-iron, ingots and semi-products, tinplates, etc., " the precise demarcation being a technical matter which would be determined by those who are charged with the direction and conduct of the industry. Each of these sections should have a considerable degree of internal antonomy ", and should, where necessary, have regional sub-divisions.

ately from the rest of the industry, would naturally be made at those points in various industrial processes, where only arms can be intended to result. If we begin to take account of possible "convertibility" of plant, we shall embark on an indefinite extension of the field.

Arms manufacture is certainly ripe for socialisation. The iron and steel industry as a whole is ripe, at any rate, for the setting up of the outer framework of socialisation, though, within this, there may need to be a series of gradual adjustments rather than an immediate reorganisation, as in the case of coal.

But all deposits of iron ore in this country should pass into public ownership, and the mining section of the industry be co-ordinated with the manufacturing sections.

Shipbuilding and heavy chemicals have both reached a high stage of unification and, from this point of view, may be deemed suitable for early socialisation. Engineering, on the other hand, is much less concentrated, both technically and geographically, and would probably require preliminary reorganisation under public direction.

Similarly with the cotton industry which is still an unco-ordinated medley of units, most of which are relatively small, with a large surplus of productive capacity over any possible demand under the changed conditions of international trade. To socialise it at one blow is obviously impracticable. It must first be reorganised through the agency of a Cotton Control Board, both in respect of production and of marketing, larger units created, the contraction in its export markets met by a planned contraction in the scale of its production through the scrapping of the least efficient plant, the recruitment of new labour checked, and special provision made for the superannuation of its older workers.

The woollen and other branches of the textile industry would presumably require similar reorganisation, though their problems of surplus plant and labour are much less acute.

Insurance in its various forms is mainly concentrated in a comparatively small number of large businesses. From this point of view it is ripe for socialisation, which would bring many advantages to insured persons, remove many notorious abuses, and enable the investment of the large funds now held by the Insurance Companies to be properly co-ordinated through the National Investment Board.[1] The economies of unification are obvious, but these should not be sought too quickly at the expense of those now employed in the insurance service.

Flour milling is another industry increasingly concentrated in a few large units. It has often been suggested as very suitable for public ownership and control.

Food distribution, both wholesale and retail, offers large possibilities of economy, especially by better organisation of retailers, and of narrowing the gap between wholesale and retail prices, thus reducing the cost of living, while keeping the general level of wholesale prices steady. Here, as also in the case of flour milling, the Co-operative Movement must be brought into consultation and its legitimate interests safeguarded in any scheme of reorganisation.

The list of cases mentioned in this chapter is illustrative, not exhaustive. On some of these, further investigation is required, before the precise lines of appropriate action can be decided. The Reorganisation Commission, which I have suggested above, would be a suitable instrument for this. But it is evident that a Labour Government would have a wide range of choice in the continuance of its socialising pro-

[1] See Chapter XXII.

gramme, after the more urgent cases had been dealt with.

There are few important private industries or services in this country, which do not require, at the least, a publicly controlled measure of reorganisation.

CHAPTER XVI

THE LAND AND AGRICULTURE

THE land, which no man has created, but which forms the physical basis of our life, should belong to the community, not to a few favoured members of it. That private ownership of natural resources should give the right to large idle incomes, to profit-making by speculation in land and by holding up the public to ransom, and to the capricious private use of great areas, often in clear conflict with the public interest, is not defensible, except by sophistry. Any dramatic rise in land values is easily seen to be due, not to the activities of landlords, but to the work and needs of great populations. The value of all forms of property is socially created. But this truth is most easily recognised in the case of land.

To permit land to become private property is one of the greatest historical errors committed by governments. But it has been committed in almost every part of the world. Under the feudal system in this country lords held their lands from the Crown, in return for the performance of certain public duties. Their tenure was thus doubly conditional. The drift of law and custom, registering self-interested pressure by strong social groups, has made it absolute. The private landlord has ousted the Crown as ultimate owner, and the duties, once the condition of every " freehold ", have lapsed. The aggrandisement of sectional interests at the expense of the Crown, though often represented by historians against a rosy light of growing popular liberties, has not always been a clear social gain. Such Crown lands as survive to-day are, in effect, public land, controlled by Public Commissioners and bringing in an annual revenue of a million and a quarter pounds to the Treasury.

Private property in the land of Britain, immortalised by inheritance down the generations, has been an enduring cause of social inequality and domination. But the large agricultural landlord, in his latest phase, has generally abandoned even the function of providing capital for the upkeep and improvement of his estate. He has become only a passive, and often a plaintive, rent receiver. Recently many large agricultural estates have been broken up by sale, often to the embarrassment of tenants, and the number of owner occupiers, owning more than one acre, rose in the eight years following the War from 49,000 to 147,000.

Looking backward we can ruefully survey lost opportunities. Even so comparatively conservative an economist as Alfred Marshall was of opinion that, " if from the first the State had retained true rents in its own hands, the vigour of industry and accumulation need not have been impaired, though in a few cases the settlement of new countries might have been delayed a little ".[1] In the long run such delay would have cost nothing. It might even have helped the building of firmer social foundations in some new countries.

To hold land not as a freeholder, but as a tenant of the State, either on long lease, or on short lease with reasonable rights of security and compensation for improvements, makes little difference to the holder. But a vast difference to posterity.

Consider how British public finance would have been

[1] *Principles of Economics* (fifth edition), pp. 802–3.

transformed, if, as wealth and population and cities grew in the nineteenth century, an ever-swelling revenue had accrued to the State from its rent rolls. The rise in urban would have swamped any decline in agricultural rents. Taxation could have stood at permanently lower levels, public debt been paid off rapidly, public expenditure on social objects started much sooner and pushed much farther. And can it be supposed that, with the State as universal landlord, the idea of Town and Country Planning would not have come to life earlier, or that our industrial towns would not have grown up less, even if only a little less, drab and chaotic than private landlords were content to let them grow?

Alternatively, if land in and around growing towns had been owned by some Local or Regional Authority, rents from its leases would have replaced local rates. If the land on which London now stands had been in public ownership since even the accession of Queen Victoria, its present inhabitants would be living practically rate free, and enjoying vastly improved amenities and public services.

But the reality is different. Out of the eight million inhabitants of Greater London, only about 40,000 own any land, and only about a score of these own really valuable slices. A few years ago the Duke of Westminster owned most of the West End, but some of this most valuable estate has changed hands recently. Eight acres of Millbank were sold for a million pounds in 1930. The total value of the estate is put at about £20 millions. It was founded in the days of Queen Elizabeth, when an ancestor of the present Duke married Miss Davies, owner of Ebury Farm, whose pastures spread over what is now Belgravia.

The Duke of Portman owned more than 270 acres of valuable West End land in 1929. This estate also was founded on a farm, purchased 170 years ago when a sickly Portman was ordered a diet of asses' milk and kept a drove of asses to provide it. The Cadogan Estate in 1933 covered 113 expensive acres in Chelsea. The Howard de Walden Estate, largely sold to an Ellerman trust in 1925, covered forty acres stretching from Oxford Street to Euston Road. The price paid by the trust was said to be in the region of £3 millions. " It is only the poor individual Londoner who lives there, who has nothing to say about his city. It isn't his." [1] But a few noble families have here stumbled, prematurely, upon the Celestial City whose streets are paved with gold.

With land in public ownership and inalienable, land values, in the sense of capital values, would have no practical significance. But rising annual values would be reflected in rising public revenue from rents. Under private ownership land values, realised on transfers of ownership, have great significance. Progressive nineteenth-century opinion, shocked by the spectacle of great unearned increments, took a wrong turning. The agitation for the taxation of privately-owned land values followed a false scent. It led away from public ownership and made even some Socialists forget Socialism. For every dozen speeches made by Lord Snowden, for example, on the taxation of land values, I doubt if he made one on public ownership. Henry George, the Land Taxer, had a greater influence, unfortunately, than Arthur Russell Wallace, the Land Nationaliser, a stronger and clearer thinker, but a less eloquent evangelist.

If, when we socialise land, we must accept the practical necessity of paying a fair price, though not more, to private owners—and I shall argue later that we must—it is beyond our power, by socialisation alone,

[1] Mr. A. P. Luscombe Whyte, in an article in the *Evening Standard*, May 30, 1934, from which I have taken the preceding particulars.

to restore to the public the unearned private increments of the past. That restoration can only be made by taxation, and in particular by Death Duties. But we can secure for the public all future increments ; and we can control in the public interest the use of land, and so plan future development.

These are the two great arguments for socialising land. But they do not apply with equal force to all land. To socialise all land in Britain at one blow is a policy which has obvious attractions. But its superficial simplicity hides complex administrative problems which, if it were urgent to solve them, could indeed be solved, but only by diverting energy from more urgent tasks. A programme of practical Socialism must weigh priorities in a delicate balance. It is important to extend the public ownership of land, and to extend it rapidly. But it is much more important to extend it in some directions than in others.

In the nineteenth century it was the combined action of two forces, increasing population in a small island and increasing wealth, even though most unequally distributed, which forced up British land values, most of all in those areas where population and wealth were most highly concentrated. With the prospective decline in our population, it is doubtful whether the aggregate value of the land in Britain will continue to increase, even though average wealth should increase greatly and be better distributed. Certainly it will not grow at the old rate.[1] The abnormal chapter of the nineteenth century is closed. Some areas will rise, but others will fall, in value. These ups and downs may roughly balance. The argument for absorbing future increments points, therefore, not to wholesale, but to

[1] Our land values are not so high as might be supposed. Sir Leo Chiozza Money estimated some years ago that, in the aggregate, the land of Britain was worth less than it would cost to cover it with linoleum.

discriminating, socialisation, concentrating on those areas where increments, not decrements, are likely.

The argument for controlling the use of land goes wider. The more we plan, the more we must control. And one of the results of planning will be to determine what land is likely to increase in value.

Control of the use of land may be either negative or positive, either to prevent, or to enforce, a different use. To prevent building in order to preserve an open space, or a beautiful view, or a historic monument, is negative control. To schedule a site for building, whether of houses or factories, which otherwise would not be built upon, is positive control. A special case of positive control, of great practical importance, is to require land now used for some purpose to be used for the same purpose, but more effectively, as when slums are to be demolished and replaced by healthy dwellings, or agricultural land put into a better state of cultivation.

Modern legislation, culminating in the Town and Country Planning Act, has modified this problem. The need for control is now recognised, though the administrative machinery is slow and clumsy. And control is possible, under this Act, without the transfer of the land to public ownership.

These problems fall to be considered under the head of economic planning.[1] The argument for control, even more strongly than the argument for absorbing future increments, points to a large and steadily expanding, but not to an immediately universal, measure of socialisation. For, if one reflects on concrete details, it is clear that even the most ambitious schemes of

[1] See Chapters XXVI–XXVIII. One of the old arguments in favour of a tax on land values, that it " forces land into use ", is in flat conflict with the idea of geographical planning. Would that much land had not been forced, by economic motives, into its present use!

practicable planning would leave the use of a considerable part of the land of this country unchanged.

Most of the land already built on, for example, most of the area occupied by private gardens, and large tracts of the countryside.

The powers required for speedy socialisation have been clearly stated by the Labour Party in its Report on *The Land and the National Planning of Agriculture* (p. 7). " It is proposed that a general Enabling Act should be passed giving the State power to acquire any or all land, rural or urban, at any time after the passing of the Act, and laying down the basis of compensation to the owners." The basis suggested for agricultural land is the Schedule A assessment for income tax. Further,

> it should be the general policy to transfer to national ownership, as soon as administratively practical, all agricultural land, and the appropriate Minister should have power under the Act to issue orders, operative without further reference to Parliament, specifying as and when decided by him the particular land to be transferred.

As regards land other than agricultural, other Ministers should have similar powers, each in his appropriate sphere. There is in this procedure nothing new, except the absence of delay. It is the State's ancient Right of Eminent Domain, brought up to date.

Either the State should exercise these powers, on request, through the appropriate Minister, on behalf of Local Authorities and other Public Bodies, including the new Public Corporations proposed to be set up, or these bodies should be granted powers in their own right, of equal promptitude. Their present powers are slow and inadequate.

What should be the respective spheres of different public authorities in the ownership of land ? It is an easy exercise to make neat and tidy paper schemes. But this is not how things are done in this country. We live empirically and suffer inconsistencies gladly.

Socialism, as I have pointed out already, is quantitative. Here, as elsewhere, we shall not start from scratch. The public ownership of land is no new thing. A large area, in the aggregate, is already owned by various Government Departments, by the Commissioners of Crown Lands, by the Forestry Commission, by various Public Boards and by a great number of Local Authorities. To this we may add the land held by the National Trust for the Preservation of Places of Natural Beauty and Historic Interest and, for certain purposes, land held by educational and charitable bodies. We have not to invent, but to increase, our public estate. All these are nuclei that will expand.

There is much to be said for encouraging Local Authorities in urban areas, rather than any national authority, to become the owners of land within these areas and of outside zones, sufficient to cover their probable expansion in the calculable future. Compared with many foreign cities, we are backward in the municipal ownership of land. The City of Stockholm, for instance, owns land equal to more than four times the size of its present built-up area. Local Authorities in rural areas should also be encouraged to extend their estates, particularly for small holdings and housing schemes. Both the Forestry Commission and the National Trust should steadily and rapidly increase their acreage. And both should work in conjunction with a National Parks Commission, which should acquire and administer substantial areas.[1] These three would hold land as agents, for specific purposes, of the Central Government. So would the National Agricultural Commission, which would ad-

[1] See Chapter XXVII.

minister State farms under the Minister of Agriculture. Public Corporations and other Public Boards would likewise hold the land necessary for their own purposes. The Central Government itself, through its Departments, will, I suggest, do little actual administration of public lands, but will work through other public bodies as appropriate agencies.[1]

How rapidly will it be " administratively practicable " to transfer agricultural land to public ownership ? It is sometimes suggested that the title to all agricultural land should come under public ownership on an appointed day, even though, it is admitted, direct public management of all this land could not be introduced for a considerable time. It is also admitted that this procedure would involve great administrative labours, for which, for some little while, there would be nothing to show.[2]

It is sometimes argued, on the other hand, that public ownership should only be introduced, in proportion as the State can invest sufficient new capital to enable the land transferred to be farmed at a high level of efficiency. Socialisation, it is said, if it is to do good and be welcomed after the countryman has had a brief experience of it, must mean much more than a mere change of rent collectors. A Labour Government must be prepared to spend money freely on reorganising agriculture. At £10 an acre, not an excessive sum if big improvements are in view, £250

[1] And, in so far as it receives land in payment of death duties (see Chapter XXXIII), will transfer it to these bodies for administration.

[2] And what is " agricultural land " ? Does it include houses and gardens (if not, within what limits ?), land used for agriculture but having a building value, land not now used at all, but which might be used for agriculture ? These conundrums are only troublesome, but then they are very troublesome, if we abandon the selective method, and try to socialise " agricultural land " wholesale.

millions would be needed to re-equip our 25,000,000 acres of agricultural land. This is much too large a total to be found quickly. There will be a host of other claims on the available finance. Over the whole area of British agriculture the sums which could be mobilised, in the early years of a Labour Government, would spread so thin as to be hardly noticeable. Better take over a section at a time, and make a good job of that before going farther.

Somewhere between these two conflicting views, I think, practical wisdom lies. We must avoid a snail's pace of advance, and equally a stupid administrative choke-up.

But too much debate on this one point of policy is a mistake. The Labour Party must be ever on its guard against seeing agriculture through a townsman's eyes. It must cherish its growing agricultural contingent, and take their guidance on emphasis and priorities. Public ownership of the land is not well chosen as the chief theme of a speech at a village meeting. The countryman's primary interest, if a farmer or a small-holder, is in prices, especially of what he sells. Hence his interest, late though it has developed, in Marketing Schemes and his willingness to sacrifice a little of his individualism on the altar of better and steadier cheques. Nor is it hard to stir his interest in credit; what he could do with money, if he could get it cheap and plentiful; how the banks charge too much and lend too little.

But ownership is secondary. If he is a tenant, he would only be paying rent to a different landlord, who might treat him better or worse. If an owner-occupier, probably still in debt to a bank for the purchase of his land, under duress, when prices were high, he might not disapprove a change of tenure which would wipe out that debt and leave him less burdened than now. But he will be doubtful whether this is really the

Labour Party's intention. If he owes the bank nothing on his land, he will probably dislike a change.

The agricultural worker is interested in his work,— he is still a skilled craftsman, not yet, with few exceptions, a mere machine minder ;—in his wages and conditions ; in his cottage and garden, and its tenure, tied or free ; in the prices of what he buys ; and in the fact that, when he draws no wages, he draws no unemployment benefit either.[1] These interests are primary in his daily life, these and the changing weather, which rules his work and its fruits, unlike the townsman's. Through these primary interests any live political appeal must strike. But a change in the ownership of land—he owns none himself—seems a remoter question, on a lower plane of meaning. Let that come after, he will be inclined to argue, but let other good things come first.

Therefore, to press the socialisation of agricultural land too hard, relatively to other items in the Labour Party's agricultural programme, will create in the countryside a sense of unconvincing irrelevance.

This programme covers a wide field.[2] It includes the creation of a National Agricultural Commission, under the Ministry of Agriculture, to administer nationally owned land, to establish, where suitable, large-scale State farms, generally to plan agricultural development, and to work through County Agricultural

[1] It is now anticipated that the National Government will introduce in 1935 a scheme of unemployment insurance for agricultural workers. It is one of the many humiliating memories of the second Labour Government that Mr. Snowden was allowed by his colleagues successfully to resist this proposal, though Dr. Addison, at least, fought hard for it.

[2] I only enumerate here the main heads of policy, which are developed in detail in *The Land and the National Planning of Agriculture*. See also, as regards the past, an excellent pamphlet on *What Labour has Done for Agriculture*, by George Dallas (Labour Party, 1*d*.).

Committees, whose members would include, as well as other "persons of experience", farmers and agricultural workers nominated by the Minister from panels submitted by their respective organisations; the maintenance, through Marketing Boards and, if necessary, by the regulation of imports, of reasonable prices, free from short term fluctuations; the narrowing of the gap between prices on the farm and in the shop; the raising of wages, and the transfer of ultimate authority from County Wages Committees to the National Wages Board; unemployment insurance for agricultural workers; the building of a large number of houses in the villages and the abolition of the tied cottage system; adequate water supply for the villages; more small holdings; improved credit facilities for farmers and smallholders; rent courts for tenants; land drainage on a large scale; the vigorous promotion of afforestation; better and cheaper facilities for transport and electric power.

There is no impossibility in making the countryside prosperous, and giving the agricultural worker his fair share of that prosperity, against a background of more varied amenity and greater social equality than he has ever yet known. But his prosperity depends on that of the worker in the towns, who is the chief purchaser of his produce.

CHAPTER XVII

WORKERS' CONTROL OF INDUSTRY

BOTH in the socialised sector of our economic life and in the still unsocialised sector, the principle of workers' control will seek its application. It will find it, I believe, in many forms, and through a great variety of industrial constitutions, not static and final, but changing in response to practical experience and growing working-class ambitions.

A society, which fails to provide for industrial self-government, lacks one of the essential elements of economic democracy. " Nor can it be imagined," said Mr. Walter Citrine recently,[1] " that the worker will be content to remain a mere hewer of wood and drawer of water. The principal factor which has emerged in Trade Union policy over the last twenty years is the demand for some share by the workers in the control of industry. Already in such matters as recruitment, dismissals and working conditions the Unions are exercising a considerable measure of control in individual firms. Furthermore, while they recognise that technical, commercial and financial matters are primarily questions of skilled management, they have the feeling that, even in this realm, some measure of consultation is imperative."

In the non-socialised sector, these are questions to be decided primarily between Trade Unions and

[1] In a broadcast talk on " The Future of Trade Unionism ", June 28, 1934.

Employers' Associations. Parliament might, indeed, assist by requiring employers to constitute Works Councils, with defined minimum functions, and by enforcing greater publicity regarding costs and the results of trading. But it is clear that, within the framework of capitalist industry, workers' control, though it can make substantial progress along the lines indicated by Mr. Citrine, is subject to strict limits. In socialised enterprises, on the other hand, these limits are shifted outwards.

One of the strongest driving forces towards Socialism is the conviction, widely held, that only in a Socialist society can labour cease to be a mere commodity, bought and sold in the market, hired and fired at the will of the boss; that only in such a society can the worker be fully endowed with human dignity and civic status.

> During the struggle to obtain increased power over their workaday lives (says Mr. John Cliff) and to secure a progressive increase in their standard of life, the workers have learned many important lessons, the most valuable of which is expressed in their demand for the Socialisation of Industry. One of the main objects underlying this demand is the abolition of servitude and the securing of free and full citizenship in Industry.[1]

A practical issue, which in the last few years has caused some division of opinion both in the political and the industrial sections of the Labour Movement, relates to the mode of selection of the Central Board of a Public Corporation. Members of such Boards, it is agreed, shall be appointed on grounds of ability and willingness to perform the necessary duties. But who shall be the judge of ability? The responsible Minister

[1] *The Workers' Status in Industry*, p. 5 (published by the Labour Party and containing two statements, from somewhat different points of view, by Mr. John Cliff and Mr. Herbert Morrison).

alone, or the Minister in consultation with others, and in particular with the Trade Unions having members in the industry ?

Mr. Herbert Morrison has been the principal advocate of the former view, which has also been supported by some Trade Union leaders. Others have supported the latter view, and have emphasised the claim that the Trade Unions in the industry should have a statutory right to be consulted and to make nominations.[1]

In these discussions, as is natural, points of difference, rather than points of agreement, have been stressed. I doubt whether, when we reach the stage of action, any important disagreement will remain. Mr. Morrison, in my judgment, is right, when he argues that the Board, responsible for the conduct of a socialised undertaking, should not be composed of representatives of sectional interests ; that such a composition would be destructive of drive, efficiency and a unified outlook on the problems of the enterprise ; that what is needed is to pick the best men to do a big job well. Equally he is right in saying that many of these men are to be found in the ranks of the Trade Union, Co-operative and Labour Movements, a rich source of administrative ability, practical knowledge, sound judgment and constructive energy, hitherto almost untapped in the making of similar appointments.[2] And he is right in

[1] In addition to the pamphlet on *The Workers' Status in Industry*, already mentioned, see the reports of the proceedings at the Labour Party Conferences and the Trade Union Congresses in 1932 and 1933, and Chapters VIII–XIII of Mr. Morrison's book, *Socialisation and Transport*.

[2] That it remained almost untapped during the second Labour Government helps to explain the atmosphere of the present controversy. Neither Mr. MacDonald nor Lord Snowden, in particular, took trouble to become acquainted with such men. They preferred, each in a different way, other social types and other company. Lord Snowden reached his

saying that such men should be appointed on their own merits. On the other hand, I think that those are right who hold that " labour in the industry " should not be regarded as a mere " sectional interest ", but, rather, as an organic part of the industry, the foundation on which the whole productive structure rests. That some of the appointments to the Board should be made only after consultation with the Trade Unions in the industry is, I think, a reasonable requirement. But if, as Mr. Morrison fears, other interests, properly called sectional, seek to make this a precedent for special representation for themselves upon the Board, their claims should be firmly resisted.

So much for the Central Board. Similar provisions should apply to the appointments to Regional Boards, or Boards dealing with particular branches of the industry.

Wages and conditions of labour would be negotiated between the Central Board and the representatives of the Trade Unions, subject to such co-ordination as might be necessary in the interest of the Government's Economic Plan as a whole.

There should, moreover, be regular consultation between the Board and the Trade Unions in the industry, and devolution of appropriate functions to smaller local units, Works Councils, Pit Committees and the like. Through these the individual worker, manual and non-manual alike, could play his part in industrial self-government and make a contribution, in addition to that of his labour, to the efficiency and smooth running of the industry, and to the convenience and safety of those engaged in it.

climax of detachment from Labour opinion, in reappointing to the Public Works Loans Board the aged and egregious Lord Hunsdon who, in a well-remembered speech, had compared British miners, on strike against wage reductions, with Germans in war time, equally " enemies of this country ", who, he urged, should be starved into surrender.

The degree of workers' control, and the methods of securing it, will vary from one industry to another, and with the stage of socialisation reached, both in the industry directly concerned and in the economic life of the country as a whole. Neat and tidy schemes, intended to be of universal and eternal application, full of precise percentages and particulars, are the creations of theorists, soon knocked out of shape in practice.

Beyond this a wider question opens out, that of the future place of Trade Unionism in a Socialist society. In proportion as they gain a higher and more responsible status, Trade Unions will assume new positive functions. The negative function of defending the interests of their members against exploitation will, indeed, continue, though its performance, we may hope, will become much easier. But, in addition, Trade Unions will, I think, more and more become Professional Associations, concerned with maintaining a high level of qualifications and of efficient public service by their members, and with promoting research and technical training, for which, with the Governing Board of the industry and with other appropriate bodies, scientific and educational, they should share responsibility.

All skilled occupations should increasingly become professions and, with the progress of science and education, all occupations should increasingly become skilled. And the skilled manual worker should take his place in the new society, side by side with doctors and dentists, architects and accountants, scientists, teachers and lawyers, as a public servant and a professional man.[1]

Some fear that workers' control will tend to strengthen technical conservatism in industry, and that new

[1] Mr. Tawney in *The Acquisitive Society*, Chapter VI, has a good discussion of this prospective development.

and better methods of production will be discouraged. Greater efficiency by way of labour saving, in particular, will, it is said, be resisted. This fear can only be removed, if industry is so organised as to make suitable provision for men displaced, to control recruitment, to adjust the age of entry and retirement, and to ensure that increased productivity, due to new inventions, results, not in more unemployment or in higher dividends to shareholders, but in more leisure and a rising standard of life. And industry, to be so organised, must first become a public service. Nor can any single industry deal with these problems unaided. To solve them we require not only socialisation by compartments, but a General Plan the main lines of which I shall attempt to sketch in later Chapters.

CHAPTER XVIII
TERMS OF TRANSFER

THE question of the terms of transfer of property from private to public ownership is not new. But it was reconsidered at the Southport Conference in 1934, when a report entitled *Public Ownership and Compensation*, presented by the National Executive, was accepted by an overwhelming majority.[1] It had also been approved by the General Council of the Trade Union Congress, with whose Economic Committee it had been discussed by representatives of the National Executive.

The argument of the report, now the accepted policy of the Labour Party, may be briefly summarised as follows.

Property rights are derived from the State and based on the law, which may at any time be changed. The community is fully entitled to demand the surrender to itself, in the public interest, of any part of the property rights of any of its members. Taxation, whether assessed on income or capital or local rateable value, is a constant illustration of this principle.

When, therefore, the community decides to perform an act of socialisation and to transfer to itself any part of the capital wealth of the country, it has the right to require individuals to surrender some part of the privileges which the State has hitherto accorded to them. But the choice of method is fundamentally

[1] See pp. 247-50 of the *Report of the Southport Conference* for the text of the Report, and pp. 191-9 for the debate.

important, in order that the transition to Socialism may be effected as smoothly, efficiently and rapidly as possible. For this purpose it is essential that, as between individuals, the State shall act in a way which appears to the ordinary man and woman reasonable and just. This is the argument which turns the scale against proposals for confiscation, either complete or partial, of private property rights in any particular undertaking which is to be socialised.

To such confiscation, large numbers of people, and not only those directly affected, would take violent objection. A state of mind would be created among property-holders, both large and small, which would prevent the Government from raising loans, either for ordinary Government finance or for national development and employment.[1] The conduct of all industry and trade still left in private hands would be seriously disturbed, additional unemployment created, and all new development checked. Further, the confiscation of property belonging to foreigners might cause grave international trouble, might result in the economic boycott of this country by foreign States, and might even lead to war.

These are major objections, all severely practical. But there are others. The method of confiscation both discriminates unfairly between individuals, and unfairly fails to discriminate, where it would be right to do so. As between two individuals of equal wealth, one holding property in an undertaking selected for socialisation, the other holding property elsewhere, confiscation discriminates unfairly. The latter's pro-

[1] I argue at some length in Chapter XXV that only by a vigorous policy of national development, which must for practical reasons be mainly financed by loans at the outset, can a Labour Government hope to make a large and rapid impression upon unemployment, and to create favourable conditions for the successful start of newly socialised undertakings.

perty is untouched, the former's is confiscated, in whole or in part. The ordinary person will see in this something flagrantly unjust. Nor can any good reasons be advanced for favouring an investor in a boot factory, a rubber plantation, a diamond mine or a night club—none of which are likely to be early objects of socialisation and some of which represent investments outside the country,—as against the investor in a railway or a colliery company.[1]

Again, as between two individuals of unequal wealth, where there should be discrimination in favour of the poorer, the method of confiscation fails to make it. All railway shareholders, for example, would suffer confiscation equally, including railway workers, many of whom have, in fact, put their savings into the enterprises in which they work, " widows and orphans ", Trade Unions and Friendly Societies. All these would suffer, equally with the large private shareholder.[2]

These are some, though not all,[3] of the grave disadvantages of the method of confiscation. It might be necessary to face them, if socialisation by any other method were impossible. But it is not. There is an alternative method, which starts with the payment of compensation on fair and equitable terms,—the pay-

[1] As Major Attlee, reported in the *Daily Herald* of May 28, 1934, truly said in a speech at Birmingham : " by confiscation you do an injustice to the holders of the particular class of property that you want to nationalise. We have to carry the mass of the people with us, and the people are very sensitive to any actual injustice ".

[2] There are no fewer than 820,000 shareholders in the railways, a high percentage of whom may be classed as " small investors ". Even in the Bank of England there are more than 14,000 stockholders, more than half of whom own less than £500 of stock.

[3] Those who both proclaim their fear of the growth of Fascism in this country and advocate Socialism with confiscation as a means of preventing such growth, lack all sense of reality.

ment, in other words, of a reasonable price, but neither more nor less than this, for property which is socialised.

> The compensation to be paid [the report proceeds] must depend on the general circumstances prevailing at the time of socialisation. The basis of compensation might well be the reasonable net maintainable revenue of the undertaking concerned, having regard also to any financial benefit already conferred upon it by tariffs or any other form of Government assistance. . . . The basis of compensation having been arrived at, the former owners will be paid not in cash, but in bonds or other form of scrip on which they will be entitled to receive interest. But this interest will not go on in perpetuity, so as to create a permanent rentier class claiming for ever from the community a tribute of a large share of the productive effort of the people. In some cases compensation may be paid in the form of terminable annuities. In others suitable arrangements will be made for amortisation, so that the financial liability may be cancelled after a term of years. The State will be able to assist in extinguishing this liability by applying part of the proceeds of the death duties, or other taxation on capital, to this purpose. Such taxation will be graduated according to the total amount of capital held by individuals, and not according to the form in which it is held. It should be understood that the bonds or scrip would not give voting power or any form of control over the socialised undertaking; nor would they confer on the owners any power to exercise any right of foreclosure.[1]

And thus

> a newly socialised industry will immediately secure the benefit of the improved credit due to its status as a public undertaking and this will result in reducing over-

---

[1] The phrase "reasonable net maintainable revenue" is further explained on p. 250 of the *Report of the Southport Conference* and on p. 15 of the Labour Party's Report on the *National Planning of Transport*.

head charges. As time goes on and the industry grows and the process of amortisation described above takes effect, the financial position will be further improved. When the extinction of all outstanding scrip is finally completed, the whole proceeds of the industry will become available to be used as may be considered best, in improving the conditions of the workers, in giving better service to the public, and in building up publicly-owned reserves for the development of the industry and of the economic life of the nation as a whole.

Having thus summarised the policy of the Labour Party, I proceed to add some comments of my own. This policy will reduce to a minimum the chance of serious political and economic " sabotage ", and will raise to a maximum the opportunity of quickly stimulating employment in the non-socialised, as well as in the socialised, sector. These are two very weighty considerations. Neither the idea nor the practice of compensation is new. Public Authorities in this country have always paid for private property acquired for public use, and the Labour Party, in resolutions passed at its Annual Conferences from time to time, has accepted the necessity for such payments. Socialisation is not a glorified snatch-and-grab raid, first on this industry and then on that. It is an orderly process of rebuilding our economic life.

The practice of confiscation, unfortunately, is also not new. It has often been practised by property owners against the community. Public Authorities have often paid far too much for private property acquired, especially for land.

We must stop such confiscation by private interests and see that future terms of transfer are " fair and equitable ", not only to the previous owners but to the community.

The terms of transfer, or methods of compensation, may be of several alternative types. It would be a mistake to select at this stage any one of these as always preferable to the others. The Labour Party's policy is wise in leaving the choice open, to be determined, when the time for action comes, in the light both of the general circumstances of that time and of the particular circumstances of the various undertakings to be socialised.

The terms of transfer, in particular cases, may take some time to work out in detail. They may be the subject of negotiation with the interested parties, or of examination before some form of Arbitration Tribunal. Such a Tribunal should be composed of persons of appropriate experience, e.g. in accountancy, acting within general instructions given by Parliament. As socialisation proceeds, precedents will be established and the work of such a Tribunal will be accelerated and simplified.

We should not grudge time spent in getting a good settlement, fair both to the community and to the various groups directly affected, including the workers in the socialised industry, whose prospects of improved conditions of employment will be compromised, if compensation is excessive.

But we should grudge time spent in delaying the essential act of socialisation, and the reorganisation to which this act should be the prelude. When, therefore, it is decided to socialise any particular undertaking, the effective transfer of authority should be made as soon as possible, even though the financial terms of transfer may not have been settled in detail. Pending such settlement, the property owners affected should continue to receive the same income as before, measured by their average receipts over a preceding period of years.

Payment of compensation may take four forms, or any combination of these four. First, a lump sum down; second, a lump sum deferred; third, a terminable annuity, with no repayment of principal at the end of the term ; fourth, a perpetual annuity, or, what amounts to the same thing, an annual payment for a term of years, plus repayment of principal at the end.

The first method is only of limited application. But it might be applied, for the benefit of small property owners only, in cases where other methods were adopted for the rest ; also in suitable cases for clearing off comparatively small blocks of equity shares.

The second method relieves the socialised industry of all burden of compensation for a term of years. A deferred lump sum payment, due to be made at some future date, has of course a present capital value, and the prospective recipient could sell it, if he wanted ready cash, or a present lump sum to invest. But the deferred lump sum would naturally be larger, by the amount of compound interest during the period of deferment, than the lump sum down. This amount measures the cost of deferment, that is to say, of throwing forward the burden of compensation to a future date. This method has received less attention than, in my opinion, it deserves. It might be used occasionally.[1] The lump sum might, in suitable cases, be made payable on the death of the private owner, and set off against his death duty liability. This would mean the shouldering by the State of the compensation charge, and a loss, in the future, of some death duty revenue. But this loss could be recovered by raising the rates of duty when the lean years came.

The third method, that of terminable annuities, is superficially attractive. But, if partial confiscation is to be avoided, the annual payment, under this method, will be larger than the annual payment under the fourth method, that of a perpetual or redeemable annuity, since it will include a " redemption factor ", or

[1] e.g. when land is acquired for National Parks. See Chapter XXVII.

element of sinking fund. This method, therefore, is less elastic than the fourth method, and imposes a heavier burden on the undertaking in the early years of socialisation, which may be very inexpedient. I incline to the view that it will be better to introduce terminable annuities by another route, through a development of the death duties.[1] It is of fundamental importance, for a Socialist aiming at greater social equality, that there should be no eternity of tribute to rentiers, either in respect of compensation arrangements or of private property generally. And a reformed system of death duties is the best means of preventing this.

The fourth method is the traditional method, which has generally been adopted hitherto. But there should be power to redeem the principal or any part of it— to be determined, if necessary, by drawing bonds by lot—at any time, on short notice, so that the socialised enterprise may be able to take full advantage of any conditions favourable to redemption, e.g. any surplus available for this purpose, or any fall in the rate of interest, permitting of a favourable conversion, and bond-holders be prevented from pocketing an unearned capital appreciation.

The further question arises, whether the socialised enterprise shall meet the cost of its own compensation charges, or whether the State shall shoulder these, in whole or in part. I believe that the answer to this question also will vary according to the general circumstances of the future, and the particular circumstances of different enterprises. We should not, at this stage, lay down any rigid rule. Nor need there be uniformity of practice. In some cases, the State might properly guarantee the prescribed payments, though the socialised enterprise would be expected to make them from its own revenue. But, with this added security, the payments would be smaller and

[1] See Chapter XXXIII.

the socialised enterprise would benefit by the saving. Such guarantees, however, if put behind too large an aggregate of payments, would lose their potency, lower the national credit and handicap national finance generally.

It has been suggested that the whole of the compensation charges should be met by the State from the national budget. In the early stages of socialisation, I believe that this arrangement would be both unwise and impracticable. It would swamp the budget by heavy new charges which would necessitate increases in taxation, probably so large as to be impracticable at the outset. It would have a fatal tendency to slow down the pace of socialisation by entangling it with other budget questions. We should have to choose, for instance, between more socialisation and better social services. And it would be inequitable as between different socialised industries which would be relieved in proportion to their compensation charges, or, roughly speaking, in proportion to the capital taken over. The railways, for example, would secure a much greater relief than the coal mines.

This simple formula, therefore, should be rejected, at any rate until socialisation has been accomplished over a wide field and Socialist economic planning has become a working reality. At that stage, we should be free to reconsider the question.

But, within narrower limits, the State may, I think, make some contribution at an earlier stage. It is contemplated, in the Report setting out the Labour Party's policy, that the State might devote part of the proceeds of the death duties, or other taxes on capital, to reducing the capital liability of socialised undertakings. Part of the death duties might be payable in the bonds issued by these undertakings, to be cancelled on receipt by the Treasury, or to be replaced by bonds bearing a lower rate of interest, payable to the Treasury. This would only be an extension of the present practice, whereby death duties may be paid by handing over certain Government securities. Again, in regard to mining royalties, compensation for which has been resisted, on principle, by the Miners' Federation, any payment, which it might be found expedient to make to the royalty owners, might be made a national charge, to be extinguished within a short term of years, not by the mining industry, but by a special addition to the taxation of the rich. The equivalent of the present royalty payments could thus be released for the benefit of the mining community, for the provision of retiring pensions and for the welfare of the mine workers.[1]

In so far as graduated taxation is applied to the wiping out of compensation charges, it can be claimed that, without the inequity inherent in confiscation, the capitalists are compensating one another, and the big capitalists are compensating the small ones, just as under the present licensing law the brewers, by a levy to which they all contribute, compensate one another for the suppression of redundant licences.

The socialisation of this or that industry or service will not, immediately and of itself, do very much for greater economic equality. Let us be blunt about this.

[1] Mining royalties stand, for more than one reason, in a special position among private property rights. They have been subject since 1909 to a special national tax of a shilling in the pound and since 1926 to a further levy of a shilling in the pound for pit-head baths. In view of the past history and present condition of the mining industry, there is, in my opinion, a strong case for a substantial increase in these levies before any question of assessing compensation on the net income from royalties is considered. The Annual Conference of the Labour Party in 1927 adopted a scheme for miners' pensions, to be financed in part by a levy on royalties. This was a commitment which the second Labour Government, to the deep regret of many of us and in spite of our private protests, failed to honour.

But it will prepare the way for, and make easier, other action in this direction. By putting an end to unlimited profits and to many forms of financial manipulation, it will close some of the avenues, some of them very shady avenues, which lead towards great fortunes. It will divert future surpluses and windfall increments to social purposes, and it will facilitate a taxation programme designed to reduce great inequalities.

The Labour Party's proposals, on compensation as on other questions, will no doubt be misrepresented. Attempts will be made to frighten the electors, particularly those who are small property owners.[1] The Runciman shock to confidence trick will be played again. Some of our opponents are very frank. "Fear is our trump card," wrote a budding Conservative politician, the son of Lord Hailsham, a little while ago, in one of those gentlemanly monthly magazines, which are read in the clubs of Pall Mall. But, if the Labour Party before the next election does its educational work well, hope based on truth will be a higher trump than fear based on a lie.

[1] On October 5, 1934, the day following the debate and decision on this question at the Southport Conference, the *News Chronicle* carried a truthful headline, *Labour Rejects Confiscation*, the *Daily Express* a lying headline, *Labour Will Confiscate*. This is a foretaste of what the electors will hear from our less scrupulous opponents.

PART IV
FINANCE

CHAPTER XIX

THE FAILURE OF THE FINANCIERS

BRITISH public opinion, increasingly impatient at the long continuance of our present disorders, more and more fixes its critical gaze upon finance. Our financial institutions, the men in charge of them, and their present policies, all stand to-day on the defensive. Their critics include, not only Socialists, but large sections of less advanced opinion. They include, in particular, a growing number of the younger and more open-eyed men with practical knowledge of finance, both in the City of London and in the provinces. Old-fashioned prejudice against Socialist ideas is rapidly weakening, and bold proposals, when presented persuasively and in a practical form, find a welcome in many unexpected quarters.

> Of course there will be opposition to your proposals [wrote a well-informed friend of mine the other day], but its real strength has been undermined by recent events. Quite apart from the complete crash of the banking systems in Germany and the U.S.A.—bankers have lost all their authority in those countries—there has been unceasing criticism here. Montagu Norman has a very bad press in the City. And what is the influence to-day of the Rothschilds, Schroeders, Kleinworts, compared with what it was? After all the shocks we have had since September, 1931, there is nothing left sacred in the City. . . . Business

men to-day are prepared to go in for great experiments.[1]

British Socialists, until lately, were inclined to underestimate the importance of finance, as compared with industry. Now there is, perhaps, a danger of over-emphasis in the opposite direction. But the economic disasters of the post-war years are mainly due to financial causes and financial mismanagement. There has been no failure in productivity. On the contrary, there have been unprecedented gluts of many commodities, and a steadily growing power, through scientific progress, to create abundance. But there has been gross failure in the financing of production, exchange and distribution.

The world-wide crash in the price level since 1929, with all its disastrous consequences, is a financiers' achievement; the continuous deflation of currency and credit in this country from 1920 onwards was a long series of financiers' decisions, taken without public advertisement, or public discussion, or Parliamentary sanction, and imposed upon British industry and agriculture, either unawares or against their will.

[1] How far even hard-bitten Tories have moved, is shown by the terms of the following motion, which was placed on the Order Paper of the House of Commons by Sir Robert Horne and a number of his political associates in March, 1933. " That, in the opinion of this House, there is urgent need for a comprehensive plan providing for the organisation of national industries under the advice of industrial councils, the co-ordination of financial, industrial, and political policy, through the assistance of a representative investment and development Board, and the raising of prices to an economic level by methods which would include (*a*) controlled monetary policy, (*b*) the direction of new capital into the channels which would produce a better equilibrium in production, and (*c*) the provision of credit facilities for desirable developments for which the necessary capital cannot be readily obtained under the existing methods of banking and issuing houses." Some of these ideas bear a faint resemblance to the proposals of the Labour Party.

British policy on reparations in the early post-war period, including the fantastic over-estimate of German capacity to pay, was based on bad advice, given by Lord Cunliffe, Mr. Montagu Norman's predecessor as Governor of the Bank of England ; our return to the gold standard at the pre-war parity in 1925 was based on the bad advice of Mr. Norman himself ; the British financial crisis of 1931 followed close on the heels of the German financial crisis, which revealed that a number of leading London Acceptance Houses, acting without consultation, either with one another or with the Bank of England, had seriously overlent to Germany, and thus endangered both their own solvency and that of a wide circle of persons and institutions, who were dependent upon them.[1] They had borrowed large sums on short term at low rates of interest from France and other foreign countries, and had lent large sums on short term at high rates of interest to Germany. There was no social justification for these operations. They were neither safety first, nor Britain first, nor constructive internationalism. They were mere speculative profit seeking of the crudest and most risky kind.

Moreover, the political events of 1931 have left a deep mark on our memories. According to the testimony of Mr. Ramsay MacDonald, it was bankers, British and foreign, who dictated the financial decisions of the British Government, making their credits con-

[1] Mr. Norman, in one of his rare public speeches, stated at a bankers' dinner in the City of London on October 20, 1932, that foreign concerns " have been able to borrow on short credit sums which, had the various lenders been aware of it, would have been quite out of the question and which have come as a surprise to all of us ". He appealed for closer co-operation among the Acceptance Houses, but added " these are matters which do not concern me very directly ". Yet the big Acceptance Houses dominate the Directorate of the Bank of England and would undoubtedly expect the Bank, and in the last resort the Government, to come to their assistance, if they were in acute danger of failure.

ditional on the adoption of specific detailed economies, including, in particular, a cut in the rates of unemployment benefit.[1] It was widely felt, not alone in Labour Party circles, that such pressure, exercised upon the Government by powerful private interests, was an abuse and a provocation.

It is only fair to add that Mr. MacDonald's evidence on this subject is somewhat confused, and lacks corroboration. It has been denied that the foreign bankers, either American or French, imposed any such conditions as Mr. MacDonald alleged. It has been suggested by some that he honestly misunderstood them, and by others that the British bankers misled him as to the attitude of their foreign colleagues.[2]

[1] Asked in Parliament whether he would restore these cuts, he replied " No. That was a condition of the borrowing."

[2] There is a striking passage in Mr. MacDonald's book, *Socialism Critical and Constructive* (on p. 196 in the edition of 1924, published after the author had been Prime Minister and Foreign Secretary for nine months), which sounded in the ears of some of us in the late summer of 1931 like an ancient prophecy spoken by a Socialist voice from the grave, or from the prison house guarded by his Conservative colleagues in the newly formed " National " Government. " One can stand ", he wrote, " at a point in the City of London and be within a stone's throw of a handful of banks and financial agencies, which by an agreement come to quite legally though perhaps in defiance of a law or Government decree, would influence materially in a very short time the business operations of the country. Nor is the growing importance of American finance in international trade an assuring event. . . . Communities must protect themselves against an imperious international financial trust. . . . This country will have to watch not only Lombard Street, but Wall Street. If international finance is to combine, the slavery of labour is inevitable, and the politics of the world will become the will of finance. Finance can command the sluices of every stream that runs to turn the wheels of industry, and can put fetters upon the feet of every Government in existence. . . . No community can be free until it controls its financial organisation."

THE FAILURE OF THE FINANCIERS 185

Since then, private bankers in Germany have suffered eclipse, the State having taken over all their concerns, some of which were in a bankrupt condition, while in the United States there have been even more spectacular banking failures, a sensational Senate inquiry into banking practice, and threats of Presidential intervention to control the whole American banking system.

Add to all this the fact that an unusually large number of financial scandals, both large and small, has come to light in recent years,[1] and it is easy to understand why British opinion has moved far from its old moorings, and lost its old blind trust in the high priests of finance.

The general principles of Socialist reconstruction in finance are simple. We must socialise the leading financial institutions, enforce a proper measure of social control upon financial policy, and infuse a social purpose, as distinct from a profit-seeking purpose, into financial operations. We must take steps to prevent the continuous increase in productive power, which could transform poverty into plenty, from being frustrated by financial hindrances and restrictions, and from being subjected to intermittent booms, slumps and crises. And we must, as an important incident in our general policy, end the private monopoly of financial power now exercised by a mere handful of individuals. For such a concentration of private power in few hands, as Mr. MacDonald has so eloquently pointed out, is a danger to the State and to democracy.

These principles are simple, but their practical application needs careful study. I shall make a series of practical proposals later, but shall begin with a preliminary study of the defects to be remedied.

[1] For a study of some of these, see Mr. Thomas Johnston's recent book, *The Financiers and the Nation* (Methuen, 1934).

I shall concentrate on British conditions, and on three principal criticisms ; first, the irresponsibility of financiers ; second, the lack of social purpose in the use of financial resources ; and third, the inefficiency of the financial machine.

The irresponsibility of financiers, both to public authority and to public opinion, is more extreme in Britain than in any other country. With us, Government control over the banks is at a minimum. Parliamentary discussion of the policy of the Bank of England is practically impossible, and no Parliamentary questions can be put to Ministers regarding the banking policy of the country. One of the catchwords used by defenders of the present system is that there should be " no politics " in banking. But this is an impossibility. For the banks and other financial institutions pursue policies of their own, and their acts and decisions profoundly influence, for good or ill, our economic life —often, as recent experience shows, for ill. The choice before us is not between politics and no politics, but between public politics and private politics. To claim that the banks should be " free from political influence " is to claim that they should be free to do as they please, regardless of public opinion, or of the wider public interests.

Mr. Montagu Norman has come to personify, in our day, this system of irresponsibility. He has been Governor of the Bank of England since 1920. He has exercised immense authority over successive Prime Ministers and Chancellors of the Exchequer, as well as in the City and in the circles of international finance.[1]

---

[1] Mr. Paul Einzig has written a very interesting book, *Montagu Norman : A Study in Financial Statesmanship* (Kegan Paul, 1932), which should be read by every serious student of British finance. I reviewed this book in the *New Statesman* of November 26, 1932, and have made use in what follows of certain passages from that review.

THE FAILURE OF THE FINANCIERS 187

It has been truly said that there must be something remarkable in a man who can make three successive Chancellors, so different from one another as Winston Churchill, Philip Snowden and Neville Chamberlain, all eat out of his hand. That he should give advice to Ministers is right and proper ; that they should generally follow it is their responsibility and his success. What is wrong and improper is that they should be unable, as the law now stands, to give him in return, not advice, but general directions ; that no effective pressure of public opinion should operate upon him ; that he should be free to use the immense financial power which he controls for purposes of private politics. That Mr. Norman has so used this power is one of the grounds of his biographer's admiration. "Although Mr. Norman has never been a politician," he writes, "he has been the greatest statesman in Great Britain since the war." He has often shown his disregard of Government. Thus, when he supported the creation of the Bank for International Settlements, "it seems probable that what he had in mind was an alliance between Central Banks which could and should, if necessary, defy Government interference". But he soon discovered, to his great regret, that "the number of countries in which the Central Bank enjoys independence in law and in fact similar to that of the Bank of England is very small. In most countries Central Banks are in practice little more than Government Departments". In July, 1932, he emphasised his independence by signing a manifesto issued by the Board of Directors of the Bank for International Settlements in favour of a restoration of the gold standard by countries which had suspended it, in spite of the fact that the British Government had recently announced that it had no immediate intention of returning to gold. "A diplomatic blunder," his biographer admits.

Until this country abandoned gold in 1931, Mr. Norman was consistently anti-French and, even in his biographer's friendly record, it is clear that he badly mismanaged his personal relations with French bankers. But his love for the gold standard was ultimately stronger than his dislike of France. And in 1933 we find him, contrary to the wishes of the British and Dominion Governments, and of the great majority of British opinion, trying to tie the pound to the French franc and to line up this country with the " Gold Group ", led by France, at the World Economic Conference.

But what his biographer finds most admirable in Mr. Norman is that, ever since he became Governor, he has " firmly " pursued a foreign policy of his own, which has been " in sharp contrast to the series of feeble compromises that has characterised the official British foreign policy ". I became dimly aware of such a dyarchy while I was serving in the (official) British Foreign Office. But Mr. Einzig has made it all much plainer to me. He explains that

> Mr. Norman's attitude towards the external policy of the country has been in perfect harmony with the traditional British constructive spirit. . . . He pursued the traditional balance of power policy, but with economic and financial means. . . . Unless Germany is economically strong and prosperous, it is impossible to balance the one-sided political strength of France on the Continent. In the olden days the British statesmen supported the second strongest continental power by arranging secret or open alliances, and by granting subsidies or loans to the weaker countries for the purpose of increasing their military strength in order to counterbalance the strength of the larger powers.

Though times and methods had changed, Mr. Norman believed in continuity.

The (official) British foreign policy, under Mr. Henderson, was to seek to co-operate with all nations, and to seek to bring them to co-operate with one another, to favour none and to estrange none, to stand clear of all cliques, to work through the League. He had as firmly discarded the balance of power theory, with all its implications, as Mr. Norman had adhered to it. If Mr. Norman has in truth had any part in strengthening Germany, relatively to France, it is at least doubtful, in the present state of Europe, whether he has deserved well of his country or of Peace.[1] Mr. Norman's " foreign policy " rests on a series of well documented events. One, in particular, sticks in my memory, the Bank of England's loan to Austria at the time of the Credit Anstalt failure in May, 1931. This loan was made recklessly, without conditions, and without proper consultation. It was made at a critical moment in diplomatic negotiations, in which it had the effect of weakening the influence of the British Foreign Secretary. And two years later, when it seemed likely to become a bad debt, Mr. Norman persuaded the British Government to transfer the liability from his bank to the British taxpayer. A modern version of taxation without representation !

> No foreign countries [chirrups Mr. Einzig] have produced a Central Bank Governor who has exerted a decisive influence upon their foreign policy. The Governor of the Bank of France is practically a Government official ; as a rule he is promoted to that position from the civil service. Even if technically he is independent, he continues to act as a subordinate to the Minister of Finance.

There is an unanswerable case for the assimilation, in this respect, of British to French practice. Mr.

[1] Mr. Norman is reputed to cherish, not merely pro-German, but pro-Nazi sympathies, and to allow these to influence his policy.

Norman is an outstanding personality, occupying an outstanding post. Therefore he reflects political irresponsibility with a bright light. But more dimly, in proportion to their lesser opportunities and personal gifts, other private bankers and financiers reflect it too. It is an essential quality of our present financial order.

I turn to the second point in the indictment, the lack of social purpose in the use of financial resources. This is a fundamental Socialist criticism of capitalist institutions generally. But it has special weight in relation to finance, of which the function is to distribute limited resources between alternative uses of widely differing social value. To grant credits for mere speculation, whether in produce, or real property, or stocks and shares, may be consistent with " sound " profit-making banking. But it is not consistent with the best social use of limited financial means. Similarly with credits for trade and industry. There is, in current capitalist financial practice, no discrimination according to social utility, no semblance of a scheme of priorities within a national plan. Was it not Mr. Keynes who said that talking to a twentieth century banker about the social good was like talking to a nineteenth century bishop about the origin of species ?

Even if the financial system were highly efficient for its own purposes, it would still be necessary to modify these purposes, and to substitute social advantage, efficiently pursued, for private profit, as its goal. But the British financial system is far from being highly efficient. And this is the third point in the indictment. I shall summarise rapidly here some of the main sources of inefficiency, and shall refer to them again later in greater detail.

Our network of financial institutions, a large part of which is concentrated in the City of London, is a historical growth. British finance is not a planned system, and if it were now to be intelligently planned afresh from the beginning, it would bear little resemblance to its present form. It is full of unnecessary complication. It is incoherent, without proper contact between some of its essential parts, for example between the Bank of England and the Joint Stock Banks. It is lopsided, providing better facilities for the investment of capital abroad than at home, and very poor facilities for certain classes of home investment, for example in small businesses. As an agency for the supply of new capital on long term, it is wasteful and needlessly expensive. For the supply of short term credit at home, it is passive and unenterprising, though it lent recklessly to Germany. For credits of intermediate length it makes hardly any provision. It permits many opportunities of swindling, both inside and outside the law. It is honeycombed with nepotism, and with patronage based on family and business connections. There are too many soft jobs for influential people, too many multiple directorships, carrying fat fees without real functions, too many " guinea-pigs ", paid simply to " give their names " and so to attract custom. The City is unrationalised to an astonishing degree. If rationalisation is necessary in British industry, it is no less necessary in British finance.

CHAPTER XX

MONETARY POLICY

SOCIALIST policy in finance divides into two branches, monetary policy and the reform of financial institutions.[1]

Monetary policy, when unimportant side issues are stripped away, reduces itself to a simple problem of planning and social control. On what principle shall we regulate the value of British money? There are, indeed, two questions to be answered here, and not one only, for the value of British money has two separate aspects, its value in terms of goods and services in Britain, and its value in terms of foreign money. In other words, we have to consider both the problem of the British price level and the problem of the rates of foreign exchange. Many high authorities have held that the best principle is a passive one. We should allow ourselves to be led about, hither and thither, on a golden chain, like a dog obedient to a master whose whims are beyond his ken.

The gold standard was always, on merits, a second-rate expedient. In the minds of many who supported it, it had the strength, not of an intellectual convic-

[1] On Public Finance which is a separate, though related, subject, dealing with public revenue, public expenditure and public debts I shall have something to say in Chapter XXXI. I have drawn freely in this and the next three chapters on two Labour Party Reports, namely *Currency, Banking and Finance*, published in 1932, and *Socialism and the Condition of the People*, published in 1933.

tion, but of an inherited superstition. It gave us, indeed, a large measure of stability in rates of foreign exchange with such other countries as were also on the gold, or gold exchange, standard. But even for this advantage we had to pay a high price. For we were compelled to restrict credit and force prices down, whenever our supplies of gold were seriously shrinking under the pressure of foreigners' demand. We were permitted, on the other hand, to expand credit and let prices rise, when gold was flowing into this country from abroad. But there was no reason why these variations in credit and prices in this country, imposed by external forces, should coincide with the requirements of our domestic situation. Often we were compelled to starve industry, just when it needed credit, or to gorge it, when it was already sufficiently fed.

Stability of internal prices, or even any control over our own price level, the gold standard never gave us. During most of the nineteenth century and the first fourteen years of the twentieth, and again during the short post-war period from 1925 to 1931, when we were again on the gold standard, the world price level to which the British price level was tethered by the golden chain, heaved up and down. Its movements were determined, principally, by variations in the world's gold supply, and the credit based upon it, relatively to variations in the production of commodities. It is very hard to defend, on rational grounds, this dictatorship of gold over human destiny. Particularly hard, when this dictatorship imposes, not on one country only, but on the whole gold standard world, a falling price level, with restricted credit, restricted production and mounting unemployment. It was in such a period of distress, when man seemed to be cheated of his heritage, that the American orator, Bryan, spoke the famous words, " Thou shalt not press down upon the brow of labour this crown of thorns ; thou shalt not crucify mankind upon a cross of gold."

With every major world crisis, the gold standard breaks down. Britain had to suspend it during the Napoleonic Wars, during the Great War and again during the Great Slump. It has been remarked that our elderly bankers may find it difficult to appreciate that a new generation is growing up, which has had more experience of what it feels like to be " off " the gold standard than " on ", and has been, on the whole, and apart from the horrors of war, happier off than on. Britain kissed gold good-bye, to the horror of our bankers, in September, 1931, and many other countries, including, after an interval of eighteen months, the United States, have followed our example. I hope it is good-bye for ever.

The practical alternative to the gold standard is a commodity standard. We should take, as our measure of value, not one single metal, but a group of commodities of primary importance in trade and consumption. An average, or index number, of the prices of these commodities, weighted according to their relative importance, should be constructed, and we should use this index number as the basis of monetary regulation. The simplest, and probably the best, policy is to aim at keeping this index number stable or, in other words, at maintaining a steady purchasing power for the pound sterling, in terms of this group of important commodities.

The Labour Party declared in favour of this policy, not for the first time, in 1932 at its Annual Conference, which expressed the opinion that,

> in view of the breakdown of the gold standard, the aim of British monetary policy should be to stabilise wholesale prices at a suitable level in this country, to seek by international agreement the largest practicable mea-

sure of stability in the rates of exchange, and to safeguard the workers against such exploitation as has been inflicted upon them in recent years by speculators and manipulators.[1]

Wholesale, rather than retail, prices are taken as the basis of stabilisation for two reasons. First, because it is easier to construct a simple and reliable index number for wholesale than for retail prices, and, second, because such an index number, covering the principal commodities which enter into international trade, is better adapted to international arrangements for stabilising rates of foreign exchange. But, if the level of wholesale prices is kept steady, any large fluctuation in the level of retail prices will be prevented, and the way will be left open for appropriate measures to be taken for the prevention of profiteering by middlemen, for the better organisation of retail trade, and for narrowing the present gap, which is in many cases much wider than it need be, between wholesale and retail prices. It was pointed out in the Labour Party Report, on which the resolution just quoted was based, that " in this field the Co-operative Movement can play a very important part, and that every increase in its share of the retail trade of the country will make the problem easier of solution ".

The technique of stabilising the price level is a job for practical experts, with some help from theorists. It is not an easy job. But it has been achieved, over considerable periods, both in the United States and in Sweden, and the means of achieving it, and the difficulties to be overcome, are becoming well understood as the result of practical experience.

These means have long been recognised to include control by the Central Bank, through the discount rate

[1] It is interesting to note that Sir Basil Blackett, a Director of the Bank of England, in his book *Planned Money* (Constable, 1932) also advocates this policy of a stable price level.

and through open market operations [1], of the quantity of credit. More recent studies have shown that additional means include control of the long term rate of interest, and of the volume of investment in relation to the volume of available savings, and some guarantee that the credit created by the Central Bank is fully taken up. And in the background, of course, is the right of the State to increase or diminish the quantity of paper currency.

Even within the framework of capitalist finance, there can be no serious doubt that it is a practicable proposition to keep the price level approximately stable. But this policy can be still more effectively carried out, as the range of social control over finance extends.

Indeed, such an extension is required for the effective regulation of the long term rate of interest and of the volume of new investment. Also in order to check speculation, which assumed gigantic proportions in the United States in 1928-9 and brought about the collapse of the stable price level, which had previously been successfully maintained in that country. And some control over industry is also needed to ensure that wages, and hence consuming power, rise adequately as producing power increases.

The aim of a stable price level must not, indeed, be interpreted too rigidly. We must not imagine that the index number selected will never show any variation. The essence of the policy is that the fluctuations of this index shall be held within a narrow range.

---

[1] That is to say, by the buying or selling of securities by the Central Bank. When the Central Bank buys securities in the open market, it increases the deposits in the other Banks, and so makes possible an increase of credit; when it sells securities, it reduces deposits, and so reduces the basis of credit. But open market operations partly fail of their purpose, if the other Banks fail to vary the volume of their credits correspondingly.

When it begins to rise, steps will be taken to bring it down again; when it begins to fall, steps will be taken to raise it.

The height at which the price level should be stabilised—the "suitable level" in the terms of the Labour Party's resolution—cannot be determined, until the time comes to apply the policy and to review all the economic circumstances of that time. It does not follow that the "suitable level" will be the actual level of that time. It may be desirable either to raise or lower the actual level, before taking steps to stabilise it. At the present moment, after the precipitous fall in prices in recent years, it might well be desirable to raise the price level before stabilisation, and thereby to give a fresh stimulus to production, and to reduce the burden of fixed money charges upon the State and upon producers generally. Wholesale prices, having fallen much faster than retail, should also rise faster. And indeed it might well be that a substantial advance in wholesale prices could be brought about, and a substantial increase in trade and employment, without any appreciable rise in retail prices. Such reflation, or controlled inflation, designed to cancel part of the ruinous deflation to which we have been subjected, is wholly different from uncontrolled inflation, with which some timid minds confuse it. Control is of the essence of the policy.

It should, moreover, be emphasised that a stable price level, in a period of increasing productivity, means a continual expansion of currency and credit, roughly in proportion to the increase in production. It means, therefore, that money wages should rise.

The improvement in the wage-earner's standard of life is the same, whether prices remain unchanged while money wages rise, or money wages remain unchanged while prices fall by a corresponding percentage. And it has been argued by some economists that it would be better to aim at stabilising money wages, rather than the price level.[1] Then, as productivity increased, prices would fall. Others have argued for a steadily rising price level, so that the burden of public debts and other fixed money charges should be steadily reduced. Such policies, equally with that of stabilising the price level, would necessitate deliberate control over the monetary system, and over the volume of currency and credit.

I turn to the question of stability in the rates of exchange between sterling and foreign currencies. This is certainly desirable. But it is not worth purchasing at too high a price, even for a country whose external trade is so important as that of Britain. It is not worth purchasing at the price of a British return to the gold standard.[2]

There are few economic problems, for which an international solution, if obtainable, is not better than a purely national solution. And in this case the best solution would be an international agreement to stabilise both national price levels and international

[1] Mostly by anti-Socialists, but also by Mr. Evan Durbin, one of the ablest of our Socialist economists, in his *Purchasing Power and Trade Depression* (Cape, 1933) and his *Socialist Credit Policy* (Gollancz, 1934). It is argued by this school that a stable price level contains the germs of an unhealthy trade boom and subsequent depression and collapse. American experience is cited as a proof of this. But an alternative explanation is that American wages did not rise fast enough, and that excessive profits were dissipated in wild speculation.

[2] The suggestion has been made that the nations now off gold should return at " provisional parities ". Thus we should stabilise sterling in terms of gold at a price which would be subject to periodic revision, say at yearly or six-monthly intervals, without any charge of breach of contract or good faith, such as some foreign holders of sterling levelled at the British Government in 1931. I am not much attracted by this idea, which would leave trade nearly as uncertain as a freely fluctuating exchange. But it would certainly be preferable to a return to gold at a fixed parity.

exchange rates. One nation, acting alone, can secure only one or other of these two objectives; a number of nations, acting in co-operation, can secure both. Since Britain left the gold standard, a number of other countries have done the same, and have maintained their currencies at a practically fixed rate in terms of sterling. These arrangements should be made more precise, and a more determined attempt made to extend this " sterling area ". The danger of international competition in currency depreciation would thus be diminished, though it might well be advantageous to seek a moderate measure of depreciation by international agreement.

How large a part of the world would join in a co-operative policy of dual stabilisation, both of price levels and exchange rates, cannot be answered till the proposal has been definitely made and vigorously pursued. But it may, I think, be safely assumed that, at a minimum, we could count on the co-operation of the British Dominions, with the possible exception of South Africa, which, however, having now left the gold standard, is less likely to stand out, if the scheme is widely accepted, and Canada, whose acceptance is likely to depend on that of the United States; of Sweden, Norway and Denmark, which are all basing their currencies on sterling at the present time, and of the principal countries of South America, which are doing the same. The so-called European " gold group ", led by France, is at present hostile to the scheme, but the currency position of several of these countries is precarious, and they may be converted by the force of events.

The participation of the United States would be of immense value, both for its own sake and for its probable influence on other nations. President Roosevelt, in his famous message to the World Economic Conference on July 3, 1933, deprecated " the specious fallacy of achieving a temporary and probably an artificial stability in foreign exchange on the part of a few large countries only. The sound internal economic system of a nation," he continued, "is a greater factor in its well-being than the price of its currency in changing terms of the currencies of other nations. . . . Old fetishes of so-called international bankers are being replaced by efforts to plan national currencies with the objective of giving them a continuing purchasing power which does not greatly vary in terms of the commodities and needs of modern civilisation. . . . The United States seeks the kind of a dollar which a generation hence will have the same purchasing and debt paying power as the dollar value we hope to attain in the near future . . . Our broad purpose is the permanent stabilisation of every nation's currency."

This statement is in harmony with the arguments of this chapter and with the policy of the Labour Party. If it continues to represent the policy of the United States, the ideal of dual stability may be realised over a much wider area than at present.[1] But even over the narrower area, the policy is worth achieving, and proof of its practical success in this limited field would help its extension.[2]

[1] The adherence of the Soviet Union to an international convention for stabilising exchange rates might also, I think, be obtained. But her methods of regulating internal prices make the ideal of dual stability in her case inapplicable.

[2] It is argued by opponents of this policy that difficulties will arise from differences in the composition of different national index numbers for internal price stability. Such difficulties, as practical issues, can easily be exaggerated. There are various ways in which they can be minimised, e.g. by the general acceptance of an international index number, or by agreement within a group of nations to accept the national index number of one of the group, or by the acceptance of exchange fluctuations within defined and moderate limits.

We have passed through bitter years of monetary disorganisation. It is time to reorganise on a more solid foundation, and this task is one of the essential preliminaries of Socialist reconstruction in Britain.

CHAPTER XXI

THE BANK OF ENGLAND

I now turn to the second branch of Socialist policy in the sphere of finance, namely the reform of institutions.

Let us begin, at the centre of the spider's web in the City of London, with the Bank of England. This is a most peculiar institution. Its capital is privately owned. In practice its Governor and Deputy Governor are appointed by the Directors of the Bank, while the Directors are appointed by themselves, re-electing each other from year to year and filling vacancies in their ranks according to their own fancy. In theory all these appointments are made annually by those holders of more than £500 of Bank of England stock who present themselves in the Bank Parlour on the appropriate date. Most of the Directors are connected with financial houses in the City. They are private individuals, responsible to no public authority; and the Bank of England is a private institution, possessing its own Charter and subject to Act of Parliament only as regards the issue of currency, certain obligations relating to gold and one or two lesser matters.

Except in the most general terms, as I have already stated, the Bank's policy may not be debated in Parliament,[1] nor may Parliamentary questions be

[1] Under the Currency and Bank Notes Act, 1928, Parliament must expressly authorise any increase in the fiduciary note issue above £260 million for a longer period than two years. This is one of the few occasions when Parliamentary discussion is now possible, but it is an occasion which may seldom or never arise, and the debate is narrowly restricted.

asked of any Minister of the Crown regarding its actions. Successive Governors have carried secretiveness to a high pitch. The Bank's weekly Return is a mystery and its half-yearly Report a mockery. The public, and even the inner circles of the City, are kept deliberately in the dark.[1]

Yet the powers and duties of the Bank are very great, and fundamental to the working of our financial system. It is the Government's banker, holds the Government balances, makes advances to the Government from time to time, issues Government loans and administers the service of the Government debt. It also holds the balances of the Joint Stock banks and likewise the nation's gold reserves. By varying its bank rate, and by its open market operations, it can expand or restrict the volume of credit, lower or raise the rate of interest on gilt-edged stocks, increase or diminish employment, and bring a strong pressure to bear on rates of wages and the standard of life. These powers are even greater, now that we are off, than when we were on, the gold standard. The Governor of the Bank not only exercises high authority in the City; he also plays an important international role. Through his frequent contacts with the Governors of Central Banks in other countries and through his nominees on the governing body of the Bank for International Settlements, he has a large influence on international finance and international politics.

Such great powers and duties should be exercised in proper subordination to public policy. The Labour

[1] The late Dr. Walter Leaf, who was Chairman of the Westminster Bank, relates in his book on *Banking* (p. 45) that he was once discussing the weekly Bank Return with the Governor of the Bank of England. There was one line of it, he said, which he thought he understood, and that was the line, " Gold Coin and Bullion ". " The Governor, with a twinkle in his eye, replied, ' Mr. Leaf, I do not think you understand even that.' "

Party holds that the Bank should be more closely related to the Government, and a scheme for giving effect to this idea was adopted at the Party Conference in 1932.[1]

The Governor of the Bank should be appointed by the Crown, on the recommendation of the Cabinet Minister responsible for Finance, and should be made subject to the general directions of this Minister, on behalf of the Cabinet, on large issues of policy. Within the broad guiding lines laid down by the Minister, the day-to-day business of the Bank would continue to be carried on by the Governor and his subordinates. Here it would be inappropriate that either the Minister or Parliament should intervene. These broad guiding lines, moreover, would fall within the framework of the law, as amended by Parliament from time to time, regulating the character and volume of the currency, and other banking questions.

The Minister and the State Department, who would naturally be charged with controlling the policy of the Bank, would be the Chancellor of the Exchequer and the Treasury. But it is a matter for consideration whether a separate Ministry of Finance should not be set up to perform the new functions which Socialist financial policy will impose on Government.

It is also a matter for consideration whether the Governor of the Bank should be appointed annually, as at present, or for a short term of years, say five. There are advantages both in annual rotation and in a reasonable continuity of experience. But Mr. Norman's continuous tenure of office since 1920 is certainly too long, quite apart from any criticism which may be made of his individual performances. There is, I think, no reason why the appointment should not be made after consultation with the Board of the Bank, and the appointment would normally, no

[1] See *Currency, Banking and Finance*, pp. 8–9.

doubt, be made from among the members of the Board.

Both the constitution and the powers of the Board should, I suggest, be modified. Its members should, in future, be appointed by the Government, probably for a term of years, say five, in such a way that some retire each year by rotation. Subject to an age limit, retiring members should be eligible for reappointment. But they should represent a much wider field of experience and interest than at present, and should cease to be drawn predominantly from the merchant banking houses of the City. On the other hand, the number of the Board, now twenty-six, in addition to the Governor and Deputy Governor, appears excessive, and should be reduced.

The Board should cease to be authoritative, and should become advisory to the Governor and to the Government. It would thus become a valuable advisory organ on the financial side of economic planning.

In addition to the Governor, the higher appointments of the Bank should include a Deputy Governor, as now, and probably, I suggest, two Assistant Deputy Governors, for the performance of special duties, e.g. in connection with the National Investment Board proposed below, and with the reformed system of deposit banking. These officials should be members of the Board, and should likewise be appointed for a short term of years, with eligibility for reappointment subject to age limit.[1]

[1] In 1933 power was taken at the first half-yearly meeting of the stockholders to employ some of the Directors on full time service in the Bank. At this meeting power was also taken to increase the salaries of the Governor and Deputy Governor, which had previously stood at £2,000 and £1,500 a year respectively. These salaries, commented *The Times* City Editor, are "ridiculously small and it has meant that only gentlemen with private fortunes could afford to occupy

The mode of recruitment of the Bank's staff should be reconsidered. There should be larger opportunities of promotion from the lower ranks, and probably an element of recruitment through the ordinary Civil Service examinations. There should also be a considerable measure of interchange between the staffs of the Bank, of the Treasury, of any new Ministry of Finance which may be created, and of the staffs of the other new financial institutions proposed below.

If financial policy is to be bold, efficient, constructive and fresh-minded, we cannot afford to cultivate the mentality of the water-tight compartment. Excessive departmentalism is a danger to be avoided throughout the public service.

The existing stockholders would lose whatever nominal and shadowy powers of control they still possess and would be given, in exchange for their stock, bonds bearing a fixed rate of interest. Steps should be taken to pay off all these bonds within a reasonably short term of years.[1]

It may be assumed that the Bank would continue, as in the past, to show a financial surplus on its operations. This surplus should be used, in proportions to be determined by the Government in consultation

the position of Governor and Deputy Governor of the Bank. They are very much smaller than those payable to the heads of the big Joint Stock banks which, incidentally, are paid free of tax." This comment shows that, even in the City of London, the prestige of an office is not measured solely by the size of the salary.

[1] It might be convenient that the Government should repay to the Bank a long-standing debt of £11 millions, on condition that it was applied to paying off the bondholders, and that some of the Bank's hidden reserves were also mobilised for this purpose. These are undoubtedly considerable. The amount of Bank Stock is now £14½ million, worth, at present market values, more than £50 million. Dividends at 12 per cent, the rate which has been paid since 1922, involve an annual drain on the Bank's resources of £1,750,000.

with the Governor, partly to pay off the bondholders, partly to increase the Bank's resources, partly to contribute to the public revenue. With the passage of time, and the progressive repayment of the bondholders, the Bank's resources should be greatly strengthened, and the Treasury should draw an increasing revenue from the Bank's operations.

The Bank of England, thus reorganised on a basis of public ownership and control, should be made, even more than at present, the pivot of the British financial system. It is through the Bank that control of other financial institutions can most effectively be operated. Such control is already exercised to a considerable extent, both through financial pressure [1] and through tacit agreement; it should be strengthened and regularised.

The practice whereby banks, acceptance houses and other financial institutions look to the Bank of England for assistance when they find themselves in trouble, but are subject to no supervision or control in normal times, must be terminated.

Moreover, as the Macmillan Committee very properly recommended in 1931,[2] much more statistical and other information regarding their activities should be furnished to the Bank of England by the Joint Stock banks, the acceptance houses, British banks doing business mainly abroad, foreign banks with branch offices in this country, and other financial institutions. A large part of this information should be published in an appropriate form by the Bank of England.

The Bank should also make an annual report of its own operations, containing much fuller information

[1] In recently forcing a reduction in the excessive number of Discount Houses, for example.
[2] The Macmillan Committee recommended a number of other changes, including the amalgamation of the Issue and Banking Departments.

than hitherto. This report would no longer be made to a meeting of shareholders, but to the responsible Minister, and should be published and laid before Parliament, and an opportunity provided for annual Parliamentary discussion of the year's record and of the major issues of monetary and banking policy.

Among Central Banks, the irresponsibility of the Bank of England is unique.[1] In all other cases the Government, or Parliament, or both, exercise some constitutional influence, both on the appointment of the Governors and Directors, and on the Bank's policy.[2] In every case, except in this country, the Treasury

[1] Those who are interested in the comparative study of financial institutions should consult the standard text-book on *Central Banks*, by Sir Cecil Kisch, to which Mr. Norman has contributed a Foreword. In the 1932 edition of his book (p. 18), it is stated that " there are only two important Banks which, at least on paper, are independent of their respective Governments, namely the Bank of England and the Reichsbank ". And in Nazi Germany the Reichsbank's independence is a very thin paper fiction. Moreover it is laid down in the Reichsbank's Charter that " before the election " of the Bank President and of his Council, " the Chairman of the General Council or his deputy shall consult the Government of the Reich concerning the election ".

[2] As regards appointments, a study of the Charters set out by Sir Cecil Kisch gives the following classification. In Australia, Finland, Latvia, the Soviet Union and on the Federal Reserve Board in the United States, the Governor, Deputy-Governor and *all* members of the Board are appointed by the Government. In the United States appointment is by the President, with the consent of the Senate. In Czecho-Slovakia, France, Japan, Jugoslavia, Portugal, Roumania, South Africa, Spain and Switzerland, the Governor and *some* members of the Board are appointed by the Government. In Austria, Belgium, Bulgaria, Estonia, Greece, Hungary, Italy, Lithuania, Netherlands and Poland, the Governor is appointed by the Government. In Chile, Colombia, Denmark and Peru *some* members of the Board are appointed by the Government. In Norway and Sweden *all* members of the Board are appointed by Parliament and the Governor by the Crown. The degree of control over policy varies widely.

derives revenue from the Central Bank's operations, participating, according to a variety of regulations, in the Bank's net profits. In this country, alone in the civilised world, the Treasury receives nothing from this source. Such abnegation is not good business for the tax-payer.[1]

It should also be noticed that Bank notes are exempt from stamp duty. In respect of its financial obligations to the Government, which guarantees its many privileges, the Bank of England gets off very lightly. The Bank, it must be conceded, has managed its relations with the Revenue Authorities pretty well ! Its shareholders, drawing their steady 12 per cent dividends, owe it gratitude.

The rearrangements proposed in this chapter will call for a spirit of common sense and co-operation on the part of Ministers, Parliament, Bank officials and others. If it is to be assumed that all concerned will act unreasonably, the rearrangements will work badly. But, on this same assumption, the present arrangements will work even worse. This is not an assumption, however, which I accept, either here or elsewhere in this book.

[1] Under the Currency and Bank Notes Act of 1928 the Treasury does, indeed, receive the net profits of the currency note circulation. But this is a case of " thank you for nothing ", for before the passing of this Act it was the Treasury and not the Bank which issued the notes and took the profits. This contribution is no equivalent for a share in the net profits of the Bank.

CHAPTER XXII

CONTROL OF LONG-TERM CREDIT

THE Bank of England is not directly concerned with the supply of capital in the form of long-term credit for industry. Nor are the British Joint Stock banks, which differ in this respect from many of their foreign counterparts.

The weaknesses of our present arrangements for long-term credit are principally four. First, there are opportunities for gross frauds by financiers upon the public. These lead to the loss of capital, which might have been usefully employed, and often to the ruin of investors, many of whom are small people, whose life savings are swallowed by these sharks. Bottomley and Hatry are familiar British examples, and Lord Kylsant went to jail for deceiving his shareholders, while Kreuger has shown that foreigners can do like deeds on an even grander scale. These are among the recurrent nine-day wonders of journalism, but their lessons are soon forgotten.

Second, short of frauds legally recognised as such, there are frequent cases of excessive charges, and promoters' perquisites, politely known in the City as "rake-offs", which waste part of the new capital subscribed, to provide unnecessary profits for financial middlemen. There are also cases of insufficient information being contained in prospectuses and company reports.[1]

[1] This raises the question of the reform of the Companies Act. It has been said with truth that the present Act was

Third, from a social point of view, there is continuous misdirection of new capital. Funds flow, not in search of social advantage, but in search of profit.

Fourth, there is a failure, not only in respect of the quality, but of the quantity, of investment. There is a constant tendency, in times of trade depression, for the total volume of investment to fall short of what is socially desirable, and for unemployment to be thereby intensified. In times of boom, on the other hand, investment overshoots the mark and thereby hastens the recurrence of depression.

As Mr. Davenport has pointed out,

> the primary consideration of the market in domestic issues is not the needs of industry, but the needs of financial salesmanship. Issues are chiefly promoted which are likely to go well with the public and to give the promoters a chance of snatching a quick profit on the Stock Exchange. . . . The 1928-9 boom in industrial issues led not only to a great waste of private capital—we need not shed tears over fools parting with their money to the vendors of new inventions or bubble companies—but to the harmful disturbance of existing

---

already out of date when it was passed in 1929. There should be greater publicity regarding profits, particularly those of subsidiary companies; the form of balance sheets should be improved; in the case of subsidiaries an audited consolidated balance sheet should be published for the whole group; a prospectus should contain detailed information as to how the money to be raised would be spent; abridged prospectuses should be made illegal; the real issuer of a new loan should be prominently named on the prospectus, and should not shelter in small type under the wing of a joint stock bank, which is only a collecting agent, but is made, by this calculated printer's trick, to appear in large type, as though vouching for the issue. I am inclined to think that, in view of current abuses, private joint stock companies should no longer be allowed. No more should be formed, and those at present in existence should be required to transform themselves into public joint stock companies.

industries. The promotion, for example, of unnecessary artificial silk companies brought about such an excess capacity of plant that Courtaulds embarked on a policy of cutting prices to unremunerative levels in order to force the redundant companies into liquidation and their plant on to the scrap-heap. Much the same disturbance occurred in the safety glass and gramophone industries. The opposite extreme to the rashness and wastefulness of capital issues in a period of Stock Exchange activity is seen in a period of prolonged trade depression. Not an issue can then be made in the London capital market. No promoter will venture an appeal to the public, for no appeal would " go " in the Stock Exchange sense.[1]

The only object that an issuing house has, when it makes an issue, is to make the public take what its friends in the Stock Exchange and its private clients will not take themselves.

The third and fourth of the criticisms which I have made above, are the more fundamental, though the first and second serve also to display the defects of modern financial methods. The first and second relate, primarily, to individual losses, the third and fourth to social losses. All these losses are avoidable, and should be avoided. By what means?

In providing for the social control of long-term credit, we have to deal, not with an existing institution, but with the lack of one. The problem is not to transfer an existing mechanism from private to public hands, but to make something new. In a most rudimentary form, indeed, public control over the capital market has existed for some years, in the Treasury embargo on various classes of new issues. But this is so rudimentary and defective that it is worth little more than

[1] " The Control of National Investment ", *New Statesman*, October 10, 1931.

a theoretical admission, valuable only for debating purposes, of the impossibility of *laissez-faire* and a "free market" for capital, and of the need for a "managed" system of investment.

This embargo is doubly defective, first, because it lacks legal sanction and, second, because it is clumsy and purely negative in its operation. "It is properly speaking only a request which there is no legal power to enforce ",[1] a request made by the Chancellor of the Exchequer "to intending borrowers to refrain from coming on the market "[2] without the consent of the Treasury and the Bank of England. The original purpose of this "request" was to maintain the price of British Government securities and thus to help conversion operations. But the embargo is still maintained, for purposes which are never officially and intelligibly stated.

We need a more flexible and discriminating instrument, with legal power behind it. The Labour Party, therefore, proposes to set up a National Investment Board, whose functions and composition I shall now discuss. Opinion, both friendly and adverse, has focussed less upon this than upon many of our other proposals. But I put it in the front rank of practical importance. Such a Board will, I believe, be one of our most effective instruments of Socialist planning and national development, a powerful agency for dealing with unemployment and, even so, only the germ of what, if it succeeds, is likely to become one of the central financial institutions of a Socialist community.

The Board should be small, and its members appointed by the Government, with overlapping terms of office. They should be appointed, in the words of the Labour Party's Policy Report, " on appropriate

[1] *The Times* leading article, August 30, 1932.
[2] Official Treasury statement of the same date.

grounds of ability and willingness to carry out loyally the policy" determined upon.[1]

It might well be desirable, as I have already suggested, that the Chairman of the Board should also hold the office of Assistant Deputy Governor of the Bank of England. Possibly it would be convenient to provide for a further element of common membership between the Board and the Advisory Financial Council, which would replace the present Directorate of the Bank. The Board would need to work in close association with the Bank, as well as with other financial institutions, with several State Departments, and with the Planning Department of the Government. It would also require a capable staff of statisticians and other experts. But the details of such *liaison* and staffing can only be fully worked out, when the time for action arrives.

Broadly, the Board would have two functions. The first would be to license and direct investment, the second to mobilise the financial resources available for this purpose. It would strike, through its licensing and directing function, at the first three weaknesses noticed above, and through its mobilising function at the fourth. It would, in short, license for quality and mobilise for quantity.

The Board would exercise control over all public issues on the capital market, and its permission would

---

[1] *Currency, Banking and Finance*, p. 9. Mr. Colin Clark very sensibly remarks that " to make membership of the Board a political appointment might lead to inefficiency in working, and would certainly invite retaliatory action by any succeeding government. On the other hand it would be difficult even for the most reactionary Government to find a pretext for abolishing an expert Board which was in active operation; some of its activities might be inhibited, but over much of the field it would be very difficult deliberately to restore disorder after an element of planning had been introduced " (*Control of Investment*, p. 30).

CONTROL OF LONG-TERM CREDIT

be required before any such issue could be made. It would thus act as a licensing authority for new issues, both for home and foreign investment. It would only grant permission after it had been furnished with full particulars of the proposed new issue, and might make its permission conditional upon changes in the form of the proposal. For example, as suggested below, it might require a proposed new factory to be erected in a depressed area, which had appropriate facilities for production, but which was being allowed to become derelict. The Board would also exercise control over the Stock Exchange by refusing " leave to deal " in any issue which, having been refused a licence as a public issue, had then been placed privately.

In deciding whether or not to license a proposed new foreign issue, the Board would be guided by expert advice as to the total amount which could be lent abroad, during any given period, without unduly disturbing the foreign exchanges, and by other relevant considerations.

" In the past," to quote Mr. Montagu Norman,[1] " we were great lenders. Lending here [in the City] was practically indiscriminate. It was merely competitive. Can that continue with the same freedom in the future ? " This hesitating question suggests that the Macmillan Committee were inclined to convey too rosy a view when they stated that " we understand that important foreign issues made by these (issuing) houses are seldom underwritten in London unless the Governor of the Bank of England has first been consulted, and that any opinion he may offer will carry great weight ". His opinion will not necessarily carry the day and, as regards a large part of our foreign lending, especially on short term, it has not been the custom of the lenders to invite it. I have referred above to the German credit

[1] Speech at a bankers' dinner in the City on October 20, 1932.

crisis of the early summer of 1931, which rocked the City of London to its foundations, and prepared the way for the British credit crisis which followed a few months later, and to the fact that British financial houses had borrowed short-term funds excessively, and at a low rate of interest, from foreigners, other than Germans, and had lent these funds to Germany at a high rate of interest. This fact, and not an unbalanced budget, a luxury which most other countries also enjoyed at this time, was the effective cause of the political events of 1931, which destroyed both the Labour Government and the gold standard. The Macmillan Committee, whose report was published in June, 1931, had already given a timely warning of the " risk of financing long term investment by means of attracting short-term foreign funds of a precarious character " and had added that " to-day . . . our liabilities may be as much as double our liquid assets ".

This danger had, indeed, been foreseen by some, and there was a movement among the London financial houses themselves in 1929 to establish a credit information bureau. But this proposal was defeated by certain banks who feared that some of their foreign customers might be stolen by rival creditors, if information were pooled.

Since 1931 there has been a slight change of practice. The Bank of England is now confidentially informed by each bank and acceptance house of the total of its foreign credits and deposits. But this is insufficient. There should be compulsory pooling of such information, which should be made available both to the Bank and to the National Investment Board. Would-be foreign borrowers on long term would have to apply through their agents, and their applications would be made openly to the Board, which would have legal power to give or to refuse a licence, instead of being made secretly to the Governor of the Bank, who has only the moral power of offering an advisory opinion.

Foreign loans, especially to certain types of rulers and governments, have often been wasteful at the best, and at the worst provocative of wars and financial oppression. The British bond-holders in Egypt, buttressed on extortionate loans to a worthless monarch, are an oft-told tale.[1] Sir Arthur Salter has told some post-war stories : [2] of a Brazilian Government, which borrowed fifteen million dollars to pull down a hill at Rio de Janeiro, twenty-five million dollars to electrify the Central Railway of Brazil, which has not in fact been electrified, and twenty million dollars for a water supply scheme which has been abandoned ; and of a Colombian Government, which borrowed between 1924 and 1928 more than a hundred and fifty million dollars, principally to build an unnecessary railway to connect two valleys, each with an adequate outlet to the sea, but separated by a range of mountains 9,000 feet high. A costly tunnel through the top of this mountain range was begun by the Federal authorities, and then abandoned, the local authorities meanwhile having begun the construction of a costly road over the summit. These incidents are both humorous and instructive.

The whole question of foreign lending, indeed, raises large issues of international policy and co-operation, regarding which the Board would need to be informed of the Government's policy.

Loans to Dominion Governments, the Government of India and the Crown Colonies would, no doubt, continue to enjoy a certain measure of priority. But each application should be considered on its merits, and in relation to trade agreements between this

[1] But never told better than by Mr. H. N. Brailsford in his *War of Steel and Gold*.
[2] *Recovery*, pp. 105–6.

country and the would-be borrower. The same consideration applies to all external lending. We shall not have, in the future, such large sums to lend outside this country that we can afford to be indifferent to the willingness of borrowers to buy our goods and give employment to our workers.[1]

Loans to foreign Governments raise special problems, and the Board should be satisfied, before agreeing to any such loan, that the proceeds would not be spent on undesirable objects, such as armaments, or the mere duplication of existing British plant. Such loans may also raise questions concerning the domestic policy of debtor states, as well as the security of creditors and the development of international trade. It would be best, therefore, that they should be the subject of international consultation. For this purpose some suitable machinery, connected with the League of Nations, should be set up.

The Board's control over new foreign issues is liable to be defeated by the issue of loans abroad, followed by the sale of securities here. Money may also leak abroad, contrary to the intention of the Board or of the Government, through the purchase by persons resident in this country of existing securities held by persons resident abroad. This is just as much an export of capital as the subscription in this country of a new foreign issue. British exporters may also try to keep abroad the proceeds of their sales.

There is only one effective means of checking such undesired leakages, which might develop into a serious " flight of capital ".[2] This is to give the Government

[1] The Trustee Acts should, perhaps, be so amended as to make the grant of Trustee status to new loans raised by certain overseas borrowers dependent on the recommendation of the Board, and not automatic as at present.

[2] A " flight of capital ", which takes the form of the withdrawal of large short-term foreign balances, raises a different problem. The best solution of this is that such

power to control, if the need arose, the purchase of foreign exchange. The purposes for which foreign exchange is acquired can then be limited and selected by the controlling authority. Such control should not, in my opinion, be exercised, unless there were evidence that British investors and financiers were not playing the game. For it is a troublesome influence on international trade.

But the power should be held in reserve. It will be recalled that the National Government in 1931 took such power, but relinquished it after a few months. They have taken it again in 1934 in the Exchange Clearing Act. The most stringent control of foreign exchange dealings has been proved to be quite practicable, even in countries with lower standards of administrative efficiency than ours.[1]

> We believe [said the Macmillan Committee] that there is substance in the view that the British financial organisation concentrated in the City of London might with advantage be more closely co-ordinated with British industry, particularly large scale industry, than is now the case; and that in some respects the City is more highly organised to provide capital to foreign countries than to British industry.

This opinion has long been held by those who have watched our issue houses at work, a number of which have foreign origins and seem to have retained discriminating foreign sympathies and business con-

balances should not be in the habit of coming to London, or to any other foreign national centre. They are a constant source of financial instability and even in the City are often spoken of as "bad money". In so far as they are not kept at home, the best location for them is probably a reformed and strengthened Bank for International Settlements, which would command continuous confidence.

[1] The neatest and most interesting scheme of exchange control, worked by a country with high administrative standards, is that now operating in Denmark.

nections. It would be one of the duties of the National Investment Board to correct the tendency for an excessive proportion of capital funds to go abroad, while legitimate British needs are often starved of resources.

The historical explanation of this lop-sided development is that London, and the financiers operating there, have been primarily concerned with external trade, while British industry grew up chiefly in the North and Midlands, and was mainly financed out of its own profits and by private or family banks with headquarters in the provinces. Nor, under present conditions, are closer relations between London financiers and the industrial north always an unmixed blessing for the latter, as the post-war orgy of speculation and over-capitalisation in the Lancashire cotton industry demonstrated. The National Investment Board must here begin to write a new chapter.

In deciding whether or not to license a proposed new home issue, the Board would have several objects in view. It would aim at preventing the unnecessary addition of capital to industries which were already over-equipped, or the floating of enterprises which, though they might yield profits to investors, were anti-social or only of small social value. On this latter point it would need general guidance from the Government.

The Board would also aim at smoothing out unnecessary short-term fluctuations in the demand for capital. The orderly marketing of securities is an important factor in stabilising trade and employment.

The Board would also aim at checking, or at least postponing till a more convenient season, new issues which seemed likely to compete, for the savings available at any particular time, with the loan requirements of any programme of planned development and industrial reorganisation approved by the Government.

CONTROL OF LONG-TERM CREDIT

Particulars of such requirements, including the approved requirements of Local Authorities,[1] would be furnished to the Board by the Planning Department of the Government.

Such a programme must have priority secured to it in the capital market over all less urgent claims. Thus housing schemes should come before dog-racing tracks or cinemas; new plant for the scientific treatment of coal before new plant for the luxury trades; the establishment of a new industry in a depressed area before that of a new industry on the sprawling edge of Greater London.

The fact that a new issue, either home or foreign, had been licensed by the Board, should not be interpreted as an official invitation to the public to subscribe, still less as a Government guarantee of the interest, though such a guarantee might properly be given in appropriate cases.

It is a simple truth, sometimes forgotten, that a Government guarantee of interest, if not pushed to imprudent lengths, is for the taxpayer a cheaper form of inducement to capital development than any subsidy. Still cheaper is the conferment of Trustee status on selected securities. The revision of the Trustee Acts, already suggested, would give power to the Board to confer or to refuse such status. But no Government guarantee should in future be given without a measure of public control, or public participation in the value of the asset thereby created, e.g. through payments by the beneficiaries, in the form of cash or interest-bearing bonds, to the Treasury or to the Board. It was a scandal of the Trade Facilities Act that the State's guarantee was handed out free;

[1] The Public Works Loans Board, which now arranges loans for the smaller local authorities, might either be absorbed by the National Investment Board, or might continue in existence, acting in close co-operation with it.

a number of private interests got cheap capital, but the guarantor got nothing, except very remotely and indirectly.

This brings me to the second function of the Board, that of mobilising the funds available for investment. In order to maintain the price level and to prevent deflationary sagging and unemployment, the total volume of new investment must be kept well up to the level of available savings. It will be the Board's duty to see that there is no falling short here.[1] Available capital must not lie idle, either in banks or other hoarding places, nor be diverted, as happens now on a large scale during trade depression, from new construction to the financing of current business losses, and of unemployment rather than employment.[2]

The Board would be able to advise the Planning Department of the Government as to the financial practicability, at any given time, of the programme of capital development desired by the latter. Such advice should relate, not only to the magnitude of the programme, but also to its composition. Particularly from the point of view of employment, a well-balanced programme is essential.

It will be useful at this point to draw an up-to-date picture of the various sources of new loan funds, and

[1] Sometimes, on the other hand, it may be necessary for the Board to damp down the rate of investment, in order to prevent the development of an unhealthy inflationary boom. But this danger, at the time of writing, seems academic.

[2] It is ironical that successive British Governments, from 1924 onwards, have borrowed Post Office Savings Bank deposits to finance the Unemployment Insurance Fund, but not to finance development schemes, and it was one of the disgraces of the 1931 election that members of the National Government succeeded in scaring many electors into voting for them by the doubly false suggestion that the Labour Government had initiated this practice and that it had thereby endangered the safety of the deposits, which were, in fact, of course, guaranteed by the taxpayer.

of their relative magnitude. This picture has been changing rapidly in Britain since the War, and even some of our expert commentators have not yet accustomed their eyes to the change.

The chief changes have been (1) the diminishing importance of saving by wealthy individuals ; (2) the relative increase in the factor of undistributed profits within private industry ; (3) the rapid increase in the proportion of new loan funds furnished by public and semi-public bodies and by institutions—insurance companies and building societies being the most prominent of these—whose financial vitality is such that they have continued to grow luxuriantly even in the dry years of the depression. It is also necessary to understand clearly the true meaning of the familiar statistics regarding new issues.

The saving habits of the rich have not stood up well to the slump. They have withered in the economic drought. Whether even the rains of a returning capitalist prosperity would much revive them seems doubtful. Mr. Colin Clark deserves credit for his pathbreaking statistical studies in this field.[1]

The defenders of capitalism used to argue that a great inequality of incomes was necessary in order that a sufficient accumulation of capital might occur. A small class of very rich men was necessary, in order that they might save, so to speak, the unwanted tail-ends of their large incomes. This, it was said, enabled investment to proceed upon a sufficient scale. And, it was added, there was no other way of enabling this to be done. We must burn down the house of equality, in order to roast the pig of thrift.

Under the impact of Mr. Clark's figures, which I quote below, this argument, never very convincing to

[1] See his *National Income* and his pamphlet on *Control of Investment* (published by the New Fabian Research Bureau and Gollancz).

a Socialist, to-day lies flat on its face. He concludes that " the net savings made by the wealthy classes out of their own incomes have now become very small, and in many cases they are actually over-spending their incomes and living on their capital ".[1]

According to his estimates,[2] British savings in a normal post-war year have been about £400 millions, or just under ten per cent of the national income ; in 1929 (later years having been badly subnormal) they were about £380 millions. Of this total, about £125 millions were invested abroad, £130 millions were invested by or under the control of the State and Local Authorities, of which £45 millions were for municipal houses, and £55 millions in new houses built by private enterprise. This leaves only £70 millions—a surprisingly small sum—for home industry and commerce, apart from housing and public utility services. Since 1929 all these totals have shrivelled, that of investment abroad most, and that of housing, municipal and private, least of all.

So much for the destination of savings when turned into investment. The sources, from which these savings come, appear to be as follows : about £100 millions from the State and Local Authorities, by way of payments to sinking funds, depreciation funds, etc. ;[3] about £50 millions through building societies ; about £50 millions through insurance companies ; £25 to £30 millions through sums placed to reserve by co-operative societies, and savings through industrial insurance and savings banks ; and some £200 millions, calculated before deduction of income tax, through the undistributed profits of companies and firms. This last item of undistributed profits accounts, even after income tax has been deducted, for nearly half the total

---

[1] *Control of Investment*, p. 11. [2] *Ibid.*, pp. 9–10.
[3] It is surprising to find that Local Authorities pay as much as £50 millions a year into sinking funds for their loans.

savings made.[1] The residue of the total savings, after all these items have been allowed for, represents the net savings of the wealthy. As has already been remarked, this residue is in some years a small positive quantity, and in others is actually negative.

This analysis, both of the sources and of the destination of savings, brings out the fact that the State, Public Boards and Local Authorities play a much larger part both in saving and in investment than is yet commonly understood.[2] Correspondingly the wealthy private investor and private enterprise, apart from the factor of undistributed profits, play a much smaller part. There is already more practical socialism in the British air we breathe than either Socialists or anti-Socialists realise. This both simplifies the task of the National Investment Board and makes it more important.

Within the sphere of private industry, there is new investment (a) by new issues on the capital market, and (b) by the re-investment of undistributed profits,— partly in the business where the profits were made, partly in related subsidiary companies, partly in assets

[1] Mr. Davenport puts it at 38 per cent ("The Control of National Investment", *New Statesman*, October 10, 1931); Mr. Clark puts it higher.

[2] Credit for bringing out this fact must be given to the authors of *Britain's Industrial Future*, the "Liberal Yellow Book" of 1928, Books 2 and 4 of which contain many interesting figures, as well as certain disputable arguments. Mr. J. M. Keynes has also contributed to making clear some important relative quantities. Thus in an article in the *New Statesman* of September 24, 1932, he points out that in 1930, £109 millions were invested in capital expenditure by Local Authorities as against £21 millions in 1914, while the corresponding figures for new building financed through the Building Societies were £89 millions and £9 millions respectively. "In the two years 1930 and 1931 the aggregate finance provided by Building Societies was appreciably greater than the aggregate of new capital issues for all purposes within the United Kingdom."

independent of the fortunes of the business, e.g. in Government securities.

New issues, which were long accepted uncritically at their face value,[1] are now seen in a fresh light. " Apart from a small volume of industrial debentures," says Mr. Keynes, " the new issue market is mainly concerned with the marketing to the public of investments made some time previously." [2]

Mr. Clark has shown that " the major part of the money raised " by new issues, " when its destination is not, as is generally the case, left in complete ambiguity, is used not for real capital purposes at all, but simply for buying out existing vested interests ". It is much more a transfer of property rights than an addition to capital equipment. Moreover, " an almost unbelievably large proportion of the capital is filched in ' underwriting charges ', ' expenses of issue ' and rake-offs of all kinds." [3] It will be one of the functions, though by no means the most important, of the

---

[1] By the Colwyn Committee on *National Debt and Taxation*, for example.

[2] *New Statesman*, September 24, 1932.

[3] *Control of Investment*, p. 21. Mr. Clark goes on to quote the evidence before the Macmillan Committee of Mr. E. L. Payton, representing the National Union of Manufacturers, who said that " to get money " frequently you must " go to a man whom we will describe as a Company Promoter. He looks at your proposition and he proceeds to have every asset valued at the highest possible value that he can put on it. They do the same to the plant ; they practically write back again all the depreciation that has been carefully written off. Then they add something for goodwill. Then they say ' we will go to the public and get the money for you ', and by the time they have finished they leave you with your business and with very little extra money. They have taken out a big profit, and the costs of the operation will take up several years of good profits. . , . And you are left with an overcapitalised business, which increases the costs of production to your customers." Sometimes, as Mr. Hatry demonstrated to his clients, you are left with considerably less than this !

National Investment Board drastically to cut down these tributes paid by industry to financial middlemen, and to economise the cost of supplying new capital to all applicants, who are judged by the Board worthy to obtain it.[1]

Undistributed profits have become, in the post-war period, the largest single source of new savings in this country. We shall consider them further below.

It is not generally appreciated [says Mr. Davenport] that in the promotion of the average new company some 10 per cent of the capital goes in the expenses of the issue and 50 per cent, not in providing new capital for industry, but in making a present to the promoters and vendors of cash for the purchase of " existing rights ".[2]

This, indeed, relates only to new investment within the sphere of private industry. But there is another item of great and growing importance, namely the new capital expenditure of public and semi-public bodies.

What is not generally realised is the extent of the " socialised sector " in the economic structure. The key point, capital development, is very largely controlled by public authorities, both national and local. . . . Public works contracting alone provides occupation for more men than either the steel industry, the motor industry, or the cotton industry. This is entirely under public direction. There are very nearly as many builders as coal miners, and these are, naturally, in spite of the revival of private building, very dependent on the policy of local authorities. When to these are added the powers for expansion of plant possessed by such authorities as the Central Electricity Board, the Metropolitan

---

[1] There is little criticism of new issues in the weekly press, and still less in the daily press. I have heard of cases where strong pressure has been exercised, from interested quarters, to silence journalistic critics, who are threatened with the loss of their livelihood if they tell the public what they know.

[2] " The Control of National Investment ", in the *New Statesman* of October 10, 1931.

Water Board, and the Post Office, and the development of public utilities under municipal control throughout the country, the immense powers of public authorities in stimulating capital development become evident.[1]

All these would become clients of the National Investment Board, and so would the new Public Boards, which will be set up to conduct socialised enterprises. It will be an important part of the problem confronting the National Investment Board to determine the rate of aggregate investment of these public and semi-public bodies.

There are also to be considered the investments of the Insurance Companies, of the Investment Trusts and of the funds of the Building Societies, in so far as these are not sunk in loans secured as mortgages on house property.

The only " control " of sinking funds which the National Investment Board need exercise is the steady offer, on a sufficient scale, to persons and institutions whose old holdings are being paid off, of suitable investments for their liberated funds.

More serious questions of control arise in connection with undistributed profits, Insurance Companies, Investment Trusts and Building Societies.

In proportion as industries and services are socialised, the sources of undistributed private profits will be narrowed, and the disposal of the surpluses of public concerns will be a matter for consultation with the Planning Authorities. But meanwhile the size of this element in the national savings is so large that the question arises whether that part of it, which is in excess of reasonable requirements for self-finance in the business where it originates, should not be mobilised by the National Investment Board in aid of its approved

[1] From a recent leading article in the *Financial News*, quoted by Mr. Robert Boothby, *Political Quarterly*, October, 1934, p. 465.

programme. Possibly some remission of taxation might be given in respect of undistributed profits placed at the Board's disposal. The Insurance Companies should, in due course, be consolidated into a Public Corporation enjoying a monopoly of certain classes of insurance. But, pending this reorganisation, they might be required to inform the Board of the composition of their investments, and to hold certain proportions in prescribed forms.

A similar requirement might be imposed on Investment Trusts. Both these and Insurance Companies are in the habit of holding a considerable proportion of foreign securities. This proportion should be kept within bounds.

The function of Building Societies is to make loans, secured on mortgage, to facilitate house building and " home ownership ". In so far as their funds are used for this primary purpose, there is no occasion for control by the Board, though the location of new houses will be subject to geographical planning. But in so far as these funds are otherwise invested, control similar to that suggested for Insurance Companies and Investment Trusts might be applied. At the present time, 85 per cent of Building Society assets consist of mortgages, the remaining 15 per cent being mainly in gilt-edged securities.[1]

So far I have sketched only the minimum and essential functions of a National Investment Board. Even with functions no greater than these, the Board will be a very powerful instrument of social control.

Let it make good, justify itself in action, and win

[1] Figures quoted by Mr. Francis Williams in the *Daily Herald* of July 2, 1934. The total number of shareholders in Building Societies is now 1,748,000 ; of depositors, 631,000 ; and of borrowers, 951,000. Share capital is £395 million, or an average of £226 per shareholder ; deposits £75 million, or an average of £120 per depositor ; money advanced on mortgage £423 million, or an average of £445 per borrower.

general acceptance as a useful and familiar piece of our financial furniture, and there is little doubt that its functions will soon extend.[1]

Should the Board itself act as an issuing house? I see no objection in principle, and substantial possible advantages, especially in reducing the cost of capital supply. But this is not, in my opinion, one of the minimum essential functions of the Board. It may develop from experimental beginnings.

Should the Board receive grants from taxation to be devoted to national development? This is a question of convenience, on which we need not be dogmatic.

But whether or not part of the proceeds of taxation are actually handed over to the Board, it is an essential principle of sound Socialist finance that part of the proceeds of taxation should be used for capital development. In view of the decline of saving by wealthy individuals, the old arguments against high taxation of wealth are greatly weakened, while the need to use taxation as an aid to capital development is correspondingly strengthened.

In so far as this is done, no matter whether the funds raised by taxation for development are lent by the State, or paid out in subsidies, the need for long-term borrowing from private investors will be correspondingly reduced.

The control of investment is one of the key positions from which to launch a grand attack on unemployment. It is not enough to control credit and currency, we must also control investment, both in quantity and direction. If the Planning Department of the Government is to be regarded as the peaceful equivalent of the Committee of Imperial Defence, it is the duty of the National Investment Board to place at its disposal a financial " mass of manœuvre ".

[1] In relation to the Stock Exchange, for example.

CHAPTER XXIII

CONTROL OF SHORT-TERM CREDIT

In the execution of a Socialist financial policy, the role of short-term credit from the banks is less important than is sometimes supposed. It has been one of the faults of capitalist finance to rely too much on short-term credit.[1] Some of our basic industries and services, such as transport, have no need for short-term credit at all. They pay their way as they go and depend, for development, on long-term credit and on the reinvestment of their own surpluses. Other basic industries could, and should, be made largely independent of bank credit, and this should be done when they are financially reconstructed on Socialist lines. Fixed plant should never be financed by short-term credit, which should be confined to the provision of working capital from time to time.[2] Socialised industries, moreover, might find it more convenient, and cheaper, to finance their short-term requirements

[1] The German financial crisis of 1931, for example, was much intensified by the misuse of short term credits from abroad, which had been used in many cases to pay for the installation of fixed capital.

[2] Nor, of course, should all working capital be provided in this way. " A well-run Joint Stock Company ", as Mr. Cole observes, " keeps back a part of its profits—often a considerable part—for accumulation in the form of reserves; and these reserves are used both to provide working capital and to release the business from its dependence on bank credit " (*Intelligent Man's Guide through World Chaos*, p. 35).

largely by inland bills, based on their own credit, rather than by bank overdrafts. And an active policy of national investment, as sketched in the last chapter, will draw into long-term securities much of the money now lying on deposit with the banks, vainly awaiting short-term borrowers.

In spite of these considerations, however, short-term credit will continue to be an important element in our financial life. It is supplied at present principally through the "Big Five" Joint Stock Banks, which held between them, in April, 1933, £1,773 millions out of the £2,551 millions of deposits in British banks.[1] The Big Five, moreover, control a number of the smaller banks whose deposits are included in the latter total.

The Joint Stock Banks are to-day subject to much criticism, by no means confined to Socialists.[2] They are one of the least rationalised elements in our economic life. There is a serious lack of co-ordination between these Banks and the Bank of England, as was emphasised by the Macmillan Committee.[3] There is an equal lack of co-ordination between these Banks themselves. This is illustrated by the ridiculous and wasteful multiplication of branches all over the country. The number of branches of the Big Five increased by 15 per cent, from 7,423 to 8,538, between April, 1926, and April, 1933. Many of these are quite unnecessary and many are housed on unnecessarily expensive sites.

---

[1] These figures are taken from *Socialism and the Condition of the People* (published by the Labour Party, price 2d.), on which I have drawn freely in what follows.

[2] See, for instance, an article on *The Banks and Public Opinion*, in the Banking Supplement of *The Economist*, May 12, 1934, and the speech of Major Hills, a Conservative M.P., in the House of Commons on July 4, 1934: "I am perfectly certain that we cannot go on in our present haphazard way. . . . . There must be some control over the Joint Stock Banks."

[3] *Report*, pp. 160–1.

Often five branch banks, one for each of the Big Five, sit in a row along a main street, or face each other across a market square. In Park Lane I have counted no fewer than seven banks within a hundred yards or so, competing for the custom of the local inhabitants. Often, especially in London, the same Joint Stock Bank has separate branches within a stone's throw of each other.

Each of the Big Five has a large and highly paid directorate, many of whom, it may be surmised, are mere passengers. Thus Barclays in 1932 had a central directorate of forty-four members, Lloyds of thirty-three, the Midland of thirty-three, the National Provincial of twenty-four and the Westminster of twenty-six. In addition Barclay's had ninety-eight local Directors and the National Provincial thirty-one. The corresponding figures for the other three are not published. Directors' fees amounted to £304,624 for the year 1931 (Barclays, £93,236; Lloyds, £69,619; Midland, £50,411; National Provincial, £47,581; Westminster, £43,777). These figures do not include Managing Directors' salaries.

So heavy are the Banks' running expenses that it is understood that a minimum of 2 per cent has to be charged as interest on advances in order to cover these alone. This explains why, although the bank rate has stood for several years at the record low figure of 2 per cent, the Joint Stock Banks have refused to make any appreciable reduction in their interest charges on advances and overdrafts, which remain round about 5 per cent, though they have shown no hesitation in reducing the rate of interest which they allow on deposit accounts to ½ per cent. The policy of cheap money has thus been held up, and in large measure rendered ineffective, by this obstacle of the excessive expenses of the Joint Stock Banks. While trade and industry have been impoverished, the Banks almost alone have flourished, having maintained, by virtue of their semi-monopoly, high dividends varying from 14 to 18 per cent.[1]

There is, moreover, a lack of social purpose in the use of the Banks' resources. There is no relation between public policy and the granting of credits to industry. Advances are often made to mere speculators, and to assist businesses which have no social utility, but are often withheld from socially valuable and financially sound undertakings. The Banks have also shown a lack of enterprise in making advances. Large additional credits have been placed at their disposal, as a result of the Bank of England's open market operations. Yet in recent years, while their deposits have risen, their advances have fallen. They have pursued a passive rather than an active policy. Instead of assisting trade recovery, they have been content to buy increasing quantities of gilt-edged securities.

To remedy these defects, the Labour Party proposes that the " Big Five " should be amalgamated into a single Banking Corporation, with a comparatively small directorate, of persons appointed by the Government, on grounds of ability and willingness to carry on the work under the new conditions, in place of the five existing large directorates. A large saving would thus be effected in directors' fees, of the order of £250,000 a year. Part of this could be devoted to the creation of a really efficient statistical and research department, which none of the Big Five now possess.

The general managers, managers and other staff of

[1] " The Chairman of the Midland Bank explained that an average reduction of 1 per cent in the rate on overdrafts would necessitate either a reduction of the salary bill by one-third, or the suspension of dividend payments. Much of the force of this argument, however, was removed when Mr. McKenna, in the same speech, announced an increase in the Midland Bank's profits " (*Economist*, May 12, 1934).

the Big Five would continue in employment under the new directorate, and would probably furnish some members of it. In view of current misrepresentations, it should be emphasised that the new directorate would not consist of politicians—a number of the present directors are Tory politicians—but of energetic people with financial knowledge, including competent practical bankers. It might be convenient, for *liaison* purposes, that the Chairman of the new Board should be one of the Assistant Deputy Governors of the Bank of England. The Banking Corporation would stand, broadly, in the same relation to the Government as the Public Corporations proposed to be set up in other socialised industries and services.

If, as is very probable, it were found, after the amalgamation had come into full effect, that a smaller staff was required than at present, the reduction should be brought about, not by the dismissal of existing staff, but by checking new recruitment, and by speeding up the process of retiring the older officials on pension. And there should be a reduction in the large amount of overtime now worked. There should also be better facilities for promotion, on merit and not by favouritism, of young and active employees.

The Banking Corporation would be required to cooperate with the Bank of England and the National Investment Board in giving effect to the National Plan of Development. But it would be required to carry on the business of deposit banking efficiently and to safeguard the interests of depositors by keeping a sufficient proportion of its assets in liquid and easily realisable form. It is for consideration whether the deposits should be explicitly guaranteed by the Government, as the deposits in the Post Office Savings Bank are now. If it were generally felt that such a guarantee was necessary, in order to create confidence in the new institution, it should be given.

The Corporation should exercise a large measure of discretion in dealing with particular applications for credit, especially from private individuals and firms. It would be both physically impossible and politically undesirable for any Minister of the Crown to attempt to adjudicate between the claims of private individuals or firms to receive overdrafts, and still more undesirable that Parliament, or individual members of Parliament, should intervene in such questions of detail. On the other hand, the basic industries, particularly those organised as Public Corporations, must be assured of adequate credit, either on long term, or through the Corporation, or by inland bills or other appropriate means.

The shares in the Joint Stock Banks—which only represent 5 per cent of the Banks' resources, the rest being furnished by their depositors—would be acquired by the Corporation at a reasonable and equitable price. The shareholders would lose their present nominal powers of control and would become, in effect, debenture holders. They should be paid off as rapidly as possible. The proceeds of the sale of redundant branch premises, which should be carried out as the state of the market permitted and should realise a considerable sum, might be applied to such repayment. As repayment proceeded, it might be considered whether an agreed part of the surplus of the Corporation should not be paid over each year to the Treasury.

A new credit institution should also be created, as recommended by the Macmillan Committee, but under public ownership and control, to grant intermediate credits to approved industries and to agriculture.[1] This institution should take over, at a fair valuation, the frozen credits which the Banking Corporation will inherit from the Joint Stock Banks, whose liquidity they have so seriously impaired.

[1] Possibly there should be a separate credit institution for agriculture.

Of the banks and financial houses, other than the Big Five, which now receive deposits, some would most conveniently be merged in the Banking Corporation. Others, for special reasons, would continue to operate outside it. Branches of foreign and Dominion Banks, those Merchant Banking Houses which now receive deposits, and the Co-operative Wholesale Bank, would fall into this category. Deposit banking, outside the Banking Corporation, should, however, only be carried on in this country in future on the grant of a licence from the Government. And it should be a condition of such a licence that there was no transfer to the licensed bank of any substantial quantity of deposits from the Banking Corporation.

This scheme of reorganisation, which I have outlined, would rationalise British deposit banking and bring it into efficient relationship with other financial institutions and with trade and industry. Differing opinions are held within the Labour Party as to the urgency of this change, relatively to others. It is held by some that it should be made by the next Labour Government at an early stage. Others would postpone it, until we have progressed some distance with the socialisation of industry.[1] My personal opinion is that events, impossible to foretell now, will largely determine this and other questions of priority. If, in spite of clear statements of what we intend, our political opponents perversely misrepresent "the nationalisation of the banks" as meaning confiscation of bank shares and deposits, and the control of banking by incompetent politicians, and if, by the propagation of

[1] See, for example, Mr. Thomas Johnston's *Financiers and the Nation*, Chapter XX, for an interesting argument along this line, concluding that "so long as private industry run for profit continues, and to the extent to which it continues, its banking system may well continue also as a private enterprise".

such lies, they start a flight of capital, or a run on the banks, they may create conditions in which a newly elected Labour Government will have no choice, but to deal resolutely and speedily with this question. If, on the other hand, such misrepresentation is either not attempted, or, being attempted, falls flat, and if the present directors of the Joint Stock Banks show a willingness to co-operate loyally with a Labour Government in its policies of development and employment, and in so handling their investments as to maintain the national credit, it may well be that other constructive tasks will seem more urgent than the creation of the new Banking Corporation.

It remains to consider the discount houses and the acceptance houses. Control over these will be secured through the socialised Bank of England and through the Banking Corporation. A discount house cannot function, unless it is able in case of need to discount its bills at the Central Bank, or to borrow on them from the Central Bank. An acceptance house, in the same way, cannot function, unless its bills are taken by the Bank of England, for, unless they are so taken, they will not be bought by discount companies or by the banks. All these institutions now show their balance sheets to the Bank of England and render returns of their foreign deposits. Moreover, they are at present dependent for part of their funds on the Joint Stock Banks, and would be similarly dependent, under the new system, on the Banking Corporation.

There is at present a much closer relationship between the Bank of England and the acceptance houses than between the former and the Joint Stock Banks. The acceptance houses, or merchant bankers, do three classes of business—acceptance business proper, issuing business and the holding of foreign deposits. The acceptance business is essential to the carrying on of British foreign trade. It also plays an important part, through the "Bill on London", in trade between foreign countries. For the reason given above it is directly under the control of the Bank of England. Any control of British foreign trade, whether quantitative or qualitative, which a Labour Government might institute could, therefore, be operated through the Bank of England's control over the acceptance houses. As explained in the last chapter, the permission of the National Investment Board would be required for all new issues, and in many cases the intervention of the acceptance houses, and the charging by them of a commission, would no longer be necessary.

PART V

PLANNING

CHAPTER XXIV

THE NATURE AND OBJECTS OF ECONOMIC PLANNING

PLANNING or drifting, looking ahead or living from hand to mouth, are two different styles of conduct. I should define Economic Planning, in its widest sense, as the deliberate direction, by persons in control of large resources,[1] of economic activities towards chosen ends. Planning is not, of course, a good thing in itself. It will be good or bad, according to who directs, towards what chosen ends, by what means, and with what skill. But a good plan, well executed, is always better than no plan at all.

Economic Planning is to be contrasted with *Laissez-faire*, Free Competition, Free Enterprise, the Free Play of Economic Forces, Service through Profit-seeking, Automatic Adjustments through the Price Mechanism. These are the soothing phrases, or some of them, which do duty in this controversy.

Anti-planners worship the God of the Free Market, in which all prices, including wages, move freely under the influence of ever-changing demand and supply, and by their movements bring a double stream of blessings

[1] The qualification " in control of large resources " is necessary, if we are to exclude from the definition the little economic " planlets " of small firms, or individual producers or consumers. These are each too small for variations in the doings of any one of them to have any appreciable effect on prices or on total production or consumption.

to mankind : employment, on appropriately changing terms, not only to all labour, but to all capital and land as well, and satisfaction of consumers' preferences, for all who have money to spend, whether much or little. This stream, they tell us, will flow ever more abundantly, as capital accumulates and knowledge grows and profiteers adventure, always on one condition. Man must not tamper with the divine machine, nor defy the inexorable laws which rule the economic universe. All the world's woes to-day—poverty, unemployment, crisis—arise from such defiance. Man has tried to plan, and brought down ruin on his impious head.

Much time might be spent in examining these doctrines of Individualism. But I have neither space nor patience, in a book devoted to positive proposals, for so negative a task.[1]

I desire to make only three points, in passing, on the individualist theory of the anti-planners. The "freedom" which they worship has strict limits, which they seldom emphasise. The free play of economic forces, which is to bring salvation, is to operate within the legal framework of capitalism. And this, as has been said already, frames social inequality. Though he resents State interference in general, it is no part of the individualist's creed that the State should cease to interfere in one most important particular, namely to enforce the law, which in its turn enforces grave inequalities of wealth, status and opportunity. The policeman and the judge are not to be abolished. Private property in the means of production, most unequally distributed and perpetuated by inheritance ; the sanctity of contract ;

[1] I commend, however, Mrs. Barbara Wootton's admirable discussion in her book, *Plan or No Plan* (Gollancz, 1934) of the respective achievements and possibilities of an Unplanned and a Planned Economy.

the maintenance of law and order; the stiff class structure of society; these things would stand. In freedom and opportunity all citizens would be equal in law, yet grossly unequal in fact.

In the second place, the "free enterprise" of the individualists' theory is not, as some seem to argue, a present possession, to be defended at all costs against the planners. It belonged to a short and peculiar phase in our history, which has already passed away. Freedom to compete implied also freedom not to compete, but to combine. Private monopoly, in all its variations of degree and form—running from huge trusts and combines to mere unwritten "gentlemen's agreements"—is both the child and the destroyer of freedom. Not only is this true within national frontiers. The understandings of financiers and industrialists cross frontiers and limit "free enterprise" internationally.

Free enterprise, therefore, is not a phrase which accurately describes modern capitalism. In a large measure, free enterprise has vanished. But private enterprise, by no means the same thing, remains the dominant type of economic organisation.

Thirdly, a word as to price movements. The individualist of the more intellectual type makes a great parade of these. He shows, with great elaboration of argument, that they perform an indispensable function in an unplanned economy. They secure the most economical distribution of limited supplies of goods, and also of "the agents of production". "Most economical", in this context, means most closely in accord with effective demand, whether of consumers, or of business men, no account being taken either of inequalities of income, or of the social utility of rival demands. It is a pretty picture. Planning, individualists think, would smudge the picture, and be "uneconomic". Some go so far as to maintain that a

Planned Socialist Economy could not be " rational ", since it could not reproduce, in their completeness, these indispensable price movements of " free capitalism ".

Such arguments against Socialism—and they apply equally against the privately planned Monopolistic Capitalism, which is developing around us—overreach themselves. They prove too much.

The practical application of this worship of price movements is illustrated by the following historical incident.[1] A famine was anticipated in an Indian Province. The Government was advised to build up a reserve supply of grain, but refused, on the ground that, if it were known that grain was being stored, speculators would be inactive and prices would fail to rise in anticipation of a coming shortage and that, if prices failed to rise, the most economical use of grain would not be promoted. The Government, therefore, laid up no reserves, the famine came, and the people died like flies. This was *laissez-faire* in action.

What is it, of practical importance to a Socialist, which emerges from individualist disquisitions on price movements ? Only this, that, in so far as we retain prices at all in our economic system, and a price mechanism—and on grounds of practical convenience we shall certainly retain it, though possibly its range will be narrowed—we must study the working of this mechanism, lest its unanticipated movements defeat our purposes.[2]

I turn from these reflections on Individualism to the consideration of Planning.

Planning is not the same thing as Socialism.

[1] Related by Professor Jacob Viner of Chicago in a lecture at the London School of Economics in 1933.

[2] It is one of the great merits of Mrs. Wootton's book, *Plan or No Plan*, that she makes this study, and relates it to the Planned, as well as the Unplanned, Economy.

Socialism is primarily a question of ownership, planning a question of control or direction. Planning is not necessarily in the public interest, nor are those who direct it necessarily the agents of the State. There is private planning towards private ends and social planning towards social ends. And these are quite distinct in theory, though in practice we find hybrid forms. [1]

Privately planned capitalism holds many ugly possibilities, some of which in various parts of the world have already begun to be experienced. Private monopolies may ruthlessly exploit the labour of vast populations and the natural wealth of great areas. Private monopolies may grow into giants, link arms with other giants, and tread the earth as masters, making their profits as much from buying governments, including judges and officials, as from selling goods. Their chosen ends are power and plunder. Their means are manifold. Sometimes they aim at building up demand by bribery, false statements or law breaking. Thus some armament firms and some drug traffickers, to take only two examples, have been known to collect business.

Sometimes, demand being given, they limit output in order to raise prices and bring profits to a maximum. These are the elementary economics of monopoly. And clearly, when output is deliberately restricted, below what would be forthcoming under competition,

[1] Logically there are five alternative systems—extreme types between which, in reality, lie many intermediate, or mixed, arrangements. These five are Unplanned Capitalism, Privately Planned Capitalism, Socially Planned Capitalism, Planned Socialism and Unplanned Socialism. The last of these is, I think, of theoretical interest only, combining public ownership of the means of production with free movement of all prices. In practice this is a most unlikely combination. But perfectly possible, if any society chose to adopt it. See Professor Cassel's *Theory of Social Economy*.

employment is likewise restricted. In this and other ways private planning under capitalism often creates unemployment. Thus " rationalisation " schemes, justified at first sight on grounds of efficiency and lower costs, but pursued wholly without regard to social ends or any socially designed plan, make whole townships and industrial areas derelict, deserts from which the waters of enterprise have drained away, leaving behind them populations without work or hope and social capital—buildings, public services, public amenities— falling into ruin. The ghost towns on Tyneside, in South Wales, and other devastated districts, bear witness to these processes of private planning. A society, subject to such influences, it has been truly said, is " more planned against than planning ".

Since, therefore, private planning is, at the best, non-social and in many cases plainly anti-social, and since, in any case, it is not an instrument strong enough to change chaos and poverty into order and prosperity, the minds of many who would not call themselves Socialists turn towards social planning, or towards plans, part private and part social.[1]

There are difficulties in the application of social planning within the framework of capitalism. But these are not, as some theorists allege,[2] " inherently " insuperable. Such beginnings, moreover, may accelerate the transition to Socialism.

The practical Socialist will hold that, both in the expanding socialised sector and in the dwindling private

[1] There is a growing literature in England on this subject. Sir Arthur Salter's *Framework of an Ordered Society*, Sir Basil Blackett's *Planned Money* (a title too narrow to describe the book, which discusses also planning in industry), Mr. Harold Macmillan's *Reconstruction, a Plea for a National Policy*, are examples of it. Rathenau in Germany was a forerunner. See his book *In Days to Come*.

[2] Here some individualists and some communists are found chanting in unison.

NATURE OF ECONOMIC PLANNING 249

sector, there should be social planning. In the chapters which follow, I am concerned only with social planning, that is to say with the deliberate direction *by agents of the community* [1] of economic activities towards ends, chosen on grounds of social, not of private, advantage.

What are these chosen ends? " Plan for what? " —our critics ask. There need not be only one object in our planning. There may be several, jointly pursued. And these may vary with circumstances. The two outstanding examples of planning on a large scale in recent times are furnished by the World War and by the Soviet experiment. The object of the former was to win the war. That and nothing else. And it is on record that the reluctance of British business men to abandon profit-seeking and the pursuit of " business as usual " in the supply of shipping, food and munitions nearly lost the war.

The main objects of planning in the Soviet Union I have tried to summarise elsewhere as follows.

> To avoid the economic crises and trade fluctuations of capitalism; to keep the whole working population in continuous employment and to raise their standard of living, without permitting the growth of large inequalities, to a level higher than that of the workers in capitalist countries; to achieve a large measure of economic self-sufficiency and, as a means to this end, to stimulate to the utmost the industrialisation of the country.[2]

For Western Socialists, in peace time, the general object of planning is the maximum social advantage. Our particular objects are to wage peaceful war on poverty, insecurity, social inequality, and war itself.

[1] Men sometimes act, in effect, as agents of the community without express appointment. Those, for example, who founded and carry on the work of the National Trust for the Preservation of Places of Historic Interest and Natural Beauty, as to which see Chapter XXVII.

[2] *Twelve Studies in Soviet Russia*, p. 31 (Gollancz, 1933).

The surrounding conditions of British planning, and many of its methods, will differ widely from the Russian, but we shall have many objects, though not all, in common.

I have argued in an earlier chapter that in every modern community there is a nucleus of Socialism, a socialised sector, wide or narrow, in its economic life. Likewise in every community there is a nucleus of social planning, chiefly within the socialised sector, but extending also into the private sector. Social progress in public education has been planned, and in public health. No " invisible hand " of the God of the individualists brought these public services. No mere " price movements " created them. Likewise the State Budget is, within its limits, a rudimentary form of planned economy.

Plans are seldom exactly realised, and should be always in process of revision. Planning is only a method of trial and error, an alternative to the trial and error of Unplanned Capitalism. Planners will make mistakes, miscalculate the future, sometimes waste wealth and opportunities, often change direction. But they, at least, have their eyes fixed, not on abstractions, but on realities.

Social planning may be considered in four stages, two national and two international. First, the national planning of particular industries or services, each considered separately ; second, national planning covering a number of different industries or services, and co-ordinating the national plans for each ; third, international planning covering the same industry or service in a number of different countries ; fourth, international planning, co-ordinating a number of national plans, each of which covers a number of different industries or services.

In Part III of this book I have been concerned with planning in the first stage. In Part IV partly with the first and partly with the second stage, as illustrated by the control and direction of financial resources. I shall now consider some further problems of planning in this second stage.

International social planning is still largely in the future. The cults of national self-sufficiency and national sovereignty do not help to promote it. But I shall touch on it in Chapter XXIX.

CHAPTER XXV

EMPLOYMENT THROUGH PLANNED DEVELOPMENT

UNEMPLOYMENT is the greatest unsolved problem of capitalism; in terms of human values by far the greatest. In Britain in the autumn of 1934, as these words are written, the total of registered unemployed still stands above two millions. Since 1921 it has never, save for a few weeks in 1926, fallen below one million. Without a large dose both of Planning and of Socialism, I believe that no approach to a solution is possible.

The point is often made that there is no unemployment in the Army, but great unemployment in private industry. The Army falls inside the planned and socialised sector of our national life and outside the profit system. Inside the profit system we can only do what " pays ". It does not " pay " to let all men work and grow rich, as science now makes possible. Therefore, many millions must stay idle, and many more millions poor.

The primary task of the next Labour Government must be to make a large and rapid reduction in unemployment. By its success or failure in this task it will be judged. We must prove that we can plan away a great mass of unemployment. Unless we are reasonably confident that, within the lifetime of a normal Parliament, we can do this, we had better not take office again, even with a Parliamentary majority.

The humiliations of the last attempt, in 1929 to 1931, will bear no repetition.

" Work or maintenance " is a famous slogan, and a moral precept which must be honoured. But we have talked and thought much more of maintenance than work in these despairing years. It is time to take the Unemployment Problem and stand it on its head, transform it into the Employment Problem, and do our best to solve *that*.

To secure a large and rapid reduction in unemployment, we must pursue concurrently five lines of policy. We must slow down the entry of the younger generation into the field of employment ; speed up the exit of the older generation from this field ; reduce the hours of labour ; plan and push national development ; plan and push international trade.

Some critics say that the first and second, and even, some would add, the third of these policies are only juggling with the unemployment figures, that they do nothing to increase employment, but only put a new label on some of the unemployed, and redistribute an undiminished total of unemployment in a different way. It is even argued that they will increase the total, by imposing new burdens on "industry" and on the taxpayer. Paying for younger people to stay longer at school or college, or paying older people to retire, or sharing the same amount of work, or possibly a less amount, among more workers, does nothing, it is said, to diminish in any true sense the volume of unemployment.

But let us be clear what we mean by unemployment. Unemployment is unwilling idleness. The unemployed man is an outlaw, against his will, from the productive process going on around him. But leisure is not unemployment ; education is not unemployment ; rest from toil, in the evening of life or in time of sickness or physical incapacity, is not unemployment.

We seek to create full employment, for all who are able and willing to work, within the age groups defined by public policy as the working years of life, and for the hours laid down by law or determined by collective bargaining. It seems natural that, as productivity grows, the age of entry into employment should be raised, and the age of exit lowered, that hours of work should be reduced, and the good social habit of holidays with pay extended. These would indeed, in a well-organised community, be the natural consequences of economic progress and of " labour-saving " invention. But under modern capitalism these consequences do not follow, production lags behind productivity, and " labour saving " assumes grim and unnatural forms. Regarded from this angle, Socialism is a planned return to nature.

I shall deal in this chapter with the fourth line of policy indicated above, that of national development.[1] A National Plan must provide for a large and varied programme. This should be the strongest of all the forces, which we can quickly set in motion, for increasing employment. It is not difficult to make a long list of desirable developments, which would confer great social benefit on the community. Here are some leading items in such a list.

Building, including houses,[2] schools and hospitals,

---

[1] I have drawn some arguments and examples in the paragraphs which follow from the Section on " Planned Development of National Resources " in the pamphlet, *Socialism and the Condition of the People.*

[2] The Labour Party's programme in regard to housing is set out in detail in the pamphlet *Up with the Houses ! Down with the Slums !* accepted at the Southport Conference in 1934. One of its principal features is the establishment of a National Housing Commission, to be appointed by the Minister of Health to act as his agent in planning and executing, either through the Local Authorities or, if necessary, directly, a large scale building programme. This Commission, if

worked out in accordance with regional plans; electrification, including the electrification of the railways; the erection of plants in the mining areas for the extraction of oil and other by-products from coal; land drainage and water supply, to be worked out in conjunction, and based on regional plans; agricultural development, including a vigorous extension of afforestation and forest holdings; roads, bridges and harbour and port improvements; municipal developments of many kinds; the re-equipment of socialised industries, and also of certain industries not yet ripe for socialisation, but requiring drastic measures of reorganisation under public control.

Such a programme would provide additional employment in a large number of different industries, in many different parts of the country, and mostly within the socialised sector, or within the range of early additions to it. It must be a varied and well-balanced programme. Ambitious schemes of public works have sometimes failed, in other countries, to produce the anticipated results, not because they were too ambitious, but because they were insufficiently varied in their composition.[1] Not too many eggs, but too few baskets.

We must restate the theory, and reshape the prac-

suitably composed, will, in my judgment, supply a central driving force which has often been lacking in the past. The Minister of Health himself is too heavily burdened with other duties to be able to give proper attention to housing, in respect of which his Department has established as yet no conspicuous tradition of positive activity. A slow and sleepy interchange of letters with Local Authorities, and a presumption that " No " rather than " Yes " is the correct Whitehall answer, are not sufficient.

[1] In post-war Germany, for example. See Mr. Brinley Thomas's account in Part II, Chapters VI and IX, of *Unbalanced Budgets, A Study of the Financial Crisis in Fifteen Countries*, by myself and other authors (Routledge, 1934).

tice, of public works, viewed as a remedy for unemployment. The old theory, propounded by many economists, including some Socialists, was as follows. When private works failed, more conspicuously than usual, to employ the working population, then public works should be called in, to restore and stabilise the demand for labour. Public works were regarded as a balancing factor, to be expanded in times of depression and contracted again in times of boom, in order to " iron out fluctuations in the demand for labour ". And this demand for labour, under capitalism, always fell far short of the supply. Except during the Great War !

In practice, the normal field of private works was the whole field of private industry. Public works were warned off this grass. There must be no trespass on the preserves of private property, no " unfair competition with private enterprise ".[1] Public works must be fed on the scrag ends of economic activity. The socialised sector must not be extended. This limitation, imposed as much by the timid and antiquated opinions of influential individuals as by the political conditions of Minority Government, was accepted by the Second Labour Government as a whole, though resisted by some members of it. " We have done all we can on roads, and schools, and telephones, and paddling pools for the children in the depressed areas," it was said. "What more can we do?" Some Ministers added, first quietly in private, then, as " the crisis " developed, more loudly, and finally in public, " unemployment is still going up. That means that we have carried these public works too far. Many of

[1] Housing in this country is on the borderline between private and public works. Private enterprise and its advocates resent the activities of public authorities. Hence the miserable see-saw of British housing policy since the war.

them are uneconomic anyhow. We must practise economy and cut them down ".[1]

Even so, the Second Labour Government's public works policy, limited in scope and slow, muddled and half-hearted in execution as it was, was not a failure. " During the years 1929–1931," as Mr. Colin Clark has pointed out,[2] owing to causes outside British control,

> the number of those employed in the export trades was almost halved, putting an extra million men and women on to the unemployment register, not counting the indirect effects on other trades. But we were able to battle with some success against this terrific tide, and actually to increase the number working for the home market. By 1931 expenditure on public works was some £600,000 a week in excess of what it had been in 1929. Even though a certain amount of this was frittered away in contractors' profits, etc., it represents directly and indirectly the employment of some 250,000 men. The National Government has cut public capital expenditure to below the 1929 level, and has thus increased unemployment by more than this amount.

The Labour Government's policy was not a failure, in spite of Mr. Snowden's too tight grip on money and Mr. MacDonald's and Mr. Thomas's too loose grip on ideas. But it was far less of a success than it might have been.

We must move to a new point of view. Public

[1] Public works were only palliatives. He would rather put ten men into permanent work than forty into work which would not last. This statement, made by Sir Wyndham Portal (*The Times*, Sept. 10, 1934), whom the National Government appointed to inquire into the distress in South Wales, is a perfect expression of the old-fashioned views. Why should public works give only temporary employment ? And why make the absurd suggestion that private capitalism gives " permanent work " ?
[2] *The Control of Investment*, pp. 8–9.

works must be started and expanded, not as mere supplements to private works, but on their own merits, as projects of public development, hitherto neglected, and of employment. If they extend the socialised sector, so much the better. The useful work waiting to be done is practically unlimited. Our available resources are very great, and a large part of them is lying idle. Let us marry the one to the other. The full employment of all our resources in men, material, machines and money is the road to higher standards of life and greater public wealth.

This seems and, in my judgment, is the plainest common sense. But there are some, including very high and respectable authorities, who see it otherwise. These may be divided into two schools. One sees in such proposals, not the road to wealth, but the road to ruin. The other sees no road at all, no road to anywhere, but only a turning round and round in our own tracks.

I will deal shortly with these two schools of objectors, beginning with the second. This represents the famous so-called " Treasury view ". " It is the orthodox Treasury dogma, steadfastly held, that whatever might be the political and social advantages, very little additional employment and no permanent additional employment can, in fact, and as a general rule, be created by State borrowing and State expenditure." These are the words of Mr. Winston Churchill in his Budget speech of 1929. Either borrowing or taxation to finance public works will merely divert money and labour from private works. It will lead to no additional investment or employment. It will only substitute one form of investment and employment for another.

This Treasury view would be correct, only if there were no unemployed resources, or practically none. And then it would be true of all new works, private not less than public. Every new demand, no matter from what source, for labour or goods or money, would then be a diversion from, not an addition to, other demands. Every private employer, who built a new factory, would prevent another private employer from doing the same. The only place in the modern world where the Treasury view is even approximately true is Soviet Russia, where a planned economy has practically banished unemployment. And this is both a result of planning, and a strong reason for its continuance, so that an intelligent choice may be made between what really *are* alternative employments, both of labour and of other resources.

Our fundamental choice is different. It is a choice between employment and unemployment. In the presence of unemployed resources, human, material and financial, on the scale to which we have, to our discredit, become accustomed, the Treasury view is quite untenable.[1] This " orthodox Treasury dogma ", if really " steadfastly held ", leads to the absurd conclusion, contrary both to reason and experience, that, however great unemployment may be, it can never be diminished. For if no public borrowing or expenditure can diminish it, neither can any private borrowing or expenditure. There is no valid ground, *in this connection*, for distinguishing between new public and new private works. Both lead to a demand for labour, materials and money. Both, when these are available and not in use, reduce unemployment.[2] Common sense, therefore, triumphs over the Treasury view.

[1] Sir Basil Blackett, himself an ex-Treasury official of some distinction, is reported in *The Times* of September 22, 1934, as saying that, " in present circumstances, the Treasury has been unduly influenced by old-fashioned orthodox views ".

[2] As the quantity of unemployed resources shrinks, the chance that new demands will be diversions, not additions, grows. When the quantity is small, diversions will be relatively large. When the quantity is zero, all new demands will be diversions.

I turn to the other school of thought which rejects the policy of public works, regarding these as the road to ruin. This school, again, has two main branches. The first is simply anti-Socialist, opposed to public works and public enterprise as such. Against this doctrinaire opinion the whole argument of this book is directed. There would be no advantage in summarising it at this point. The second branch admits that some public works might, if we could afford them, bring additional employment and some social advantage, but argues that we cannot afford them on any considerable scale and that, if we spend much money on them, we shall be ruined. This argument I believe to be plainly wrong.

What a man can " afford " depends upon his income. The larger his income, the more he can afford. He may be living in poverty, because his earning powers are rusting unused. Could he but bring them into use, he could afford many things now beyond his reach. As with a man, so with a family, so with a community. These thoughts are elementary. But they are none the less true.

This is a comparatively wealthy country. The wealth is very badly distributed, a few being very rich and many very poor. But, at this stage in my argument, the distribution of wealth is not the most important point. The most important point is that our wealth is far less than it might be, because more than two million people are unemployed, are producing no wealth, and are being kept alive, at a miserably low standard of life, out of the wealth produced by the others, and because much land, many machines and large stocks of goods are also not being used. We cannot afford to allow all this unwilling idleness of human beings and all this wastage of material things to continue. As a community we should be much wealthier, and as individuals we could afford to buy many things which we lack now, if we set our idle workers to produce new wealth, with the aid of our idle material resources.

The critics, whose doubts we are now examining, ask : Where is the money to come from to pay for all these things ? In one sense this is a foolish question. Money is only a convenience to assist exchange, a lubricant of the economic machine. Fundamentally men live by exchanging the products of their labour, though, in a capitalist society, a large part of the products go to those who have not laboured, some to private property owners and some to unemployed workers. If there are more products to exchange, then, unless, as often happens, capitalists destroy them before they can be exchanged, so as to profit by artificial scarcity, wealth will be greater, and if the greater wealth is more equally distributed, human well-being will be greater still.

But the question admits, after all, of a series of quite simple answers. The money to pay for all these things will come, partly from the money which is now being paid to the unemployed, who will be reabsorbed in useful work ; partly from the savings which are now running to waste, financing losses instead of new investment ; partly from the new money which will be created, in the form of additional currency and additional bank credits, in pursuance of the monetary policy outlined in Chapter XX, whereby the general level of prices is kept steady and purchasing power expanded in proportion as production expands.[1]

From this digression, in which I have been discussing

[1] Any reader, who finds this discussion too simple or too summary, may be interested to read also Mr. Keynes's *Essays in Persuasion*, Part II, Sections 4, 5 and 6, Mr. Colin Clark's pamphlet on *The Control of Investment* and his article in the *Economic Journal* of June, 1933, and the American Report of the Columbia University Commission on *Economic Reconstruction* (Columbia University Press, 1934).

objections to any large programme of national development and employment, I return to the actual programme which I have already outlined. There will, of course, be a limit to the total programme which can be financed during any given period. But this limit will be elastic, rather than rigidly fixed. It will depend on the savings, both individual and corporate, available for investment, the corporate savings including those of public bodies and socialised undertakings. It is essential that the programme should be big enough to ensure the absorption of all these savings and prevent any wastage. It has been truly said that Socialists have to consider, not only the problem of providing savings for enterprise, but also the problem of providing enterprise for savings. Principally, and increasingly as the socialised sector and the range of public works extend, it will be public enterprise which will take care of new savings. But private enterprise will continue, for a considerable time to come, to be a not unimportant factor. In addition to individual and corporate savings, there will be another source of finance for capital development, namely taxation. Some forms of public capital expenditure, such as afforestation and roads, are to-day financed by taxes. There is no reason for disturbing this practice, which may indeed be extended to other suitable cases. A Development Fund, fed from taxation, should be set up and applied, probably by loan and revolving credits, to selected public developments. This element of taxation helps to give elasticity to the limit of the total programme of development in any given period. Its magnitude must be determined by the Government, which must take decisions from time to time on the relative importance of consumption and construction, enjoyment in the present and provision for the future.

The financing of any really large development programme must be mainly by loan. For this programme must begin at the beginning of the next Labour Government's life. It cannot wait till this industry or that has been socialised, and has acquired a surplus. And loans must come from persons and institutions possessing loanable funds. This will be the initial situation, which no rambling rhetoric can alter. We must borrow from those who have money to lend. Even borrowing from socialised banks would only be borrowing, in effect, from their depositors.

In all projects which are being financed by loan, including cases where money raised by taxation is lent through the Development Fund, the cost of the projects will depend on the rate of interest charged. Every fall in the rate of interest will make a substantial difference to the cost of big schemes.[1]

It is essential, therefore, to keep down the rate of interest, both long and short term, to the minimum. Our socialised banking policy both should and can promote this end.

The short-term rate is largely within the control of the banking system itself and of the Treasury, especially if we keep free from the shackles of the gold standard. The Bank of England can keep its own bank rate low, and by open market operations on a sufficient scale can increase the resources of the clearing banks sufficiently to enable them to lend large sums at low rates.

But, as I have argued elsewhere, it is a mistake to exaggerate the importance of short-term credit, and of the clearing banks, in the national economy. The long-term rate of interest is more important than the short-term rate, especially in relation to a programme of development which should be financed by long-term investment, not by short-term credit.

In 1932 the long-term rate on British Government

[1] I have illustrated this in Chapter XIII from the case of the electrification of the railways.

securities fell sharply from 5 per cent to $3\frac{1}{2}$ per cent. This was the result, not of "natural forces", but of steps taken by the Bank of England, in consultation with the Treasury, to facilitate the conversion of the 5 per cent War Loan. The Bank in that year undertook open market operations on an unprecedented scale, increasing the resources of the London clearing banks by £246 millions, of which they invested £176 millions in British Government securities, thus raising their price and bringing down the rate of interest. Some critics argued that a rate of $3\frac{1}{2}$ per cent was "artificially low" and could not last. They have proved wrong. The rate on Government securities has since fallen below 3 per cent and the rates on other securities have moved downwards correspondingly. The fear is sometimes expressed that, if economic activity revives, interest rates will rise. This fear is based on the belief that the banking system will unload large quantities of securities upon the market, in order to lend the proceeds of such sales to industry.

But there is no reason why this must happen. It can be prevented by the continuance on an appropriate scale of open market operations by the Bank of England. New credits could thus be furnished by the clearing banks from the additional resources which would thereby be created for them, and by some reduction in their reserves, now unduly high. They would not need to unload their present gilt-edged investments. Moreover, increased economic activity requires, much less than of old, advances from the clearing banks. Other methods of finance, as I have pointed out above, are becoming increasingly important.

Given anything approaching full employment of our human and material resources, the funds available for new investment would be very much greater than to-day, and would create conditions favourable to the maintenance of a long-term rate of interest even below the present level.[1] It makes no difference to this argument whether these funds are put on loan, or directed increasingly, by way of taxation, into new investment. In the latter case, the Government, or the body in charge of the Development Fund, could, of course, determine its own rate of interest. This, if we choose to call it so, would be a " managed " rate of interest. Already, however, we have to-day a " managed " market for loans. Management through open market operations, embargoes on foreign lending, etc. keep the rate of interest below what it would be in a " free " market. The market should be managed still more actively, with the same end in view.

Another weapon of " management ", to this end, is the giving of a State guarantee of interest and principal on selected loans. This, for the Treasury, is the cheapest of all forms of subsidy to employment. Even if some guarantees are sometimes called, this method may still show a substantial balance of advantage. I have already suggested the conditions under which such guarantees should be given, including a public share in any assets created. An amended Trade Facilities Act should be passed and freely used. Export credits also should be extended.

The effect of a programme of national development on our public finance is exceedingly important. It would make itself felt on both sides of the national budget. It would reduce expenditure on the maintenance of the unemployed, through reducing their number, and it would increase the yield of taxes at given rates, by increasing incomes and the consump-

[1] On all this, see an interesting speech by Mr. Keynes, some of whose arguments I have here summarised, reported in the *New Statesman* of February 24, 1934, to the Annual General Meeting of the National Mutual Life Assurance Society.

tion of taxed commodities.[1] It would thus relieve budgetary stringency and make possible further programmes of social development and extensions of social services which, owing to the effects of years of trade depression, are at present out of our reach.[2]

Not everything can be done at once. But our financial resources, properly handled, are ample to support a big development drive. And, given good planning, the harder the drive, the faster our national wealth and financial resources will grow.

When the next Labour Government takes office, a large and varied programme should be put in hand quickly. We must get a flying start in overtaking unemployment.

[1] Moreover, every fall in the rate of interest increases the yield of the death duties by increasing the capital values on which they are assessed.

[2] Mr. Keynes in his pamphlet, *Means to Prosperity* (pp. 9–15), estimates that, in present circumstances in this country, every £150 of new loan expenditure gives employment, directly or indirectly, to one man for one year, and hence that a loan expenditure of £3 millions will employ 20,000 men, directly or indirectly, for one year, and so save £1 million a year in unemployment benefit (at the rate of £50 a year for each man employed); and that the revenue will benefit from the new expenditure to the extent of £450,000 a year, so that the net benefit to the two sides of the Budget is nearly £1,500,000, or close on half the new loan expenditure. Similarly £100 millions spent on housing would benefit the Budget by close on £50 millions. These figures may be thought too optimistic, but, even if they are scaled down considerably, they show the budgetary possibilities of a bold programme.

CHAPTER XXVI

GEOGRAPHICAL PLANNING

BY geographical planning I mean the deliberate social control of the distribution within this island, and within smaller areas forming part of it, of houses, factories, agriculture, forests, open spaces, roads, etc. ; or, in other words, the deliberate social control of the use of the land, and of its allocation to different purposes.

Within so small an island, so heavily populated, past neglect to exercise such control has been a crime committed against this generation by its predecessors. We have inherited a squalid anarchy. We must pass on to our successors an ordered design, a civilised framework of health, beauty and power.

Mr. John Burns's Housing and Town Planning Act of 1909 dates the rebirth of an idea which, in this country, had long been dead. Town planning had become a lost art in Britain.[1] But Wren, after the great fire of London in 1666, had planned on paper a new and spacious and beautiful city, which, had it taken concrete shape, would have set an example for other British cities and towns to follow. But Wren was defeated by the conservatism of shopkeepers and the greed of vested interests.

In the disordered rush of the industrial revolution

[1] A good introduction to the study of this subject is Professor Patrick Abercrombie's *Town and Country Planning* (Home University Library, 1933).

there was no town planning. "To-day," in the words of Mr. Thomas Sharp, "the Victorian era is not so memorable for its prosperity and Empire-building, as for the legacy of sordid and ugly towns that it left us."[1]

The need for town planning, and for some measure of geographical planning outside the towns as well, is accepted now, in principle, by a practically unanimous public opinion. But the acceptance, as yet, is passive, rather than active. This is partly due to the weakness of existing legislation, and to the lack of visible evidence of its possibilities.

Let not Socialists deceive themselves with easy phrases. The public ownership of the land would not, of itself, solve this problem of geographical planning, though every extension of public ownership will make its solution easier. But if a public authority, owning all land within its area, were blind to the needs and conditions of planning, or clumsy in its handling of them, or if it aimed simply at getting the maximum revenue from its estate, there would be little improvement. The question is much larger and more complicated than that of mere ownership. On the other hand, even while a large part of the land remains in private ownership, planning by public authorities is both practicable and urgently necessary.

Let us start from the simple case of town planning.

> It is essential to town-dwellers that they should be appropriately and decently housed, that they should be able to get about their city in reasonable comfort, that light and air and provision for out-of-door exercise and recreation should be assured them, as well as such services as sanitation, gas, electricity and water. If we look at our great cities . . . as machines, we shall find

[1] In his excellent book, *Town and Countryside* (Oxford University Press, 1933), p. 3.

that they do not function as they ought. The inhabitants, except for a fortunate few, are inadequately and uncomfortably housed, and traffic is a chaos. There are, as regards the buildings, a few picturesque survivals and a mass of fine eighteenth-century architecture, but for the most part the existing structures are mean and unworthy. The whole urban scene is one of wasted opportunities and inefficiency.[1]

The scandal of the slums is notorious. But we must feel deeply ashamed also of the interminable miles of more " respectable " streets built during the last century after the eighteenth-century tradition of good building had been lost. Under Queen Victoria the more pretentious specimens were trimmed in what has been aptly named the " Gaspipe Gothic " style ; under King George V " Ye Olde Tudor " is preferred. These hideous creations of the speculative builder are tightly packed, without regard to the planning of the streets or the provision of open spaces. The housing activities of Local Authorities, especially since the war, have brought some improvement, both in design and layout. Council houses are not all they might be. But they are immeasurably superior to the cheap products of the jerry builders. Though they sometimes suffer, particularly in the areas of the smaller authorities, from failure to employ an architect, they show, as a rule, a democratic simplicity of line and an absence of the snobbish, fussy, meaningless ornamentation of

[1] Mr. Frederick Etchells, preface to the English translation of Le Corbusier's *City of To-morrow and its Planning* (Rodker, London, 1929), pp. v and viii. This is a book which every planner should read. Whether or not we approve its detail, or think it practicable in this hidebound world, it opens out a wonderful imaginative vision of what a great modern-city might be, and leaves us stimulated both by its Gallic boldness and clarity of thought, and by its power and charm of phrase.

the jerry builder, which is a relief to the eye ; and they have space for little gardens round them.

But, though the housing programmes of many Local Authorities have done something to relieve overcrowding by moving numbers of families to healthier houses and surroundings, the more fundamental problems remain untouched. The continuous drift of population into the large urban areas, and the uncontrolled growth of these, is the negation of all planning. London, worst of all, " sprawls ", as Professor Abercrombie puts it, " in shapeless confusion ". The population of Greater London rose between 1921 and 1931 by nearly a million, from 8,230,000 to 9,150,000. This increment is equal to ten towns the size of Halifax or Wolverhampton, or twenty towns the size of Carlisle or Worcester. And the rate of increase is still accelerating.[1]

As this haphazard and sporadic " development " proceeds, green fields and open country are continually pushed farther and farther away from the great majority of town dwellers, while the traffic problem grows ever more intractable.[2] As multitudes come to live farther and farther from their work, sleeping in " dormitory " suburbs, hours are subtracted from leisure, and heavy costs incurred in money and in physical and nervous strain, merely in travelling to and fro. The gains of progress, and especially of a

[1] For a very valuable study of this problem and a number of practical suggestions for handling it, see the two *Reports of the Greater London Regional Planning Committee*, prepared by Sir Raymond Unwin, and published by Knapp, Drewett & Sons, 1929 and 1933.

[2] Some individualists are madder than others. One, a well-known publicist, met me some years ago in the Strand. There was an exceptionally bad traffic block. " Look ", he said, " at the result of State interference. This is what happens when you try to interfere with the laws of supply and demand."

shorter working day, are eaten up by the monster of
" transport facilities ".[1]

In the centre of London and other great cities, large
new blocks of flats and offices are built in narrow
streets, making the traffic congestion worse than ever.
100,000 people still inhabit London basements and
only 37 per cent of London families live in single occupation of structurally separate dwellings, either separate houses or separate flats. Meanwhile, owing to the
lack of open spaces, the children must play in the
streets, and some Local Authorities are praised for
restricting traffic in certain streets, in order that these
pitiful substitutes for playgrounds shall not be children's death-traps. Every month that passes makes it
more difficult and costly to secure land for playing
fields and other open spaces, while uncontrolled building
encroaches on the outskirts of every town.

The approach to London by any of the main line
railways is an object lesson in planlessness. The
houses of the poor, and even their schools—such as
the large elementary school just outside Paddington
station—are seen strung along the railway, the worst
possible site, spoilt by smoke and noise, either for
dwellings or schools. Yet even in recent years many
Council houses have been built alongside railway lines.
Even some Local Authorities, apparently, think that
any site, however disagreeable, is good enough for
working people !

Smoky skies we have long accepted, with a tame

[1] Major Harry Barnes (*The Slum, its Story and Solution*,
pp. 290–4) gives particulars of the distances between the
London railway termini and the principal housing estates
now being developed or acquired by the London County
Council. The average is ten to eleven miles. After these
termini are reached, bus or tram rides must be taken. A
man living outside and working near the centre will be lucky,
if travelling takes him less than two hours a day or costs him
less than five shillings a week.

submission that does us no credit, as a necessary evil of our modern civilisation. It is no such thing. The emission of smoke from factory and domestic chimneys and from railway engines can be stopped, whenever we choose to stop it, at a trifling price, in money or changed habits, compared with the benefits which it would bring us. Electricity, gas, oil, central heating, or smokeless fuel burnt in open grates, all lie ready to our hand.

To-day a pall of smoke cuts off the sunlight, blackens our homes and lungs, erodes the stone of our buildings, including those most worth preserving, and injures vegetation within a radius of a hundred miles round our industrial areas.[1] But, if we choose, this filth and ruin can be ended, and our black country become green again. And, with effective smoke abatement, we could use the roofs in our cities, for gardens, rest and recreation, building our separate dwelling houses and our blocks of flats and offices with flat roofs, as men did in Sir Thomas More's *Utopia* and as many of the best modern architects do now.

> The desire to rebuild any great city in a modern way [says M. Le Corbusier] is to engage in a formidable battle. Can you imagine people engaging in a battle without knowing their objectives? Yet that is exactly what is happening. The authorities are compelled to do something, so they give the police white sleeves or set them on horseback; they invent sound signals and light signals; they propose to put bridges over streets or moving pavements under the streets; more garden cities are suggested; or it is decided to suppress the tramways, and so on. And these decisions are reached in a sort of frantic haste in order, as it were, to hold a wild beast at bay. That Beast is the great city. It is

---

[1] According to Sir John Stirling Maxwell, a high authority on forestry, speaking at a meeting of the British Association at Aberdeen on September 10, 1934.

GEOGRAPHICAL PLANNING

infinitely more powerful than all these devices. And it is just beginning to wake. What will to-morrow bring forth to cope with it ?[1]

There is more than one possible solution. M. Le Corbusier's conception—of skyscrapers sixty floors high for business premises, cruciform and so without inner wells, each with a tube station and car park beneath it, surrounded by public gardens, sports grounds and bathing pools, these open spaces occupying 90 per cent of the superficial area ; of residential blocks, less high than the business premises, but similarly surrounded by open spaces ; of public buildings, schools, places of amusement, cafés and restaurants, relatively low, close to the skyscrapers ; of industrial establishments set in a zone apart ; with garden cities, for those who prefer them, in an outer zone : most of this is probably too revolutionary for twentieth-century minds.

A more modest alternative is to set a limit to the growth of our great cities, gradually to replan and reconstruct the central areas, and to organise the dispersion of industry and population in smaller centres.

In 1928 the average density of population within the County of London was 60 persons per acre ; within the Metropolitan Police area 3 persons per acre ; within the Greater London area only $1\frac{1}{4}$ persons per acre.[2] Owing to large outward movements from the centre combined with still larger movements from the rest of the country into the Greater London area, the first of these three densities is slowly falling, but the other two are rapidly rising. More than a fifth of the whole population of this island is now living in the Greater London area.

[1] *The City of To-morrow*, pp. 164–5.
[2] *First Report of Greater London Regional Planning Committee*, p. 8.

It is a horrifying thought that this whole population could be housed within the Greater London area, within a radius of twenty-five miles from Charing Cross, at an average density of only eight houses, or less than forty persons, per acre. This is a low density, measured by mere housing standards, and illustrates vividly the relatively small amount of land which is required for building. But a low average density of continuous building over a large area is quite consistent with a shocking deficiency of open spaces. And it creates inevitably a transport problem which defies all tolerable solution. Towards this awful climax of metropolitan concentration we are now drifting. It is still some distance away from us, but we have allowed our rudderless boat, carried by the tides of economic individualism, to bring us much too near it. We have let our cities grow too large. The near prospect of a slowly diminishing population will make it easier to stop their growth, to make them less populous, and to plan a healthier distribution of our people over this island.

London is by far the worst case. Cobbett christened it the Great Wen a hundred years ago, pronounced it overgrown and called for its dispersion. But a number of our other cities also have outgrown their strength and the maximum size which is socially desirable. An attractive proposal has been made,[1] based on a project of Mr. Trystan Edwards, for a Hundred New Towns. These would be built in appropriate localities, planned for an average population of 50,000 each, or five millions in all. They would be built where land was cheap, and where facilities for transport and electric power

[1] In a letter to *The Times* of February 24, 1924, signed, among others, by Professor S. D. Adshead, Mr. Colin Clark, Mr. R. Coppock, Professor Gowland Hopkins, Sir Edwin Lutyens, General Sir Frederick Maurice, Rev. H. R. L. Sheppard and Sir Squire Sprigge.

were good, often around the nucleus of an existing small town or village.

They would relieve the congestion in our existing industrial centres, which could gradually be transformed into far pleasanter places of habitation ; and they would gather to themselves a large proportion of the new buildings which, but for such a scheme of urban development, might tend to spoil the countryside. They would give facilities for the expansion of many industries now being conducted in cramped and inadequate quarters, while to those who are devoting themselves to education, science or the arts, these hundred model towns might afford an opportunity of establishing new and vital centres of cultural activity.

If each of these towns had an average diameter of two miles, they would only occupy less than one-half of 1 per cent of the total area of Great Britain. Such an idea as this, worked out in greater detail, might form a most valuable element in a National Plan.[1] Far better build new houses and new factories in such a framework than on the outskirts of London and other great cities. And let the further growth of these be checked by reserving round them a broad green belt of permanent open spaces and agricultural land.

In London at last things are moving. The Labour County Council, elected in March, 1934, decided by a resolution passed on July 10, 1934, to prepare a plan for the whole administrative county.[2] But much time

[1] In the *Second Report of the Greater London Regional Planning Committee*, p. 106, it is suggested that " the Government might promote two or three complete industrial satellite units ", as part of its programme for creating employment, and that this would be " a sound financial proposition, if carried out through a suitable expert business board, with the support and co-operation of Government and Local Authorities " and a guarantee of interest on the necessary loan.

[2] This decision was warmly welcomed by the *Architects' Journal*, among others, which on August 30, 1934, in an open letter to Major Harry Barnes, Chairman of the L.C.C. Plan-

is likely to elapse, under the slow and cumbrous procedure of existing legislation, before this plan can be completed and begin to take effect.[1]

At this point we may usefully examine the present law on Town and Country Planning.[2]

The Act of 1909, a pale copy from German models, made a timid beginning

> to ensure by means of schemes which may be prepared either by Local Authorities or landowners, that in future land in the vicinity of towns shall be developed in such a way as to secure proper sanitary conditions, amenity and convenience in connection with the laying out of the land itself and of any neighbouring land.[3]

But only land in the vicinity of towns. Both built-up areas and the countryside were left outside the range of planning powers.

Procedure was complicated and progress slow. The Act, moreover, though it had introduced a new principle into British law, or at least a new form of social control over individual liberty, suffered from the defect, so common in our social legislation, that it was only per-

ning Committee, wrote : " May we finally congratulate you, Sir, and your Council on their civic-mindedness in undertaking this gigantic enterprise, and on their courage in accepting this terrific responsibility ; and may we hope that the confidence you have expressed in the adequacy of your Council's preparations will be fully justified by the results ? "

[1] It is anticipated that the sanction of the Ministry of Health for a plan to be prepared will not be obtained till March, 1935, i.e. eight months after the passing of the resolution ! And this is only the first stage in a long process.

[2] In the following account I owe much to Mr. W. I. Jennings's admirable book on *The Law Relating to Town and Country Planning*. I have found no better guide, either to the history of the subject, or through the " terminological tortuosities ", to adopt one of the author's own phrases, of the Town and Country Planning Act of 1932.

[3] Circular issued by the Local Government Board on December 31, 1909.

missive. Few Local Authorities showed energy enough to wield these new powers. Here, as elsewhere, " legislation ", in this permissive form, " has outrun administration. More powers exist than are exercised." [1]

The Housing and Town Planning Act of 1919 made a few minor improvements, and the Town Planning Act of 1925 consolidated the existing law. But by now this problem, like many others, had been changed by the rapid growth of transport facilities. The problem of planning was seen, even by Conservative eyes, to have widened and to include, not merely the undeveloped portions of urban districts, but the whole country. The need for " regional planning ", over wider areas than those of small and separate Local Authorities, grew obvious. The Local Government Act of 1929, which in several directions extended the effective areas of local government, nibbled at this problem. The Town and Country Planning Act of 1932 took another nibble.

This Act, in spite of all its imperfections, " represents ", as Mr. Jennings puts it, " one more stage in the supersession of the Law of Property by Administrative Law ".[2] It imposes further limitations on the right of the owner of land to " do what he likes with his own." " Property ", in an old phrase, " is a bundle of sticks." This Act pulls out a few more sticks and hands them to Local Authorities. Very considerable public interference with the use of land is now permitted. A large part of the initiative for planning passes from the private landowner to the Local Authorities.

The Act of 1932 applies to all land, whether developed or not, and whether in town or country. Local Authorities, or a joint committee of several authorities,

[1] Major Harry Barnes, *The Slum, its Story and Solution*, p. 315. [2] *Op. cit.*, p. vi.

may prepare schemes regulating the use of any, or all, land within their areas and, provided a number of conditions have been complied with, such schemes become legally binding on all concerned. This is the essence of the Act. It opens out wide vistas of hopeful expectation. The growth of towns may be controlled, or even halted. Green belts may be thrown round them. The unspoilt country may be saved from spoliation. Objects of natural beauty and historic interest may be preserved. Ribbon development, hideous, uneconomic and physically dangerous, may be checked. Existing built-up areas may be planned and gradually rebuilt, transformed and beautified. Separate zones may be set aside for factories, for offices, for dwellings, for open spaces, parks and playing fields. The elevations of new buildings may be controlled.[1] All these things become possible, many for the first time.

But the Act is much too long. It has 58 sections, 198 sub-sections and 6 schedules. It is a good example of what I have called in an earlier chapter a legislative monstrosity. How can the staffs of small Local Authorities, such as the District Councils which in rural areas are the planning authorities, be expected to cope with all this legal mumbo-jumbo ? The Act gives us the worst of all the worlds : a complex statute, in which the lawyers will probably discover or manufacture many lucrative ambiguities ; costly, cumbrous and slow-moving procedure ; some powers of delegated legislation, indeed, but in combination with vexatious and purely destructive forms of Parliamentary inter-

---

[1] Control of elevations is sound in principle. In practice it is of very doubtful value, when used, as in several recent instances, to prevent architectural innovations, simply because they seem shocking to the old-fashioned eyes of elderly gentlemen, while leaving unchecked the atrocities, to which these eyes have become accustomed, of the jerry builders.

ference. A critic might not unfairly describe it as an Act for the promotion of delays, with a view to the prevention of planning and the enrichment of lawyers.

It is in many respects more complicated and more reactionary than the Act of 1925. Those supporters of the National Government who represented vested interests on the Standing Committee of the House of Commons did their work well, and overbore on several important points the Tory Minister of Health himself. Sir Hilton Young, had he cared enough for his Bill, might, even so, have marshalled the dumb, obedient hundreds of Government supporters, to repair, when the Bill returned to the floor of the House, the damage done in Committee. But he did not care enough. In this, as in his other Ministerial performances, he remained an icy failure, frozen in self-esteem.

I will now summarise briefly some of the provisions of the Act.

(1) Before a Local Authority, or joint committee of Local Authorities, starts to prepare a scheme, it must first pass a resolution, which must obtain the approval of the Minister. This is a new restriction, not in the Act of 1925. It was inserted in Standing Committee of the House of Commons against the Minister's advice.

(2) Before passing the resolution, the authority must consult with every other authority or committee which may be affected by the scheme.

(3) After the resolution has been passed, the Minister must, before approval, satisfy himself on various points set out in Section 6 (2).

(4) After the resolution has been approved by the Minister, the authority must advertise in the press that a scheme is to be prepared, and must serve notices to this effect on all owners and occupiers of land within the area affected.

(5) After the scheme has been prepared, it must be submitted to the Minister for approval.

(6) If approved by him—and it may be disapproved or varied—it must be laid before both Houses of Parliament, by either of which it may be rejected, in whole or in part. This is an entirely new restriction, not in the Act of 1925. It is particularly objectionable, in that it brings the House of Lords into the picture on an equal footing with the House of Commons.

(7) If approved by the Minister and by both Houses of Parliament, the authority must then advertise the fact that the scheme is about to come into force, in order that its validity may be challenged, by any person desiring to do so, in the High Court. This again is new. There was no such provision in the 1925 Act.

This is a long-winded procedure, and I have only given a summarised account of it.[1] It is safe to assume that several years at the least will elapse between the passing of the initial resolution and the coming into force of the scheme. In view of this, there is provision in the Act for the issue of " Interim Development Orders ".

The Act also makes very complicated provisions for compensation to be paid by Local Authorities to owners who suffer loss through the operation of a scheme, and for the recovery of betterment, up to three-quarters of the added value of the land, from owners who benefit. It appears that securing the payment of betterment will be a lengthier and more difficult task for the authority, than securing compensation for the owner. Provision is made for acquisition of land, either by agreement or, with the approval of the Minister, by compulsion.

The Minister *may* require an authority, which has

[1] Mr. Jennings in his *Law Relating to Town and Country Planning* gives a list of 44 steps which have to be taken between the original resolution to plan and the final approval of the Minister!

not done so, to prepare a scheme. And he *may*, in the case of Urban or Rural District Councils with populations of less than 20,000, turn over their planning powers to the County Council. If this were done as a general rule, it would remove one of the weaknesses of the Act. Urban and Rural District Councils which, outside London and the County Boroughs and Boroughs, are the planning authorities under the Act, are too small for the job. In the Lake District, North Wales, Dartmoor, and other areas suitable for National Parks, they are much too small, and for some of these areas, forming part of more than one county, even County Councils are too small. But, at any rate, County Councils will have larger and presumably more efficient staffs, and less parochial minds, than the Councils of small Urban and Rural Districts. Moreover, the small authorities are often too poor to pay the compensation necessary to make a really good scheme.

Joint Committees *may* be formed and *may* be made executive. On these, County Councils affected must, if they wish, be represented.

In one respect the present law is surprisingly drastic, considering the political colour of the Parliament which enacted it. It gives power to " sterilise " land, that is to say to prohibit all building and other development upon it. This power, which does not affect the private ownership of the land, may yet reduce the private owner's rights to an empty shell.

It is essential to cut a path through this jungle of legal requirements and delays. The following amendments to the Act of 1932 are obviously necessary.

(1) All planning authorities should be required, not merely permitted, to prepare a scheme, and a time limit should be set within which the scheme must be submitted to the Minister, failing which he should be

required to make a scheme himself, and charge the cost to the defaulting authority.

(2) Such schemes should cover, without exception, all land within their area.

(3) The requirement of the Minister's approval of a mere resolution to prepare a plan should be cut out.

(4) Planning powers should be transferred from Urban and Rural District Councils to County Councils, the Minister being authorised, as now, to group together two or more adjacent planning authorities into a regional planning authority. This power to group should be freely used.

(5) The submission of schemes to Parliament should no longer be required.

(6) The power to challenge in the Courts the validity of a scheme approved by the Minister should be cut out.

(7) Provisions for compensation and betterment should be simplified, and betterment payable raised to 100 per cent. Consideration should be given to the possibility of adopting a procedure, whereby the planning authority stands aloof from these financial transactions, and all compensation is drawn from a pool fed by payments for betterment, one section of private owners compensating another.

Yet even at present much can be done by energetic Local Authorities. An illustration is furnished by the regional planning scheme for the City of Aberdeen and adjacent parts of the counties of Aberdeen and Kincardine, which was prepared before the Act of 1932, and went into force in 1933 by virtue of a special Act of Parliament. This scheme covers an area, mainly rural, of 62,000 acres. It provides for road planning, including road widenings and the building of new roads, for the establishment of zones for industrial and residential development respectively, for the creation of large open spaces and the preservation from all building of the whole stretch of coastline and of long stretches of the banks of the Dee and the Don, two rivers entering the sea at Aberdeen. Under the arrangements made with private landowners the Local Authorities paid no compensation.[1]

But geographical planning should not be left entirely to local, or even large regional, authorities. We need a Master Plan, national in scope, into which local plans shall be fitted. Local plans tend to be made without knowledge of national conditions. Estimates, for example, of the future growth of population or industry based on local patriotism and local optimism, in ignorance of the trend of national vital statistics, are often wildly in excess of what is possible. The Central Government, moreover, acting through the Minister of Health or other appropriate Ministers, should have powers, concurrent with those of the Local Authorities, to sterilise land, or to schedule it for specific purposes, such as afforestation or national parks.

These last two examples lead on to another aspect of the question.

[1] This scheme was described at a meeting of the British Association held at Aberdeen on September 7, 1934.

CHAPTER XXVII

NATIONAL PARKS AND FORESTS AND THE NATIONAL TRUST

THE Town and Country Planning Act has great potentialities, and its value could be much increased by the amendments sketched in the last Chapter.

But the nature of the control which can be exercised under this Act is subject to three limitations. First, it is local or, at best, regional, both in initiative and scope. Though liable to overmuch peddling interference from Whitehall and Westminster, planning on a national scale is beyond its reach. Second, it is largely negative. Bad uses of land may be prohibited, and undesirable development prevented. But the promotion of good uses and of desirable development can only be partially achieved. Third, the control is often general, rather than particular. A residential or industrial zone may be delimited, but there is no assurance that population or industry, much less that any particular industry, will settle in it. We need, therefore, to supplement the operation of the Town and Country Planning Act by positive and detailed action on a national scale.

It is a good rule that geographical planning should proceed by setting aside ample but relatively small tracts for building upon a large background of open land, rather than, as under the old Town Planning procedure, by setting aside small tracts of open space upon a large background of built over, or potential building, land. The former method makes for a healthier degree of concentration in building development, for economy in the cost of social services, and for wider unspoilt country spaces for recreation and enjoyment. This is a good rule of action, both under the Town and Country Planning Act and under larger schemes of National Planning. I shall now consider some of the immediate steps to be taken under such larger schemes.

A Labour Government should schedule certain areas as National Parks, and other areas for the National Forests of the future. It should support and rapidly extend the present activities of the National Trust. And it should guide and direct movements of industry and population, giving particular attention to the most grievous case of the depressed areas.

This programme will mean a large increase in the national ownership of land, additional to the increasing area of public ownership by Local Authorities.

Wide circles of opinion, including many persons who would be surprised to be called Socialists, are for social planning of this kind. A number of voluntary societies have come into existence to support these ideas. They exercise a healthy and increasing influence. Their common aim is the preservation and extension of public amenities. The Council for the Preservation of Rural England, the National Trust for the Preservation of Places of Historic Interest or Natural Beauty, the Commons, Open Spaces and Footpaths Preservation Society, the various local societies supporting the National Parks Movement, the National Playing Fields Association, the various associations of nature lovers, walkers, climbers and campers, the Youth Hostels Association, and many more, will be strong allies of any Government which boldly pursues this aim.

Such questions lie a little off the beaten track of party politics. No political party has ever given them their proper emphasis.[1] Politicians do not always know what the public really wants, and sometimes miss the obvious. Because he was an outstanding exception to this tendency, George Lansbury became, for a large section of the public, the best known Minister of the Crown in 1929–31. " Lansbury's Lido " in Hyde Park was much the most popular achievement of the second Labour Government in London.

The Labour County Council in London in 1934, by finishing off the job of snatching the Foundling Site from the claws of building speculators and providing money to maintain it for ever as a playground for the children of central London, has shown a like appreciation of simple human values.

On the subject of National Parks a strong and healthy public opinion has grown up. The report of the National Parks Committee, of which Dr. Addison was Chairman, published in 1931, contains not only positive proposals, though these are much too modest, but also summaries of much valuable evidence presented by societies and individuals, and an account of what has already been done in other countries.[2] Here Britain has lagged badly behind.

National Parks are found in nearly every civilised country but our own. Only in the New Forest, owned by the Crown and administered by the Forestry Commission, have we anything even approximating to such a possession. When in the United States, having

[1] But the Labour Party, at any rate, has declared that " the proper utilisation of the land extends far beyond the re-organisation of agriculture—profoundly important though that is—and involves . . . the preservation of natural beauty and the provision of national parks and facilities for recreation " (*For Socialism and Peace*, p. 46).

[2] Cmd. 3851, price 2s. Of course, like all the Committees appointed by Mr. MacDonald as Labour Prime Minister, it contained only a minority of political supporters of the Government, none, indeed, except the Chairman.

seen something of their splendid public reservations, I expressed to a Middle Western College President my sense of shame at our national poverty in this form of wealth, he asked me : " have you enough real estate to do it ? " But the fact that our national area is relatively so small, and so thickly populated, makes public reservation far more urgent and important here, and our lazy neglect more culpable.

What is a National Park ? It should satisfy three conditions. First, it should be an area containing important elements of unspoilt natural beauty ;[1] second, it should serve as a place of public recreation in the widest sense ; third, it should be large enough and important enough to justify the direct intervention of a national authority. For the creation of National Parks is not to be regarded as a substitute for the activities of Local Authorities in providing open spaces, including playing fields and " parks " in the narrower sense, for the enjoyment of their populations, nor, except in the National Park areas themselves, as a substitute for the work now done by the National Trust.

On what principles should areas be selected as National Parks ? First, on the ground that they do contain those elements of unspoilt natural beauty which it is important in the national interest to preserve. Nothing that is beautiful in nature is safe from early spoliation in this little island, if the profit-seeking individualist is permitted to go on working his ugly will. He is destroying our heritage of natural beauty

[1] As Mr. John Bailey, the Chairman of the National Trust, said in evidence before Dr. Addison's Committee, " a National Park must have enough of the untouched in it, whether of forest, mountain, moor or water, to give the sense of nature as she is in herself, alike undisfigured and unadorned. It may include much else, much that is not wild or primitive, but if it does not include that, it falls short of the ideal of a National Park."

day by day, without any justification of social necessity, while we stand idly by, gaping and grumbling. There are many different forms of natural beauty in this country, some uniquely English,—such as the Lake District, the Downs, the Broads—which it should be a legitimate object of our national pride to save from ruin.

The second principle of selection must be the accessibility of the selected areas from the point of view of those who are to enjoy the use of them. This suggests the selection of a number of areas in different parts of the country, easily accessible to different centres of population. What areas should we choose? There is no need for lengthy argument, or for further " surveys" and investigations. These only waste our fleeting opportunities for action. All the essential facts are perfectly well known. Let us act at once in the most obvious cases, and follow on with others.

Much the most obvious case is the Lake District. Practically the whole of this should become a National Park. In this area an unceasing defensive battle has been fought for years, by little groups of public spirited and decent minded people, against jerry builders and advertisers and landowners eager to sell to the highest bidder, and against those who wish to drive new motor roads over high passes, to carry people who have lost the use of their legs. The National Trust now owns more than 10,000 acres in the Lake District in forty separate properties, some of them mere rocky summits. It has borne the brunt of the battle gallantly and long enough. It is time the State threw in its reserves and made victory sure. All those parts of the shores of lakes which have not yet been built upon, and all the higher ground within the Lake District, should be included in this National Park.

Hardly less obvious is the creation of a National

Park for Scotland in the Cairngorms.[1] This great *massif* of 200 square miles comprises mighty hills, a large number of separate peaks, several small lochs, and numerous glens, corries, rivers and burns. The grandeur and wild nature of the country could easily be kept unspoilt, and the area forms a complete unit of characteristic Highland scenery on a magnificent scale, fit to be preserved intact for all time.

Enlightened Scottish opinion expressed itself strongly in favour of this project before Dr. Addison's Committee. The local landowners opposed it. They saw " no reason for proposing that the privilege of access freely granted by proprietors should be converted into a public right ", and argued that " the establishment of a National Park would be detrimental to flora and fauna and the present amenity, which are now adequately protected by proprietors." But the protection furnished by a national authority could, and should, be still more adequate.

In England and Wales there are a number of other areas with strong claims.[2] Outstanding among these are Snowdonia, Dartmoor, the Norfolk Broads, the Forest of Dean, the Peak District and Dovedale, an area of what still remains " undeveloped " on the South Downs, the Berkshire and Wiltshire Downs, an area round Ingleborough and Pen-y-Ghent, an area along the Scottish Border, including the Roman Wall, and " coastal parks ", such as parts of the coastline of Cornwall, including the extreme Western peninsula, and of Pembrokeshire. From these an early selection

[1] The case for this was admirably stated by Professor F. G. Bailey of Edinburgh, acting as President of the Engineering Section of the British Association in 1934, at Aberdeen.

[2] See the evidence submitted to Dr. Addison's Committee, particularly that of Mr. John Bailey, and of Dr. Vaughan Cornish and Professor Patrick Abercrombie on behalf of the Council for the Preservation of Rural England.

should be made, giving an appropriate geographical distribution.[1] And it should be the aim of public policy steadily to increase the number of areas thus selected. Meanwhile all areas suitable for selection within a reasonable term of years should now be scheduled and sterilised.

How should our National Parks be administered? Probably through a National Parks Commission, composed of experienced enthusiasts. These would not be hard to find. This Commission should set up a local Committee in each National Park area, to be responsible, subject to the supervision of the Commission, for all arrangements regarding preservation and regulation, access, camping sites, mountain huts, etc., and for the safeguarding of agricultural activities within the area. For these activities, it is important to emphasise, need not be disturbed.

The Commission should receive an annual Treasury grant. Dr. Addison's Committee modestly suggested an annual grant of £100,000 for five years as the maximum to be expected. They had a Treasury official as their Secretary and doubtless, acting on instructions, he damped their ardours. But this job, if it is worth doing at all,—as it certainly is—is worth doing properly. It would probably be convenient to vest the ownership of all land situated within National Park areas in the Commission, acting as trustee for the nation. As a general rule, nothing short of public acquisition is satisfactory.[2] But, where the National

[1] As regards undeveloped coastline, which is rapidly dwindling, most of those sections not included in National Parks should, with the aid of the Town and Country Planning Act, be preserved against " development ". This would be popular with the Local Authorities in seaside resorts.

[2] But compensation to private landowners within a National Park area might take the form, suggested in Chapter XVIII, of a postponed payment at the owner's death, to be set off against his liability for death duties. This mode of payment

Trust is owner now, there is no need to alter this arrangement, unless the Trust preferred to hand over small scattered properties within the larger area of a National Park, and concentrate its future activities outside these areas.

The Commission should be responsible for general direction, though not for detailed administration, to some Minister of the Crown. Preferably, I think, to the First Commissioner of Works, who now exercises functions, analogous though on a much smaller scale, in respect of the Royal Parks and of Ancient Monuments.

The term National Park should be reserved for areas of considerable size. But a great number of smaller areas should also be reserved for the use and enjoyment of the public, and protected permanently against " development ". The care of such smaller areas can be safely left, for the present at any rate, in the hands of the National Trust. This body is a characteristically English creation, which has acquired a nucleus round which not only National Parks, but a great National Estate, may grow. Founded in 1895 and given statutory recognition in 1907, it now owns more than 60,000 acres, made up of nearly 200 separate properties, varying in size from less than an acre to more than 6,000 acres on Exmoor. In addition to open spaces, it owns a number of historic buildings and monuments. I witnessed in September, 1934, the handing over to the Trust of the Martyrs' Tree and adjoining land at Tolpuddle, to commemorate for ever the seven Dorsetshire farm labourers who were sentenced to transportation for forming a trade union in 1834.

The rate of acquisition of land by the Trust has been rapidly rising in recent years, due to a quickening of

seems specially suitable here, since National Parks are not intended to be revenue producing in the narrow sense, and since their benefits will accrue undiminished to future generations.

public interest in its activities and increasing financial support for its purchases. It is a non-profit-making body, deriving its income partly from regular subscriptions and partly from donations towards the cost of specific acquisitions. It has acquired some of its properties by gift, but most by purchase. It will acquire, under bequests in wills not yet operative, a number of additional properties in years to come. I give Lord Snowden, whom I criticise elsewhere in this book, credit for his action, when Chancellor of Exchequer, in permitting the exemption from death duties of property left by will to the Trust.[1] Under the Act of 1907 half the members of the Council of the Trust are appointed by such bodies as the Universities and the Trustees of the British Museum and by such persons as the President of the Royal Academy, the President of the Royal Institute of British Architects and the President of the Linnean Society.

The National Trust is an example of practical Socialism in action. It has behind it a fine record of public service, and commands a widespread public good will. A Labour Government should give it every encouragement greatly to extend its activities. Whether or not, if it became more closely associated with the Government, any modification in its constitution would be desirable, is, I think, a question of minor importance, to be settled by amicable discussion when the time came.

For open spaces smaller than National Parks and not controlled or owned by a Government Department or by Local Authorities, the National Trust is an ideal owner. Many of its present holdings are too small and should be enlarged, and it should be enabled to acquire a large number of new holdings. Land, for both these purposes, should, I think, be scheduled by the Govern-

[1] But this concession does not go far enough, for permission may be refused, in particular cases, by the revenue authorities.

ment, probably through the Office of Works, acting in consultation with the Trust. Powers of compulsory purchase should be given to the Trust over such scheduled land on the same basis of valuation as for compulsory purchase by public authorities. Extortionate prices are now often extracted from the Trust by private owners under the threat of imminent destruction of public amenities. Such robbery should be stopped. Power should also be given to remove disfiguring features which have been created near the boundaries of the Trust's properties. This would be a valuable form of retrospective planning.

As regards beautiful and historic buildings and private parks and gardens, the Trust is likewise an ideal owner. These may now be bequeathed to it free of death duty.[1] I hope that many owners of such property, who are apt to make public lament of their " poverty " and of the burden of death duties, and to suggest various forms of public assistance for themselves, will take advantage of this provision. Better still to present such properties to the Trust in their own lifetime, on condition that they became tenants of the Trust, and perhaps even had the right, subject to the approval of the Trust, to name their successors in the tenancy, and that the public had reasonable access to the property, payment for which would go to pay for its upkeep. In any case, there is much to be said for scheduling a large number of such properties, and giving the Trust priority of right of purchase at a fair valuation.

It is for consideration whether an annual grant from public funds should be made to the Trust to enable it to increase its National Estate. Such a grant might bear a fixed proportion, subject to a maximum total, to the income raised by the Trust from private sources.

[1] Subject to the limitation mentioned above, which should be removed.

I turn now from National Parks and National Trust properties to National Forests. These will not be wholly separate areas. Parts of the latter will lie within National Parks and, perhaps, also within National Trust properties. But the aims are different. National Forests are primarily for the growth of timber, though they are nearly always objects of natural beauty and may, with proper safeguards against fire and other damage, be places of public recreation.[1]

National Forests are an essential part of a National Plan. In this country private enterprise has a very poor record in forestry, especially in recent years. We have many beautiful small patches of woodland and many lovely individual trees.[2] But the aggregate is small, especially of timber having commercial value. We import more timber, and grow less, than any other important country and, with the exception of Portugal, we are the worst wooded country in Europe. The profits from growing timber are too remote in time to tempt the private planter. The State, taking a wider and longer view, must, therefore, intervene. Many, who are not Socialists, admit that this is necessary.

The Forestry Commission was established in 1919, in order to make good the failure of private enterprise, to lay the foundation of State Forests, such as exist

[1] It was announced in May, 1934, that proposals had been framed by the Forestry Commission to increase the facilities for public enjoyment of large areas of forest and mountain land and to provide camping sites and car parks. Among the areas which it was hoped to develop on these lines were part of the Snowdon Range, Thetford Chase, the North Tyne Valley and the Rendlesham area. Fifty per cent of the fires reported by the Forestry Commission are caused by sparks from railway engines, a further small argument in favour of railway electrification !

[2] Under Section 46 of the Town and Country Planning Act provision may, for the first time, be made for the preservation of single trees and groups of trees and for the protection of woodlands.

on a large scale in nearly every other civilised country, and to repair the serious destruction of our meagre timber supplies during the war. Within the limits, and subject to the caprice, of Treasury assistance, it has made a good beginning. But the time has come for a larger and better sustained effort.

At present the Chairman of the Commission is the only full-time paid member. It would be better to have a small body of paid Commissioners, of whom at least the Chairman and Vice-Chairman should be full-time.

The Commission should probably be subject to the general direction of the Minister of Agriculture. Its powers of acquiring land should be strengthened. It is dependent at present on the chance of suitable land coming into the market. Many proposals for acquisition are abandoned, because the terms of voluntary purchase are unsatisfactory, or because, while the Commission is negotiating, someone else buys the land, often merely for sporting purposes. The Commission should have powers of compulsory purchase at a fair valuation over all land scheduled as suitable for afforestation, as and when required. All such land should be scheduled, as part of the National Plan, and no use of any part of it, inconsistent with subsequent afforestation, should be permitted. Estimates of the land suitable for this purpose vary between four million and nine million acres, excluding land on which good timber could be grown but which is more suitable for food production. At least the minimum area of four million acres should be scheduled. Allowing for the area already planted—including 233,000 acres of State forests, 63,000 acres of Crown forests administered by the Commission, and nearly 100,000 acres planted by Local Authorities and private owners with financial assistance from the Commission —our present pitiful little planting programme of some

20,000 acres a year will take nearly 180 years to cover even the minimum area.[1] And this, moreover, on the assumption that replanting to replace future fellings is additional to the annual programme. This programme should be steadily, but rapidly, increased.

State Forestry in this country carries no loan charges. It is financed by an annual Treasury grant and by the sale of forest products, which in the near future will expand rapidly. The present Treasury grant is only £450,000 a year, while the proceeds of sales brought in £160,000 in 1932–3. This sound practice of finance from revenue should be continued; but a substantially larger grant should be provided and fixed, probably on a rising scale, over a term of years, to allow for planning ahead. Since 1919 the Commission's programme has twice been "axed" in economy panics, first in the Geddes panic of 1921 and again in the May panic of 1931. The second was the more serious, a whole plan of development being dislocated and the Commission being forced by the Treasury to destroy no fewer than fifty million young plants, which it had cost £50,000 to grow.[2]

Various estimates have been given of the employment provided by forestry operations. Mr. David Grenfell, himself a Forestry Commissioner, with access to official information, has stated that "there is no public industry which gives so much advantage for an

[1] The total net area acquired by the Commission up to September 30, 1933, was 727,000 acres, of which 455,000 acres were classified as plantable. A further 121,000 acres of Crown Woodlands, of which 63,000 acres were under timber, had been transferred to the Commission (*Fourteenth Annual Report* of the Commission, p. 17).

[2] See an interesting debate on the Forestry Vote in the House of Commons on July 3, 1933. Members of all parties spoke in favour of increasing the Commissioner's planting programme, though one Conservative expressed the individualist view that "it would be far better if this money were spent naturally instead of by the Forestry Commission".

expenditure of a million pounds as forestry. No fewer than 7,400 people could be found employment for the expenditure of that sum ". This estimate refers to direct employment only, while another Forestry Commissioner, Sir George Courthope, has pointed out [1] that, as a forest matures, and still more as subsidiary industries, such as sawmilling, arise in its neighbourhood, the volume of employment continuously increases.

The Commission has created 1,200 forest workers' holdings, averaging eleven acres each and accommodating about 5,000 persons, including women and children. The forest holders are guaranteed by the Commission a minimum of 150 days work a year in the forests. They now own livestock on their holdings of a total value of more than £40,000. Many of these men are miners from the distressed areas, who have found a new home, new hope and a healthy life above ground in the service of the State and in the production of food. The number of forest holdings should be rapidly increased, and as large a proportion as possible of the workers employed by the Commission should be settled upon them.

There is an exceptionally strong case for pushing on vigorously with afforestation in the neighbourhood of the mining areas. New forms of employment are specially needed here and for all the work required the mining population, which has always remained much nearer to the land in spirit and in fact than the dwellers in industrial and commercial towns, has special aptitudes. Much suitable land is available and cheap in such areas. And, as these forests grow, the mining industry will have a source of supply of pit-props conveniently near at hand.

Here is a case, and there are many others, where the large scale importing habit indicates, not as some theorists too easily assume, the most economical

[1] In the Parliamentary debate mentioned above.

international division of labour, but rather a failure by private enterprise to develop the full economies of national production.

National forests, efficiently built up and administered, will stand us in good stead if the fears, now widely held, of a coming world shortage of timber within the next two generations, should come true. In any event, they will be a valuable addition to our national resources, give additional beauty and amenity to our national landscape, and occupation amid healthy surroundings to a growing number of our people.[1]

---

[1] Chiefly because of their shorter life to maturity, leading to earlier cash returns, the Forestry Commission have hitherto concentrated on conifers. They have 218,000 acres now under conifers and only 15,000 acres under hardwoods. A higher proportion of hardwoods should be planted to give a more varied beauty to the State Forests of the future.

CHAPTER XXVIII

THE LOCATION OF INDUSTRY

IN earlier chapters I have argued in favour of the deliberate planning of the location of industry.[1] The advantage for industrial purposes of one site over another, within the comparatively small area of this island, is often much less than might be supposed.[2] Cheaper and more easily accessible power and transport have already reduced the relative advantages of many sites, and encouraged the movement of industry into new districts, not previously industrial, where land is cheap, rates low and labour unorganised and tame.[3]

The mining industry is immobile. It must be located at the mines. But even here, as argued in Chapter XIV, the rate of progress or decline of different areas should be nationally planned. Heavy industry is a little more mobile, but cannot move very far from

[1] An excellent discussion of this problem is contained in Mr. Colin Clark's pamphlet on *National Planning*.

[2] Sometimes the choice of one site rather than another is due merely to the preference of some employer, or managing director, for living in or near London, or some other large city, rather than in a small town or a depressed area; or for drawing his labour from a large rather than a small pool. Such individual preferences reflect no social advantage.

[3] Captain Harold Macmillan, speaking in the House of Commons on November 22, 1934, expressed the view that improved Trade Union organisation in the South of England would be of national advantage in helping to check the present drift of industry from North to South.

either minerals or its most convenient form of transport, often by water. But light industry, increasingly important in our national life, is very mobile. Within wide limits it can settle anywhere.

A policy of national planning, therefore, can easily change the relative advantages of different sites, and hence the geographical distribution of industry, especially light industry, and of population. Such a policy should guide new industries away from London and its outskirts, and away from the larger cities, to selected smaller towns, to garden cities, both new and old, and into the depressed areas. And it should check the present drift from North to South.

The present movements involve a double waste. In those areas, from which movement is now taking place, particularly in the depressed areas, there is a serious waste through social capital — houses, schools, roads, public services, etc.—becoming derelict. Likewise, and worse, with human capital, subject to mass unemployment lasting for years on end. And in those areas, into which movement is taking place, there is waste, through the provision of houses, schools, roads and public services which, but for this movement, would be largely unnecessary, with the added evil, on the edge of London and other large cities, of the intensification of the traffic problem and of other disadvantages described in Chapter XXVI. Continual movement, of course, there must be, both of industry and population, but recent movements have been too rapid for social adjustment and often in wrong directions.

By what methods should these movements be corrected and these wastes be avoided ? The location of socialised industry can be planned directly. The location of private industry can be planned indirectly, through pressures and inducements. The equalisation and cheapening of charges for electricity and transport, as explained above, will be a powerful factor. We might, indeed, go farther and use our socialised electricity and transport services to discriminate, temporarily at least, in favour of undertakings established in selected areas.

The National Investment Board, as explained in Chapter XXII, should, in appropriate cases, make its sanction of a new capital issue dependent on the suitable location of a new factory. Similarly with other financial inducements, the grant of short-term credit, for example, or of a guarantee of interest. Land for new factories in selected areas might be compulsorily acquired by the State and let rent free, or very cheaply. And it might be well worth while for the Treasury to make a substantial contribution in aid of the rates of new industrial enterprises in the depressed areas.[1]

New industries entering an area are a primary source of new employment. But they also bring in their train much secondary employment, in building, transport, commerce, distribution, entertainment and public services generally.[2]

In addition to the planned development of new towns, including satellite towns and garden cities, in other parts of the country, it is even more urgent to create a number of these in the depressed areas.

It is here that the regional replanning of Britain should begin. Each depressed area should be taken

[1] The Northern Ireland Government, in its New Industries (Development) Act of 1932, gives power to the Minister of Commerce to grant free sites, in the form of annual payments equal to the reasonable annual rent of the site for a period up to 20 years, to " substantial undertakings " establishing new industries in Northern Ireland, and permits Local Authorities to exempt from rates any factory erected on such sites. This is a good precedent.

[2] Mr. Clark points out (*National Planning*, p. 17) that these secondary occupations now employ nearly 70 per cent of all workers covered by Health Insurance.

in hand as a whole; existing industries should be reorganised; suitable new industries introduced;[1] land settlement and afforestation stimulated; where existing housing is bad, it should be replaced by new accommodation.

Thus the depressed areas could be transformed into well-planned modern communities, with modern factories and modern houses, with private and public gardens and playing fields, and with good facilities for general and technical education and for a healthy and varied communal life.

These regional plans would be instalments, and would form part of the Master Plan referred to in Chapter XXVI for the geographical planning of the whole national area.

[1] Including, in the mining areas, publicly owned oil-from-coal plants, as well as new light industries, some publicly and some privately owned, and some, it is to be hoped, providing employment for women.

CHAPTER XXIX

EXTERNAL TRADE

SINCE the start of this century the controversy over Tariffs versus Free Trade has had a prominence in British politics out of all proportion to its importance. Neither the acceptance nor the rejection of a general tariff on imports has greatly mattered, at any stage of this tedious, long drawn out debate, to the general body of the population, as distinct from sectional interests. Under Free Trade there were still slums, poverty and unemployment.

But it suited those, whether Conservatives or Liberals, who were equally opposed to more fundamental changes, to keep political attention concentrated on this essentially secondary question.

On the narrow issue of new tariffs under private enterprise versus a continuance of free imports under private enterprise, there could, indeed, be little doubt as to the Labour Party's attitude. It was opposed to tariffs. But this issue was too narrow. If tariffs were to be given, not as an unconditional gift to private enterprise, but on condition of reorganisation, or of some recognition of the public interest, the answer would be less clear. It would turn on how much reorganisation or recognition, and of what kind.

There will, in my opinion, be three reasons why a Labour Government will find it inexpedient to scrap forthwith our present tariff.

First, it may find, in existing import duties, powerful

levers for persuading industries to reorganise themselves. Second, a tariff in operation changes the channels of trade and employment. To scrap it, wholesale and suddenly, would cause dislocation and fresh unemployment. Third, a Labour Chancellor of the Exchequer could not afford, at the outset, to sacrifice so much revenue.[1] Far better spend it on new and hopeful projects, than fritter it away in a multitude of small remissions—many in respect of luxuries—which will be slow and uncertain in reaching consumers.

What, then, should be our policy? " Back to Free Trade " is a dead slogan. Public opinion, particularly since the old Liberal Party has split and shrunk and split again, is no longer stirred by this old battle cry.[2] Free trade, in the old sense, is a denial of planning; tariffs, in the old sense, are a caricature of planning.

The Labour Party stands for a planned expansion of our external trade. As a means to this end, many present import duties may be reduced or abolished. But, in taking such action, we should seek reciprocity.

It would be worth our while to join a multilateral agreement to reduce trade barriers—both tariffs and other obstacles—provided enough other Governments were willing to join. But it seems doubtful whether world opinion is yet ripe for this. The late William Graham failed in his tariff truce effort in 1929, and the World Economic Conference failed much more conspicuously in 1933. Economic nationalism still triumphs over international good sense. But we should watch for any change of sentiment, and should do our best to encourage it. The recent shrinkage in the

[1] In 1933-4 duties on imports, leaving out of account alcohol, tobacco, the " breakfast table duties ", oil and silk, brought in more than £37 millions.

[2] Even Sir Walter Layton, at the Liberal Summer School of 1934, declared against " a return to unilateral free trade ".

volume of world trade is a stupidity and a general disaster, not least for this country.

It seems more likely that we can make progress by bilateral, or group, agreements. But these should aim at expanding, and not restricting, the flow of trade. Quotas, absolute or relative, are appropriate instruments of planning. But the idea of quotas has been prejudiced by the fact that they have been introduced as a means of trade restriction. We should aim at a policy of expanding quotas over the periods covered by bilateral, or group, trade treaties.

The aim of " balanced trade " in a bilateral treaty must not be pushed too hard. But, in the present state of the world, it is not unreasonable that we should agree to buy most from those who will buy most from us.[1]

The Anglo-Soviet Trade Treaty of 1934 is an interesting, but imperfect, model. It provides that Soviet purchases from Britain—of all goods and services, including the use of British ships—shall rise year by year, relatively to British purchases from the Soviet Union, until after five years the value of the purchases on either side is approximately equal. But this equality, under the terms of the treaty, may be approached either through an increase of Soviet purchases from Britain, or through a decrease of British purchases from the Soviet Union. This is a defect in the agreement, which should have operated to increase the flow of trade both ways.

Trade treaties between groups are illustrated by the Ottawa agreements, now generally admitted to be very unsatisfactory. But this method, whether within the British Commonwealth or within other groups, holds possibilities.

[1] See, on all this, the brilliant pamphlet *America Must Choose* (Foreign Policy Association, New York, 1934), by Mr. Henry Wallace, President Roosevelt's Secretary of Agriculture.

The Most Favoured Nation Clause, in its old interpretation, must be modified. It hampers our own negotiations, while we hamper, often with no real gain to ourselves, the negotiations of others, e.g. in the Danube Basin. But it is an advantage of quotas, as compared with tariffs, that, whereas the Most Favoured Nation Clause forbids differential rates of duty, it allows differential quotas.

External trade in a British planned economy must still be substantial, unless we are to suffer much lower standards of living. But it cannot, and should not, be so predominant as in the past. In the late nineteenth, and early twentieth, century the proportion of our external to our home trade had risen dangerously high, too high to last.

Some things we must import—tea, raw cotton, oranges—because we cannot grow them here at all. Others we must import in part—wheat, for example—because we cannot at reasonable cost grow all our requirements in this island.

But there is a wide margin of doubt, in particular cases, as to how far it is better to produce at home or to import, and pay by exports.

During the Free Trade era in Britain the benefit of the doubt was nearly always given in favour of external trade. This was partly due to the urge towards foreign, rather than home, investment. Many of our financial houses, as I have pointed out above, were created, and exist, only to export capital. And this activity was overdone.

On the other hand, there was an important factor limiting British exports, namely bad marketing. Too proud or lazy to learn the languages of their customers, or to travel among them, or to study their requirements, British exporters threw away many orders. This conservatism in business methods is not a good advertisement for private enterprise. The selling agencies of our future Public Corporations must improve on this performance. We cannot hope, in view of changed conditions abroad, to restore the old volume of our exports of coal or cotton. But, as against this, a large expansion should be possible in the exports of our light industries.

Conversely, bad and ill-organised marketing at home has been a factor limiting domestic production, especially in agriculture. Dr. Addison's Marketing Act of 1930 aimed at removing this handicap, but not, as some of his successor's schemes have done, at fleecing the consumer. Given good organisation, there is no reason why, in respect of many agricultural products, we should not greatly increase our national production, at reasonable prices.

Where, for any reason, there is a marked social advantage in producing part at least of our supply of some commodity at home, even though it could more cheaply be imported from abroad, we should make our plans accordingly.

Illustrations could be multiplied, but I will give only three, agriculture, iron and steel, and oil from coal. Agriculture and an iron and steel industry, both on a considerable scale, are essential elements in our national life. We could not, as a nation, afford to see them disappear under the pressure of imported supplies, however cheap. Therefore, we must take steps to maintain them. The extraction of oil from coal is a new industry, still in its infancy. Equally, on national grounds, its development is essential. Partly as a better use of coal than burning it raw, partly to bring back prosperity to our coalfields, partly because, the present state of the world being what it is, it is prudent to produce some of our oil at home. I did not find the distant view, through a Foreign Office window, of the Anglo-Persian Oil Company, or of pipe lines from Iraq crossing desert sands, very reassuring.

The mechanism of planned external trade must be experimental. The Labour Party will institute Import and Export Boards, and attach selling agencies to Public Corporations doing export trade. These instruments will operate within the terms of trade treaties, bilateral, or group, or multilateral, and of any quotas which these may allocate. And I have already noted the possible use, by the Bank of England, of the acceptance houses as the agents of quantitative trade regulation.

CHAPTER XXX

THE MACHINERY OF PLANNING

IN preceding chapters I have discussed a number of separate activities of economic planning. What central machinery is required to co-ordinate these activities and make them fully effective ? The Labour Party, I think wisely, has given no dogmatic answer to this question. We must proceed experimentally, guided by the light of experience rather than by any elaborate preconceived theory. The practical suggestions made in this chapter are tentative and individual.

At the beginning we should create only the necessary minimum of new machinery. Otherwise we shall be in danger of becoming choked with delays; all machinery and no planning. At the beginning Ministers should be able to get quickly off the mark with the first stages of their Departmental programmes, as soon as the necessary financial or legislative sanction has been given. We need not wait to raise the school age, for example, or to accelerate housing programmes. There will be plenty of obvious jobs to be done quickly. But, as our legislative and administrative programme takes effect, the importance of co-ordination will grow.

Let me here recapitulate some of the principal planning problems indicated in earlier chapters, and some of the agencies proposed for dealing with them.

There must be a plan within each socialised industry

or service, for its efficient organisation, conduct and development. The primary agency for this is the governing body of the enterprise—ultimately responsible through a Minister to Parliament—consulting with the appropriate Trade Unions and with representatives of consumers and users, and dependent for new finance on the appropriate financial institutions.

As the number of these socialised enterprises grows, there must be a plan for their relations to one another, including, in particular, some machinery for determining the prices at which they sell their products to one another and to other purchasers. This machinery can, I think, best be supplied through the Supreme Economic Authority described below.

There must be a monetary plan, for the controlled expansion of credit and currency in relation to increasing production. The primary agency for this is the Central Bank.

There must be a plan for that part of national development which is to be initiated by Government action. The primary agencies for this must be the Ministers concerned with the various sections of the programme e.g., as regards housing, the Minister of Health working through the National Housing Commission. But here, too, the financial institutions and, after the initial impetus has been given, the Supreme Economic Authority must play important parts.

There must be a financial plan, for distributing credit —long term, intermediate and short term—between the various items in this development programme, between the various socialised undertakings, and between claimants for credit from the private sector. Here the primary agencies are the financial institutions e.g., as regards long-term investment, the National Investment Board. But the Supreme Economic Authority must give certain directions.

There must be a supplementary financial plan, in so far as development is financed from taxation. Here the primary agency must be the Treasury, which is responsible for the plan of the Budget.

There must be a geographical plan, for the allocation of land to different uses and for a suitable distribution of industry and population. The primary agencies for this must be the Departments concerned with the various uses of land, the Ministry of Health in respect of housing and Town and Country Planning, the Ministry of Transport in respect of roads, the Ministry of Agriculture and the Forestry Commission, the Office of Works in respect of National Parks, and other Ministries in lesser degree. But here the need for co-ordination by the Supreme Economic Authority, though not for delay in the taking of obvious first steps, is evident.

There must be a plan for agriculture, and another for external trade. Here the primary agencies are the Ministry of Agriculture and the Board of Trade respectively, subject to the control of the Supreme Economic Authority.

Finally, there must, before long, be a plan for "labour supply", in the broadest sense of the term, for regulating the distribution of the working population, and especially of new entrants, between different occupations. This is a fundamental problem, bounded by the fact that, in a year or two, the population of this island will reach a maximum and will then slowly diminish.[1] It is related to unemployment

[1] This turning point of population will be reached, if present trends of births and deaths continue, in France before 1937, in this country before 1940, in Germany before 1950 and in the United States before 1960. No country in Europe, west of the Soviet border, is now exempt from this tendency, and none of the white populations in the British Dominions. Perhaps within another generation no part of the world will still be exempt from it.

and to education, general, technical and professional. It should be studied, through the Supreme Economic Authority, with the aid of the Trade Unions, Professional Associations and educational bodies.

These planning problems overlap. They will change their shape as socialisation proceeds. They will look different at the moment when the third Labour Government takes office, and when, after several years, it has got into efficient socialised working order an important central group of industries and services.

As socialisation proceeds, the machinery of planning will necessarily become more elaborate. But not the machinery of our economic life as a whole, for many present elaborations, which serve no social purpose, will disappear. In many directions Socialism will simplify, not complicate, the present arrangements of capitalism. Within the growing socialised sector, a multiplicity of separate private concerns, competing private agencies and unnecessary middlemen, both in finance and trade, will vanish.

Clearly we must create, at an early stage, a Supreme Economic Authority, which must satisfy two principal conditions. It must be democratic, in the sense of being responsible, on large issues, to the Government and through the Government to Parliament, and of providing for regular consultation with the legitimate interests affected by its decisions.

And it must be efficient, in the sense that it applies well understood and intelligently formulated rules to the material with which it deals, and is competent both for current administration and for fresh thinking and research.

Such an Authority should be based, I think, upon an Economic Committee, or Planning Committee, of the Cabinet, consisting of a small permanent nucleus of Ministers, but bringing in other Ministers from time to time, when the work of their Departments is relevant to its discussions.[1]

What Ministers should form this nucleus will depend on personal, as well as Departmental, considerations. And it should probably include one or more of the non-Departmental Ministers.

This Committee of the Cabinet should be served by a supra-Departmental staff, which would be a specialised extension of the Cabinet Secretariat. This staff should consist, partly of permanent Civil Servants, drawn from existing Departments; partly of experts, in economics, finance, labour conditions, etc., brought in from outside the Civil Service, but with a view to permanence; partly of supporters of the Government, possessed of energy, tact and special knowledge, but intended to serve only temporarily, and to disappear with a change of Government.

This staff would perform a variety of functions, which would tend to increase. It should be organised and subdivided accordingly, with a habit of frequent interchange of personnel, both within its own subdivisions and between itself and Government Departments and socialised enterprises.

It would be a State Planning Department, or National

[1] Mr. Herbert Morrison (*Socialisation and Transport*, Chapter XV) proposes that a single Minister should be in charge of all socialised industries and services, with a Department appropriately organised for this purpose. This is a possible, though I am not sure that it would be the best, arrangement. If it were adopted, such a Minister would, in the scheme which I am proposing, be one of the most important members of the Economic Committee of the Cabinet, and his Department would perform some, but not all, of the functions which I attribute to the staff of this Committee. I do not understand Mr. Morrison to propose that this Minister should also be in charge of socialised financial institutions. This, I think, would be quite an unworkable addition to responsibilities which in any case would be in danger of becoming excessive for efficient discharge by one man.

Planning Board, which would both prepare detailed plans to carry out the general directions of Ministers and, on its own initiative, suggest plans for Ministers' consideration. In practice, this is not a sharp distinction. It could be set up without legislation, simply by charging certain additional salaries and other expenses on the Cabinet vote.

It would be a co-ordinating body, to pull together at the centre sectional plans, e.g. in making a geographical Master Plan, or a national plan of investment, and to accelerate inter-Departmental decisions, e.g. on such related problems as land drainage and water supply.

It would be an intermediary between Ministers and such a body as the National Investment Board, whose function would be to advise on total possibilities and to execute, with a measure of discretion, instructions given in the light of this advice.

It would be the agency for securing from all socialised enterprises the data of " measurement and publicity ", by which their efficiency would be gauged, and for settling questions of the relations of such enterprises with one another, e.g. as to prices.

It would provide a link between the process of planning and the execution of approved plans, supervising, on behalf of Ministers, their speedy application, and working through regional offices and skilled regional staffs.

It would help to furnish Ministers with an Economic General Staff, to keep under constant survey problems of policy and the changing economic situation. On this side it would be closely related to any advisory and consultative bodies which might be set up to assist in the work of planning, e.g. to a National Economic Council,[1] on which, I suggest, the Trade Union and

[1] But this must avoid the faults of composition and procedure which have made Mr. MacDonald's Economic Advisory Council a dreary and time-wasting farce.

MACHINERY OF PLANNING

Co-operative Movements should be represented, as well as other elements in industry, both socialised and private; and to the Advisory Financial Council, into which I have suggested that the present Directorate of the Bank of England should be transformed.

Deliberately I have sketched, only very lightly and provisionally, the form and functions of this Supreme Economic Authority. As we go forward, experience will be the best teacher.

I make, however, one final observation. Just as a Public Corporation, in a particular industry, should stand a little detached from, though ultimately responsible to, a Minister and Parliament, so, in my judgment, should the State Planning Department. It should gradually acquire from Ministers a wide range of delegated action, and from accumulating experience a large authority over detail. If the machine of economic planning is to work at its best, both the public and the politician must be prepared, as a general rule, to stand back from the machine in its daily working. But this principle can only win acceptance, if Parliament can review periodically the results of its work, and if the public is reasonably satisfied that it works for public, and not for private and sectional, advantage.

PART VI
EQUALITY

CHAPTER XXXI
TOWARDS SOCIAL EQUALITY

SOCIALISTS seek, by the abolition of poverty and the establishment of social equality, to build a prosperous and classless society.

Complete economic equality—in the sense of absolute equality of individual income, or of individual " outgo " in the form of effort—is neither practically possible, nor ideally good.[1] Nor is it necessary to the attainment of social equality and the classless state. But what *is* necessary is a very great reduction in our present economic inequalities.

This implies that, while the average level of wellbeing must be greatly raised, the rich shall become poorer and the poor richer. The span of individual incomes in this country runs from well over £50,000 a year to much less than £1 a week, a ratio of much more than a thousand to one. This is grotesquely wide.

But when we propose the reduction of economic inequality, we meet at once a whole procession of silly arguments. It is suggested that, once we admit absolute equality to be impossible, there is no more to say ; or it is pretended that present inequalities of wealth correspond to inequalities of service, or merit, or intelligence, or " social standing ", and should not, therefore, be disturbed ; or that these present in-

[1] Because, to mention only two reasons, it makes no allowance for individual differences, either of need or performance.

equalities are inevitable, because men are not " equal in nature " ; or it is claimed that, under capitalism, all men of exceptional ability can rise from humble beginnings to proud endings ; or it is observed that a few gifted children of the poor have, in fact, climbed our steep and narrow educational ladder to the high roof of commercial and professional eminence.

The wealthy " self-made man " is a familiar advertisement of the virtues of individualism. And

> it is possible [as Mr. Tawney says] that intelligent tadpoles reconcile themselves to the inconveniences of their position, by reflecting that, though most of them will live and die as tadpoles and nothing more, the more fortunate of the species will one day shed their tails, distend their mouths and stomachs, hop nimbly on to dry land, and croak addresses to their former friends on the virtues by means of which tadpoles of character and capacity can rise to be frogs. This conception of society may be described, perhaps, as the tadpole philosophy, since the consolation which it offers for social evils consists in the statement that exceptional individuals can succeed in evading them.[1]

Why is social equality desired by Socialists ? Because Socialism means comradeship, and comradeship means social equality. Because great inequality is both unjust and ugly. Because it gives cake to a few, while many lack bread. Because it breeds servility, wastes talent, and restricts the sources of initiative and leadership.

Finally, because it makes a mockery of freedom. We have no freedom to spend money we have not got.[2]

[1] *Equality*, p. 142. I know no better book on this whole subject.

[2] Intellectuals are apt to put too much stress on freedom of opinion and its expression. Even more fundamental is freedom to eat sufficient food, to occupy sufficient house room, to possess sufficient clothes, to enjoy sufficient comforts and amenities, to be able to live like a human being.

The millionaire and the coal miner are equally free, in theory, to drink champagne or travel round the world ; their wives equally free to hire a lady's maid or to cook their husband's dinner with their own hands ; their sons equally free to go up to the University or to go down the pit. But, in practice, wealth opens the gates of freedom and opportunity, and poverty closes them.

Social equality must rest on equality of opportunity, and this in turn upon equality of environment, especially in childhood. Great social inequality looks its ugliest, when we see it strike the young.

What practical framework, of laws and institutions, does social equality require ? The elements of such a framework

> belong [as Mr. Tawney points out] to one or other of two principal types. There are those, in the first place, such as the extension of social services and progressive taxation, which mitigate disparities of opportunity and circumstance, by securing that wealth which would otherwise have been spent by a minority is applied to purposes of common advantage. There are those, in the second place, such as trade unionism and industrial legislation, which set limits to the ability of one group to impose its will, by economic duress, upon another, and thus soften inequalities of economic power. The co-operative movement and the extension of undertakings carried on as public services, with their practice of returning profits to the consumer, and their recognition of responsibility, not to investors, but to the community, combine, in some measure, the benefits of both.[1]

Of the so-called " social services ", some are destined to assume increasing importance with the advance of Socialism, others, one hopes, to dwindle into insignificance.

In the first class are public education and public

[1] *Equality*, pp. 165–6.

health services, including the provision of houses.[1] Likewise State pension schemes. All these are permanent functions of the State.

In the second class are unemployment benefit and poor relief. In proportion as Socialism succeeds in curing unemployment and poverty, these forms of provision will become unnecessary, as with many physical diseases now extinct among civilised nations. But, while these economic diseases continue, not to succour their victims is a social crime.

The rapid extension of education and health services is essential, not only as a step towards social equality, but as a social investment in human capacities, which we can ill afford to neglect. Educational advance is one of the main roads towards the abolition of class privilege. The Labour Party has declared that " it stands for complete educational equality and for the final abolition of the system under which the quality of the education offered to children has depended on the income or social position of their parents ".[2] Such equality is not an unrealisable dream. But it looks remote, when to-day the proportion of children in England and Wales entering secondary schools is less than one-seventh, and in some areas less than one-tenth, of those leaving elementary schools, and when three-quarters of the children reaching the age of fourteen plunge immediately into an overcrowded labour market.

The raising of the school leaving age to fifteen forthwith, and to sixteen with the least possible delay, is urgent both on educational grounds, including grounds of physical health, and as a blow at unemployment.[3]

[1] Some speak glibly of " revolution ". But what a revolution it would be, if every family were decently housed !

[2] *Labour and Education*, p. 20. This pamphlet contains a sketch of immediate policy, approved at the Party's Annual Conference at Southport in 1934.

[3] See R. H. Tawney, *The School Leaving Age and Juvenile Unemployment* (Workers' Educational Association, 3*d*.).

Complete equality requires not merely more, but better and more varied, education. For it is important to insist that, for a variety of inclination and ability, equal opportunity means variety of opportunity. In concrete terms, there must be, for all children under eleven, better buildings, smaller classes, ample facilities for practical work and for play, with nursery schools, especially in the towns, as the preliminary stage.

For children between eleven and sixteen, standards of staffing, building equipment and amenities, including playing fields and provision for physical training, must be levelled up to the present standards of the better secondary schools. And fees in secondary schools should be abolished.

For young people over sixteen there must be such an increase of scholarships to Universities and other centres of higher education and professional training as shall secure that no advantage, in respect of entry to such institutions, remains with wealth, but that appropriate abilities alone decide the question. I have stated these concrete requirements of educational equality in unemphatic words. But if they could be fully realised, we should have made a real revolution in the lives and outlook of the young, and in the future form of our society.

It is an important item in the Labour Party's policy that maintenance allowances should be paid to parents, in respect of children kept at school beyond the age of fourteen. Personally I regard this as the thin end of the wedge of a national scheme of family allowances, which, by adjusting family income more closely to family needs, would be a bulwark of social equality. There is no sanctity, nor finality, in maintenance allowances only starting at fourteen. But such a national scheme, starting at birth, is not financially practicable yet, though I hope that we shall move steadily towards it. The same is true of the more ambitious national pension schemes, whose cost runs into hundreds of millions of pounds annually.

Health, it is often said, is a purchasable commodity, of which, within wide limits, a community can buy as much or as little as it cares. In this commodity we are practising criminal economies. Preventable death, disease and general ill-health bulk large in our national heritage.

A constructive health policy is many-sided. It includes an ample and efficient State medical service, which will care for men, women and children alike, without the discriminations of the present system of National Health Insurance. It is closely linked with housing, with the provision of more open spaces and playing fields, with the abolition of unemployment and low wages, with shorter hours and healthier working conditions. Most closely of all it is linked with the schools, with more frequent and thorough medical inspection, to be followed in all cases by the prescribed treatment,—specially valuable if continued for all children until the age of sixteen,—with the provision of school meals and of a regular milk ration.

Chiefly to help the farmers, the National Government has done something to encourage milk drinking by school children. But the Board of Education has laid it down that free milk may only be given to children certified by a doctor as showing visible symptoms of "malnutrition". A cruel and ignorant pedantry! As Dr. Somerville Hastings has observed, "the effects of under-nourishment are by no means easy to detect by physical examination".[1]

> Unfortunately [writes another high authority] we cannot make a sensational story out of malnutrition as it occurs to-day—it produces a slow silent rot of virility, vitality and fibre from which recovery soon becomes

[1] *The Lancet*, March 25, 1933.

impossible. It takes a lot of ill-feeding to kill a child. It takes very little to sap his vitality seriously.[1]

Industrial legislation must have a prominent place in any Labour programme. In its various aspects such legislation is a powerful aid to health, to leisure, to security and to the legitimate rights of organised labour ; indirectly a powerful aid to social equality, through the levelling up of standards of life. A new Factories Act, a new Shops Act, a new Workmen's Compensation Act, an Offices Regulation Act, are long overdue. The next Labour Government should pass them into law.[2] Likewise a new Mines Regulation Act, though the socialisation of the mines would, one hopes, make the requirements of such an Act mere ordinary routine. Likewise a legislative reduction of working hours. Likewise a restoration to Trade Unions of the rights taken from them by the most reactionary Act of 1927. I have not the special knowledge needed to discuss usefully here the details of these various branches of industrial legislation. But I wish to emphasise their great practical importance,[3] and I know that in this field the Labour Party is exceptionally rich in experts.

[1] From a leading article in *The Medical Officer*, April 29, 1933. This and the preceding quotation are taken from Mrs. Barbara Drake's pamphlet, *Starvation in the Midst of Plenty, a New Plan for the State Feeding of School Children*, published by the Fabian Society, 3d.

[2] But these need not be enormously long and complicated statutes, requiring months of preparation and of detailed Parliamentary debate. They should give powers, under a comparatively simple statute, to Ministers to make appropriate orders and regulations, as proposed in Chapter VI.

[3] People who invent imaginary difficulties sometimes say that the next Labour Government must choose between the extension of social services and industrial legislation on the one hand, and the introduction of measures of socialisation on the other. On the contrary, it must choose both, and must vigorously pursue both lines of policy.

The pace at which the social services can expand and industrial legislation go forward, partly depends on the pace at which prosperity increases and Socialism goes forward. A greater flow of plenty, better distributed and safeguarded against interruption, is a necessary condition of rapid advance.

It is wrong to pitch hopes too high, or to date their complete fulfilment too early. There are limits to the practical possibilities of the redistribution of wealth based on high taxation within the framework of capitalism. Within this framework, our gains, as recent history shows, are not secure. Economy campaigns may come again, as in 1931 and 1922, intensifying inequality in the hope of reinvigorating capitalism. " Since the standard of education, elementary and secondary, that is being given to the child of poor parents is already in very many cases superior to that which the middle class parent is providing for his own child, it is time to call a halt." So spoke Sir George May, from the depths of his heart! Such extravagance necessitates too high an income tax.

The Labour Party has always preferred graduated taxation of incomes, and of property passing at death, to other sources of revenue. These must continue to be the mainstays of a Socialist Budget. But we should, I think, turn our minds also to the possibility of new taxes on luxury consumption.

The next Labour Government will need all the revenue it can gather, both from old taxes and new. There will be heavy competing claims upon it, coming from many quarters. Some of these will have to be postponed in the early years, or only met in part. Only the growth of planned prosperity, and a heavy fall in unemployment, can ease the Budget problem. But gradually contributions from the surpluses of socialised enterprises should become an important aid to public revenue.

The problem of debt charges will take on a new aspect with the extension of socialisation. Some years ago the Labour Party proposed a capital levy, on a graduated scale, on all individuals owning capital worth more than £5,000, to be applied to debt redemption. Unfortunately, this sound policy was not adopted. In the last few years the burden of the dead-weight debt, previously much increased by falling prices, has been somewhat diminished by conversions, and the debt problem has now receded to the second line of our preoccupations. But the burden on the Budget remains severe, and the opportunities of further relief by conversions are now small. It is my personal opinion that, once we have made good progress with socialisation, the policy of the capital levy should be brought to the front again, to reduce both the dead-weight debt and that attached to socialised enterprises.

Last, but not least, of the measures for achieving social equality—for a Socialist, indeed, the most fundamental—is the extension of the " socialised sector ". For this purpose, as for many others, I count the Co-operative Movement, both on its productive and distributive side, as a great public enterprise, and as a powerful engine of equality. It generates no large unearned incomes, no inflated salaries, no private profits, only a social surplus which all its members share. Between Co-operative and other forms of public enterprise, mutual goodwill should always find practical accommodation.

We must distinguish clearly between the initial act of socialisation and the subsequent process of socialised enterprise. The initial act, not being accompanied by any confiscation of private property rights, but only by a change in their form, makes no direct contribution to equality. But the subsequent process steadily promotes it. And even the change in form is significant. For the rentier is not well placed to play the bad citizen by trying to " sabotage " government. In the last resort, he is the captive of his paymaster.

But social equality does not imply the abolition of private property. Quite the contrary, as will be argued in the next chapter.

CHAPTER XXXII

SOCIALISM AND PRIVATE PROPERTY

SOCIALISM aims at a vast increase in private property. But this must be understood relatively to the form of private property and to the size of individual holdings.

> Needless to say [writes Mr. Brailsford] I have no case to urge against the private ownership of consumers' goods, nor even of houses and gardens. Such things are necessary extensions of human personality, and with economic order and peace we should enjoy them in greater abundance and security.[1]

He is clearly right. But of those who die in this rich country, under capitalism, only one in four leaves even as much as a hundred pounds' worth of individual property, less than one in thirty-four as much as £5,000, and less than one in sixty-five as much as £10,000. Such is the cold record of the death duty returns.[2]

Some defenders of our present arrangements emphasise the great aggregate "wealth of small investors". "Who can say", asks Mr. Runciman, "that a country like ours, in which 14,000,000 or 15,000,000 people hold between them at least £2,833 millions, is not a very stable industrial and financial

[1] *Property or Peace?* p. 128. Public ownership of "the means of production, distribution and exchange" is a familiar formula, and a very comprehensive one. But it does not extend to the means of consumption.

[2] *Report of Inland Revenue Commissioners for* 1932–3.

concern ? "[1] Even if we take Mr. Runciman's figures as correct—and there is reason to think that his total is too high—the average holding is only £200. This is a poor showing, for the great majority of holdings will be considerably below this average. There will, moreover, be debts to set against them, so that the average net holdings will be smaller still. The official death duty returns correct Mr. Runciman's unofficial estimates and their truthful acid eats deep into his brightly coloured picture.

If each family in Great Britain " possessed private property to an aggregate value of only £5,000, no one possessing more, this would represent a total capital wealth of £50,000 millions, or at least three times as much as all the existing private riches of the inhabitants of the Kingdom."[2] Even this modest vision of the Earthly Paradise is very far from the facts around us. Yet, in any truly civilised community, a convenient and pleasant home, books, recreation, holidays and travel should be within the reach of every family. So, too, should command of a sufficient sum of money, over and above current income, to meet exceptional needs and emergencies, and give a sense of added security.

Public provision, through the development of the social services, does not make individual or family provision either unnecessary or unwise. On the contrary, by narrowing the gap to be bridged, it makes it more effective.

Command of money may take many forms. A deposit in a bank or savings bank, savings certificates or other securities of Government or Local Authority

[1] In an address to the London Regional Conference of the National Savings Movement, reported in *The Times* of October 26, 1933.
[2] Webb, *A Constitution for the Socialist Commonwealth of Great Britain*, pp. 346–7.

or Public Enterprise, shares in a co-operative or building society, are obvious forms, yielding interest and holding the principal in reserve against contingencies. Likewise insurance policies of many types.

Outside these fields, moreover, we may take for granted that a wide and varied range of private investment will continue, though this will be gradually narrowed and increasingly subject to public controls. And, in addition, each individual or family will have a share, though not an individually separate share, in an ever-increasing mass of public property.

It is the chief historic aim of Socialism to transfer to public ownership private property rights in the means of production. But, since first this aim was formulated, the character of such rights has undergone changes which make the problem of Socialist transformation both simpler and easier.

> Property originally [says Professor Henry Clay] was the legal right exercised by the owner; then there developed a tendency to exchange this right for a money income charged on the thing, and to relinquish the use of the thing itself to the person who undertook to pay the money income; latterly property has taken more and more the form of a bare right to money payments . . . secured, not by being charged on some particular thing, which the borrower uses, but simply by the borrower's undertaking to pay. . . . Less than half the property returned for Estate Duty now consists of tangible possessions, more than half consists of contractual rights to money payments. . . . Owing to this change, property has lost the obvious *prima facie* justification that attaches to tools in the possession of their user, or land in the possession of peasant proprietors. It may be doubted whether respect for property rights, derived from a time when these were the typical forms of property, will indefinitely afford a support for the security of property rights of a very different order. . . . Property must be unstable so long as it is

so unevenly distributed. . . . The existing distribution of property is the most glaring denial of the ideal of democratic equality.[1]

These changes have strengthened the case for Socialism, by concentrating real power in the hands of a small number of men, who have come to exercise a dangerously dictatorial influence over our economic and financial life ; [2] they have simplified the technical task of socialisation, since this now involves, for the great majority of the property owners affected, only the exchange of one piece of paper, one contractual right to money payments, for another ; and they have sapped the strength of the present property system, and its capacity to resist Socialist change.

For the great majority of property owners, who to-day exercise no real control over the undertakings in which their money is invested, the change will be one

[1] *Problem of Industrial Relations and Other Lectures*, pp. 263-4.

[2] In the United States, according to Messrs. Berle and Means, " approximately 2,000 men out of a population of 125 millions were directors of the 200 largest concerns in 1930. Since many of these are inactive, the ultimate control of nearly half of industry was actually in the hands of a few hundred men " (*The Modern Corporation and Private Property*, p. 46). In this country no such complete piece of research has yet been done. But Mr. Peter Howard, writing in the *Sunday Express* on August 12, 1934, states that 170 members of the present House of Commons hold between them 650 company directorships. Sir Charles Barrie, Tory M.P. for Southampton, holds the record with 34. Mr. George Balfour, Tory M.P. for Hampstead, comes second with 26, including 16 chairmanships. Sir Robert Horne has only ten ; but " if I had my choice ", says Mr. Howard, " I would take his ten in preference to all the others ". He is a director of Lloyds Bank and chairman of the Great Western Railway. He is concerned with " navigation, mining, almost every activity ", including oil. His income from his directorships Mr. Howard puts at £20,000 a year. " No politics in business ! " cry the anti-Socialists.

of form rather than substance. As for the very rich, taxation, particularly of inheritance, will be the chief means of redressing the gross inequality which their excessive wealth exhibits.

CHAPTER XXXIII

INHERITED WEALTH

In a book first published in 1920, I wrote that

> the phenomenon of inherited wealth is at once very curious, very important and very much neglected. . . . Under almost all systems of property law, the living are allowed to step into the shoes of the dead, either under wills or under various legal rules of succession. This is a very curious fact. It is also a very important fact. . . . Within the framework of the capitalist system, the chief cause of the inequality of incomes from property is that some persons receive much larger amounts of property through inheritance and gift than others. The effects of inherited property in maintaining the inequality of incomes from work are also very great, since the children of those who inherit property inherit better economic opportunities. . . . Though very curious and very important, the phenomenon of inherited wealth has been very much neglected, especially by professional economists. . . . And in the controversy between socialism and individualism, the one side have generally lost sight of inheritance, because their eyes have been fixed upon far larger reconstructions, while the other have also passed it by in silence, generally because it has not occurred to them, but sometimes perhaps because they have felt it to be a weak point in their system.[1]

---

[1] *The Inequality of Incomes*, pp. 281, 283 and 126. In this book, and especially in Part IV, I examine the problem of inherited wealth in greater detail than is possible here. I

I should not alter these words to-day. Property is a bundle of rights, and one of these rights, as the law now stands in capitalist countries, is the right of unlimited inheritance by private individuals of wealth created by others; unlimited both in amount and in time. There is no limit to the unearned millions which one man may pocket on the death of another. And there is no limit to the number of generations, which may successively inherit the same family fortune. The fortune, indeed, may change its form, from land to securities, or from one set of securities to another, or from home to foreign investment. But in substance it remains the same, a mass of titles to wealth which the owner has not created. At each transfer by death taxation, through death duties, does something to reduce the mass, but in the intervals between transfers other forces operate to increase it—saving, lucky speculation, unearned increment of all kinds, as well as " business ability " operating under very favourable conditions.[1] Moreover, the habit of intermarriage between wealthy families is continually adding mass to mass, and strengthening the tendency towards the concentration of great private wealth in few hands. Sometimes, of course, great fortunes are diminished or even destroyed, by private extravagance, or unlucky speculation, or business misfortune. But the losses, as the death duty returns show, are far smaller than the gains.

The majority of great fortunes, in any society where there has been large-scale private accumulation for several generations, are inherited fortunes, rather than

would also refer the interested reader to Mr. Josiah Wedgwood's able and much fuller study, *The Economics of Inheritance* (Routledge, 1929).

[1] Professor Irving Fisher, the American economist, has remarked that the distribution of property " depends on inheritance, constantly modified by thrift, ability, industry, luck and fraud " (*Elements of Political Economy*, p. 513).

those of " self-made men ", who started from scratch.[1] The latter, indeed, have sometimes rendered useful services, though, where they have become millionaires, they have been grotesquely overpaid. But those, who owe their great wealth to inheritance, can make no such claim. They afford a glaring example of unearned wealth on a fantastic scale, of passive acquisition divorced from the active performance of any social function. The continued existence of these vast fortunes is indefensible, either on economic or on moral grounds. They take unending toll of industry and often demoralise those whom they enrich.

No energetic directive people [says Mr. H. G. Wells] are deeply in love with inheritance ; it loads the world with incompetent shareholders and wasteful spenders ; it chokes the ways with their slow and aimless lives ; it is a fatty degeneration of property.[2]

Private property, provided it is moderate in amount and not anti-social in form, may serve, as has been said

[1] Mr. Wedgwood, from a close study of the figures, shows that the larger part, perhaps as much as two-thirds, of the privately owned wealth in this country has come into the possession of its owners through inheritance and gift ; that " in the great majority of cases, the large fortunes of one generation belong to the children of those who possessed the large fortunes of the preceding generation "; that only a minority of wealthy men have built up their capital without the aid of inheritance, and that the large fortunes of women are almost entirely due to inheritance and marriage (*Economics of Inheritance*, Chapters V and VI). These conclusions correct vague popular opinion which is inclined to minimise the significance of inherited wealth. The press feeds this error by featuring the self-made millionaire and leaving the other type, except for a few Noble Lords, in comparative obscurity.

[2] *Life of William Clissold*, Vol. III, p. 669. And Mr. Bernard Shaw adds that " the whole propertied class is waiting for dead men's shoes all the time " (*Intelligent Woman's Guide to Socialism*, p. 456), a weary, enervating, envious occupation.

above, as an extension of human personality or as a reasonable provision for individual security. The Socialist attack is directed, not against private property as such, but against private property in excess and in socially undesirable forms. The limitation of inherited wealth is the principal gateway through which that attack must pass, if it is to carry the inner citadel of Capitalism, to complete the work of Socialisation, and to sublimate the individual justice of Compensation in the higher social justice of Equality.

The British Death Duties, gradually and empirically developed, are a recognition, in principle, of the strength of the Socialist case against great fortunes.

Every year about one-thirtieth of the privately owned wealth in this country changes hands through the death of its owners. And so, about every thirty years, death makes a clean sweep of capitalists, though not, as yet, of capitalism.

The Reports of the Commissioners of Inland Revenue show fluctuations from year to year in the total wealth passing at death, in its distribution between groups, and in the yield of the Death Duties. But the general trend is upward, both in the total and in the part of this which is left by a small wealthy minority. The years of depression have made little, if any, mark upon this picture.

Thus the subtractions made by Death Duties, on their present scale, has been more than offset by the additions, which the opportunities of the capitalist system make possible, to the wealth of the fortunate minority. The Death Duties do not, as yet, arrest the process of continuous concentration of wealth in few hands. They only slow it down. The rich in Britain are still growing richer. And in the last few years the fall in the rate of interest has raised substantially the capital value of land and securities, and of gilt-edged securities most of all.

Over the last ten years the total net capital value of estates liable to Estate Duty rose from £442 millions in 1923–4 to £538 millions in 1929–30, fell to £517 millions in 1930–1 and to £467 millions in 1931–2, rising again to £516 millions in 1932–3.[1] In 1933–4 all previous records for a single fortune were broken by the monstrous estate of Sir John Ellerman, which exceeded £17 millions ! The wealth left by millionaires alone has averaged over £31 millions a year during this period, and the number of millionaires dying each year has varied from three to twenty-two, with an average of just over twelve per year. Yet the great majority of those who die leave property so small that it is not worth the while of the Inland Revenue to value it.

The Death Duties brought in £85 millions in 1933–4, as against £77 millions in 1932–3, £65 millions in 1931–2 and £83 millions in 1930–1. Each year, even after payment of Death Duties, more than £400 millions pass by way of inheritance. There is evidently here, to put it mildly, some margin for increased taxation.

The great bulk of the Death Duty revenue comes from the Estate Duty, which is graduated according to the total net value of the property passing on an individual death. It rises from 1 per cent on estates between £100 and £500 to 10 per cent on estates between £25,000 and £30,000, 20 per cent on estates between £100,000 and £120,000, 30 per cent on estates between £300,000 and £400,000, 40 per cent on estates between £1 million and £1¼ million and 50 per cent on estates over £2 millions.

The Legacy and Succession Duties, levied on inheritances of personal and real property respectively, bring in together about £9 millions a year. They are

[1] Seventy-Sixth Report of the Commissioners, for the year ending March 31, 1933.

graduated, not according to the amount of the inheritance, but according to the relationship of the inheritor to the deceased. The rate of duty varies from 1 per cent of the inheritance in case of husband or wife, or direct descendant or ascendant, to 10 per cent in the case of distant relatives or persons unrelated.

The other Death Duties are unimportant.

The modern history of the Death Duties begins with Harcourt's Budget of 1894, which created the Estate Duty in its present form and abolished the previous differentiation in favour of landed property. To his brother, who protested against this change and told him that " you have no landed ideas," Harcourt replied, " you have the land, and may leave the ideas to me ". The *Morning Post* declared that his Budget was " introduced with the levity of a schoolboy whose knowledge of finance is limited to some socialist manual ".[1]

The Estate Duty was further increased, and its graduation steepened, in 1907, 1909, 1914, 1919, 1925 and 1930, by Chancellors of the Exchequer so varied in their outlook as Asquith, Mr. Lloyd George, Sir Austen Chamberlain, Mr. Winston Churchill and Lord Snowden. The most spectacular increase in the rates

[1] To me Harcourt is by far the most attractive of the Victorian Radicals. He stood, more firmly than any of his colleagues, both for international peace and against class privilege and inequality at home. He had wit, gaiety and courage, as well as a social philosophy far more advanced than that of his contemporaries. Some of his hardest fights were inside, not outside, the Cabinet. To Rosebery, who disliked the levelling tendency of his Budget, he wrote prophetically ; " you say that ' the masses do not appear to support the Liberal Party as much as we have a right to expect '. If that is true, so much the worse for the Liberal Party. It is probably more the fault of the Party and of its leaders than of the masses. . . . You desire to avert the ' cleavages of classes '. The hope on your part is natural, but you are too late." Mr. A. G. Gardiner's *Life of Harcourt* is one of the political biographies most worth reading.

of duty on large estates was made in 1919 by Sir Austen Chamberlain, who doubled the rates on estates of over £2 millions, raising them from 20 to 40 per cent.

It is a remarkable tribute to the strength of the case against large inheritances that, though the Death Duties have been increased seven times in the last forty years, they have never been reduced. Here at least there has been no reaction. The wealthy have often conducted successful political agitation against the Income Tax, but though they have grumbled furiously at the Death Duties, they have never ventured to agitate in earnest for their reduction. The next Labour Government should make the further development of the Death Duties one of its principal financial tasks.

I offer the following rough provisional sketch of such development, which I believe to be immediately practicable.

(1) The present scale of Estate Duty should be raised throughout a considerable part of its length. It should be more steeply graduated on the larger fortunes, but even an estate of £20,000 might reasonably be required to pay more than 8 per cent. The special treatment of agricultural land, which since 1925 has been allowed to pay at lower rates than other forms of property, should be discontinued.

(2) The present Legacy and Succession Duties should be repealed and replaced by a single Inheritance Duty, graduated according to the amount of individual inheritances. Graduation according to the relationship of the inheritor should be discontinued, but a moderate duty-free allowance might be given to a surviving wife or husband, and a smaller duty-free allowance to a son or daughter.

(3) The whole yield of the revised Estate Duty and of the new Inheritance Duty should not be treated as current revenue. Part of these Duties should be paid

in land, and a further part in specified securities, including both Government securities and those issued by socialised enterprises. Definite portions of the prospective yield of the Duties in any given year should be earmarked for payment in land and securities respectively. The power to take payment in land has existed since 1909, but has not been used.[1] We have suffered here, as elsewhere, from a narrow " Treasury view ". The Treasury wants ready cash, and is professionally uninterested in social welfare.

The power to select, from the land changing hands each year by death, those parts which it is specially desirable to bring forthwith into public ownership, would be a valuable aid to the larger policy of socialising land.

(4) At present inheritance is unlimited, except in so far as Death Duties limit it, not only in amount but in time. Though its successive owners are mortal, an inherited fortune wears an air of immortality and may pass, not once, but many times across the grave.[2]

We shall, I hope, later reach a stage when the State will only permit inheritance in the form of an annuity, terminable at the end of one life, or at most two lives, or at the end of a fixed term of years.

I do not propose, in terms of immediate practical politics, so absolute a limitation as this. But I propose a step towards it. I suggest the imposition of a Supplementary Inheritance Duty in cases where an individual receives a net inheritance, after the payment of Estate Duty and Inheritance Duty, in excess of a

[1] Under this power Lord Snowden could have acquired Loch Lomond for the nation in 1931. But he refused the offer !

[2] The Italian economist Rignano first drew attention to this aspect of inheritance, and proposed a Death Duty which should be " progressive in time ". I have discussed his ideas at some length in my book on *The Inequality of Incomes*. He was a pioneer in this line of thought.

certain capital value, say, to begin with, £50,000. This Supplementary Duty, equal to this excess or to some prescribed proportion of it, say one half, should be payable in cash or land or appropriate securities. But the taxpayer should receive from the State in exchange a terminable annuity, say for twenty years, of equal annual value to that of the property handed over in payment of the Supplementary Duty.[1] Such an annuity would, therefore, contain no " redemption factor."

By this means a steadily increasing quantity of private property rights now running in perpetuity would be transformed into terminable annuities, running off within a comparatively short period.

(5) It is worth considering whether a Gift Duty should not be instituted, to prevent loss of revenue through the tendency, which further increases in the Death Duties would encourage, for rich men to give away property to their heirs during their lifetime.[2]

(6) It will also be necessary to deal with those unpatriotic British citizens who now legally evade Death Duties by acquiring a foreign domicile, usually in the Channel Islands. Several such cases have caused unfavourable public comment in recent years. The latest is that of Sir James Knott, who shortly before his death acquired a domicile in Jersey, and is reported

[1] I made this proposal to the Colwyn Committee on National Debt and Taxation. Their chief objection to it was that " terminable annuities are an unpopular form of property ". It will, however, be necessary to popularise them if Social Equality is to be achieved. If they are " unpopular " in the sense that their value in the market falls short of their actuarial value, the State could purchase them and thus kill two birds with one stone, doing a good stroke of business for the Treasury and helping to " popularise " them by raising their market value.

[2] This proposal, and the administrative difficulties involved, is admirably discussed by Mr. Wedgwood in *Economics of Inheritance*, Chapter X.

to have left £5 millions. I quote the comment on this case of a Conservative newspaper.

> He was one of the men who made great sums out of the war, and he sold his shipping interests before the days of the slump. . . . His name is associated with no great public benefaction. His estate, he had resolved, should make no big contribution to the revenues of the country where he was born and in which his business career was spent. Under the law as it now stands a similar avoidance of death duties is possible to many men of wealth. To their credit few avail themselves of this way of escape.[1]

Clearly the law must be changed. It has been suggested that domicile abroad for a period of ten years before death should not count for avoidance of Death Duties. It would be better, I think, to go farther, and to make the total wealth of all citizens of the United Kingdom liable to Death Duties, regardless of their domicile at death. Until such duties had been paid, or proper arrangements made for their payment, no rights of inheritance should be recognised by British law for any of the beneficiaries under their will or intestacy.

The Death Duties, thus strengthened and extended —and this process will, I hope, be continuous—would become something more than an expanding source of current revenue, important though this aspect of them is. They would also furnish an auxiliary method for the socialisation of the land; a debt-clearing mechanism, or sinking fund, both for deadweight national debt and for the debts attached to socialised enterprises; and one of our most powerful instruments for the progressive achievement of Social Equality.

[1] *Daily Telegraph* leading article, June 19, 1934.

PART VII
PEACE

CHAPTER XXXIV

CROSS-CURRENTS OF HOPE AND FEAR

UP to this point in this book I have sketched a programme of Practical Socialism for Britain. But such a programme is conditional on the avoidance of war. There is still hope of this, though it has grown less bright since 1931. No decent-minded and observant person likes the present look of things. The world is in a bad phase.

> The rhythm of progress has been accelerated to such a point that man—who has created it with his small individual inventions, just as an immense conflagration can be started with a few pints of petrol and one little match—lives in a perpetual state of instability, insecurity, fatigue and accumulating delusions. Our physical and nervous organisation will soon give way, unless some energetic decision, far-sighted and not too long delayed, brings order once more to a situation which is rapidly getting out of hand.

So wrote Le Corbusier of the Modern Great City. But his words also describe perfectly the Modern Great World and the present tension of international relations.

Man, it seems, can invent, but can neither foresee nor control the results of his inventions. He has now conquered the air, but not the nationalist passions which lie thick on the ground. Chemists and bacteriologists make new ingenious plans to spread death quickly, but not yet among those rank thistles of profit-seeking, which sow the seeds of war along the wind.

Another Great War does not bear thinking about, except that thinking now may lead to action that will stop it. If it comes, it will be death for countless millions : for some, an old-fashioned soldier's death on the battlefield, but for most, death in the flames of burning cities, or by poison gas, or by plague germs dropped from the air, or in the literal anarchy of a dissolving civilisation.

> However calmly surveyed [says Mr. Winston Churchill] the danger of an attack from the air must appear most formidable. The most dangerous form of air attack is by incendiary bombs. The argument in favour of such an attack is that if in any great city there are, we will say, fifty fire brigades, and you start simultaneously 100, or even 80, fires, and the wind is high, an almost incalculable conflagration may result. . . . We must expect that under the pressure of continuous air attack on London at least three million or four million people would be driven out into the open country around the Metropolis. This vast mass of human beings, numerically far larger than any armies which have been fed or moved in war, without shelter or food, without sanitation, and without special provision for maintaining order, would confront the Government of the day with an administrative problem of the first magnitude. Problems of this kind have never been faced before.[1]

> The man in the street [says Mr. Baldwin] should realise that there is no power on earth that can protect him from being bombed. Whatever people may tell him, the bomber will always get through. Calculate that the bombing aeroplane will be at least 20,000 feet high in the air, and perhaps higher, and it is a matter of simple mathematical calculation that you will have sectors of tens of hundreds of cubic miles to defend. Now imagine a hundred cubic miles covered with cloud

---

[1] House of Commons, November 28, 1934.

and fog, and you can calculate how many aeroplanes you would have to throw into that to have much chance of catching odd aeroplanes as they fly through it. It cannot be done, and there is no expert in Europe who will say that it can. The only defence is in offence, which means that you have to kill more women and children more quickly than the enemy if you want to save yourselves.[1]

And Mr. Anthony Fokker, the famous Dutch aeroplane designer, has asked:

> What defence could there be against an attack in foggy and bad weather against aeroplanes "flying blind" with modern direction finders and guided by wireless? Do people realise that in the next war the whole system of spying would be different? Do they realise that one spy, possessing a secret sending-apparatus, could direct the entire enemy fleet over the city they wished to attack?[2]

The only defence is in offence. Rival bombing fleets will pass each other in the air, each bound on its murderous errand. They will not fight each other in the sky; each will pass on to massacre and terrorise the multitudes which sightless economic forces have drawn together into huge cities.

"Our targets are on the Thames," some foreigner will say. "And ours are somewhere in Europe," is our only technical reply. And these would be only the opening moves in the next Great War. There would be much more, and worse, to follow.

But Mr. Baldwin is the most important member of a Government which has never really tried, as I shall show, to make the Disarmament Conference succeed, and is now busily building more aeroplanes. And Mr. Churchill's only complaint is that we are not

[1] House of Commons, November 10, 1932.
[2] Press interview, August 19, 1934.

building enough. Both see the danger vividly clear, but, looking for a way of escape, they are stone blind.

Shall it be Peace ? The answer rests, of course, not wholly with the British people. But it rests with us to an extent which many of us fail to realise. There is no other nation, except, perhaps, the United States, which has so great a power to influence others, if we choose to use it. And there is no other nation, we like to think, in which a general desire for peace is so widespread. Perhaps in this we flatter ourselves. But, in any case, peace will not come through desire alone. Peace will endure, only if real desire for it is backed by clear-sighted and tough-minded preparation, and by resolute constructive action.

We must prevent war by three separate, but complementary, methods. We must smother the superficial pretexts and excuses for war ; we must root out the underlying causes of war ; and we must organise peace positively, planning international co-operation in every sphere where human relationships cross national frontiers, and setting our faces towards the abolition of these frontiers in a Co-operative World Commonwealth.

The distinction between pretexts for war and causes of war is important. Even such rudimentary international organisation as we now possess can, if skilfully used, smother the pretexts. Contrast the murder of King Alexander at Marseilles in 1934 with that of Archduke Francis Ferdinand at Sarajevo in 1914. There was a grim, almost uncanny, likeness between these two events. In both cases the murderer was a Southern Slav : a Serb in 1914, a Macedonian in 1934. In both cases he fired, through a Royal figurehead, at a hated régime. In both cases it was alleged, with dangerous passion, that the Government of a small neighbouring State, nursing an irredentist grievance,

CROSS-CURRENTS OF HOPE AND FEAR 351

had aided and encouraged the murderer. In 1914 Austria-Hungary accused Serbia ; in 1934 Jugoslavia accused Hungary.

But here the likeness ended. In 1914 the pretext flamed into an ultimatum, which ended in the Great War. In 1934 the pretext was smothered in the Council of the League of Nations, and ended in the passing of a resolution. History does not always repeat itself. The League has substituted international machinery of delay and investigation for the pre-war international anarchy, and personal contacts at Geneva for impersonal diplomacy at a distance.

Had such facilities existed in 1914, there is good reason for believing that the Great War would have been prevented—for that year ; postponed at least till the next critical pretext ; and then, perhaps, postponed again ; and such a process of successful postponement would have given time to strengthen the forces in support of peace, and opportunity to remove the deeper underlying causes of war.

The League has at least given practical proof, on a lengthening series of occasions, that it can smother pretexts for war which, had it not existed, would have enveloped the world in flames. It has, up to now, been slow to deal with underlying causes. But it has powers of growth.

The Soviet Union was welcomed, on its entry into the League on September 18, 1934, by the President of the Assembly, Mr. Sandler, the Socialist Foreign Minister of Sweden.[1] In the course of his reply Mr.

---

[1] I mention this detail because the League is sometimes called a " League of Capitalist States ". This is a sloppy misdescription. The League takes its political colour from that of its members. The more its member States have Socialist Governments, the more it is a Socialist League. And the more its member States have peace-loving Governments, the more it is a League of Peace.

Litvinov, the Soviet Foreign Minister, used these words :

> The Soviet Government could not but observe the increasing activity in the League of Nations of States interested in the preservation of peace and their struggle against aggressive militarist elements. And it noted that these aggressive elements were finding the restrictions of the League embarrassing, and trying to shake them off. . . . I am aware that the League does not yet possess the means for the complete abolition of war. But I am convinced that with the firm will and close co-operation of all its members a great deal could be done at any given moment for the utmost diminution of the danger of war, and this is a sufficiently honourable and lofty task, the fulfilment of which would be of incalculable advantage to humanity.

A few months earlier he had declared that

> we have never refused, and do not refuse, to participate in any organised international co-operation aimed at consolidating peace. Not being doctrinaires, we do not refuse to utilise existing or future international organisations, provided we have reason to consider that they would serve for the preservation of peace.[1]

What are the underlying causes of war ? They may be analysed in more ways than one. Fear, greed and armaments is one analysis.

> The real cause of war in the modern world [said Lowes Dickinson], and whenever, in history, there have existed independent States armed against one another, is, first, the desire of all States to hold what they have and to

---

[1] From a speech delivered in Moscow at the session of the Central Executive Committee of the U.S.S.R. on December 29, 1933, reprinted in a pamphlet, entitled *Soviet Foreign Policy* (containing also declarations by Messrs. Stalin and Molotov) with a preface by Mr. Arthur Henderson (Anglo-Russian Parliamentary Committee, 5 Robert Street, Adelphi, London, W.C.2, price 4*d*.).

take what belongs to others ; next, the armaments produced by that situation, which armaments then become a further cause of war.[1]

And we may add, on this last point, the testimony of the late Lord Grey : " Militarism and the armaments inseparable from it made war inevitable. Armaments were intended to produce a sense of security in each nation. What they really did was to produce fear in everybody. Fear causes suspicion and hatred." [2]

Another analysis makes, in the light of history, a fourfold classification, into religious, dynastic, nationalist and economic causes. The first of these, with the decline in religious fanaticism and intolerance, has become unimportant.[3] The second counted for something before the Great War. Both German Kaiser and Russian Tsar, by their vanity and self-assertion, had a share of personal responsibility for 1914. In the post-war world the pseudo-dynastic egoisms and ambitions of some dictators are an incalculable element of peril. And nationalism, deliberately kept in high fever in some countries, and ready, on the slightest provocation, to rise to fever point in many others, is a constant danger.

Economic causes of war are a commonplace, working through capitalist rivalries and the pursuit of private profit, regardless of the consequences to peace. Some Socialists admit no other causes. This, in my view, is a false simplification. None the less, I regard such causes as deep-seated in the capitalist order of society; infinitely varied in their operation ; often most insidious, when least visible, in the background of a

[1] *War, Its Nature, Cause and Cure*, pp. 51–2.
[2] *Twenty-Five Years*, 1892–1916, Vol. II, p. 53.
[3] Anti-Semitic barbarities, such as Nazis practise, have nothing to do with religion. They spring from diseased nationalism and from misunderstanding of the causes of economic misery.

political situation ; often masquerading under the cloak of national patriotism ; continually threatening peace ; a principal argument for Socialism. But I reject the facile fatalistic formula that " under capitalism war is inevitable ", and I reject, with even greater emphasis, the saying of half-wits with criminal propensities that " you will never do away with war, while man remains a combative animal ". We need, not these helpless theories, but detailed study of reality and energetic action based on knowledge.

War is never inevitable until it breaks out. Peace, in a world so full as ours of nationalist and capitalist rivalries, must be one long difficult improvisation. But there is no inherent impossibility in continually fending off war by adroitness and goodwill and, most surely of all, by organising peace. And, in proportion as the world moves towards international government and Socialist forms of society, this difficult technique will become easier.

When the Great War smashed into our peaceful lives, and more and more as it dragged its slow, hideous, bloody length along, I realised how few of us, in those now incredibly remote pre-war days, had troubled to make any study of international relations or to seek to understand or influence foreign policy. " My people have gone into captivity "—and worse—" for lack of knowledge." It was the conviction that politics, rightly handled, can put an end to war, which, more than anything else, drew me into the life of active politics when the war was over. In the next few years I followed international affairs closely, and made a number of journeys of political observation in Europe, to examine for myself the new conditions created by the war and by subsequent events. I visited, in particular, several of those controversial areas, concerning which, because they lie off the beaten tracks of Englishmen abroad, it is more than usually difficult to form objective and up-to-date judgments. I also visited Geneva and tried to assess the practical possibilities of the League, and to become acquainted with its mechanisms. I published my conclusions, together with a number of proposals for action, in 1928, in a book entitled *Towards the Peace of Nations, a Study in International Politics*. I have there dealt much more fully with international problems than is possible in this book. Re-reading now what I wrote then, I find little to change.

I took some share in the preparation of the programme of foreign policy, on which the Labour Party fought the general election of 1929, and I can claim that, in foreign affairs at any rate, we had clearly defined our aims in advance and that we pursued them vigorously when our chance came.

In the second Labour Government I served for twenty-seven months as Mr. Henderson's Under-Secretary at the Foreign Office, and both there and at Geneva I gained much valuable knowledge at first hand. I was proud to serve under a great political Chief and a great Peacemaker. Blessed are the Peacemakers, even in their own lifetime. The Nobel Peace Prize was conferred on Mr. Henderson in December, 1934. He had fully earned it.

While he was British Foreign Secretary, there was no war in the world, hardly any talk of war, no serious fear of war. He renewed diplomatic relations with the Soviet Union, ruptured by our Tory predecessors; negotiated the simultaneous evacuation of the Rhineland by British, French and Belgian troops, five years in advance of the Versailles time-table; committed this country, by the signature of the Optional Clause and the acceptance of the General Act of Arbitration, to predetermined methods of peaceful settlement of international disputes, and to the principle, rejected by our predecessors, of international arbitration; and persuaded all the Dominions to join with us in these two symbolic acts and give a united British Commonwealth lead, which a large number of foreign countries instantly followed. He revived public interest and faith in the League of Nations, strengthened its authority, made it the pivot of British foreign policy, initiated reforms in its organisation, and took a leading part in the creation of an Economic Commission of the League (left to rust by his successors), in order to emphasise the economic side of the League's work and to promote international co-operation with a much wider scope than hitherto. He joined in negotiating with the United States and Japan the London Naval Treaty which, though it left levels of naval armaments in all three countries disappointingly high (he would gladly have seen them lower), yet was the first example in history of a treaty limiting in every class of ship the three greatest navies in the world ; and finally, when the Labour Government fell, he was preparing a British programme for the World Disarmament Conference, of which, by the unanimous vote of all the States concerned, he had been chosen President.

In 1931, in spite of the black economic outlook, peace seemed increasingly secure, and international co-operation a growing habit. Many difficult problems still loomed ahead, but, with the assurance of a strong and constructive British lead, none seemed insoluble.

Since 1931 there has been an almost incredible deterioration. It seems a different world. There has been open war in two Continents ; there is talk of war everywhere ; fear of war everywhere ; no disarmament, but rearmament everywhere. The League of Nations is in the trough of the political depression. For this deterioration the British National Government bears a very heavy load of responsibility. By their foreign policy they have increased the danger of war. I choose my words deliberately. I do not accuse Ministers of desiring war, but of so acting, and failing to act, as to bring it much nearer.

To the best British Foreign Secretary of recent times has succeeded the worst. As one contemplates the performances and personality of Sir John Simon, one longs for even a return to the transparent honesty of Sir Austen Chamberlain. We judged his objectives to be unduly limited, and his outlook unimaginative. But he at least was not universally distrusted by foreign statesmen, and he argued his case cleanly, and without quibbling and legal sophistries.

Sir John Simon is a disaster. Nor does Mr. MacDonald, whom we often found hesitant and unhelpful in foreign policy in 1929-31, lend strength or directness to his present Foreign Minister. Our Fighting Departments have never found an easier prey than this one-time " pacifist ".

When Japan, by her actions in Manchuria, beginning in the autumn of 1931, violated not only the Covenant of the League, but several other Treaties as well, Sir John Simon adopted, and consistently maintained, an attitude of benevolent neutrality. " When he arrived at the Paris meeting of the League Council in November 1931, he made no secret of his opinion that technically the Chinese were right, but in fact the Japanese were justified." [1] On a later occasion at Geneva the Japanese representative thanked him for a speech in which, as he said, " Sir John Simon has put very clearly, in a quarter of an hour, the case which I have been trying to put for several months." By its policy in the Far East, the British Government has seriously undermined public confidence in the League and the Collective Peace System, and has allowed Japan to set a

[1] *The Dying Peace*, by Vigilantes (published by *The New Statesman*, price 6d.), p. 7. This brilliant pamphlet contains the most powerful and well-documented criticism of the foreign policy of the National Government which has yet been written.

precedent, which others have noted. "I pay my respects to the League," said Dr. Frick, Hitler's Minister of the Interior, " but I thank Japan for her example."

I turn to the British Government's record at the Disarmament Conference. Experience shows that an international conference has its best chance of success, if it starts off with a rush, and reaches a series of rapid decisions on important issues. The classical example is the Washington Naval Conference of 1922, when the Americans led off with a series of bold proposals, and Balfour, on behalf of the British Government, played up. But Sir John Simon has never played up at Geneva. The British Government produced no disarmament proposals of their own until the Conference had lasted thirteen months. And in the interval they ingeniously obstructed every good proposal made by others. The Italians, very early, proposed the all-round abolition of the so-called " aggressive weapons " forbidden to Germany at Versailles. They were supported by the Germans, Russians and many smaller States, and the Americans expressed their goodwill. Sir John Simon proposed a Commission of experts to determine which weapons were really aggressive.[1] He then left Geneva for six weeks, while a British Admiral was permitted to expound the view that battleships were " more precious than rubies " and were not aggressive weapons.

To the proposal to abolish all tanks, the British Government replied with an offer to abolish all tanks over twenty tons in weight. It was later admitted that we had only one tank above this weight, an experiment which had proved a failure.

[1] The " aggressive " weapons forbidden to Germany include capital ships, submarines, military and naval aircraft, tanks, heavy artillery and poison gas. This schedule was drawn up by high military and naval experts, including Foch, Sir Henry Wilson and Lord Beatty. What need have we of further expert witness?

The Americans next made the so-called Hoover proposals for an all-round reduction of naval armaments by one-third in the case of battleships, and one-fourth in other classes, and a low maximum tonnage for submarines; for the abolition of all bombing planes and tanks; and for large cuts in land armaments. These proposals were widely supported in the Conference. Sir John Simon damned them with faint praise. The British Government proposed to retain bombing planes " for police purposes in certain outlying regions ". They suggested that reductions might be made in the tonnage of capital ships and cruisers to be constructed in the future. But the Americans had proposed reductions in the number of existing ships.

The French proposed a concrete scheme for internationalising civil aviation, for creating an international air police force, and for abolishing national air forces. These proposals again had very wide support. The British Government first opposed them all. Later they changed their ground and said that they were favourable, in principle, to abolition of military and naval aircraft, provided there were guarantees against abuse of civil aviation. But they put forward no constructive proposals, but only raised innumerable difficulties in the Air Committee of the Conference in February and March, 1933, when the French proposals were under discussion, and in March finally caused the Committee to be adjourned. After leaving this Committee in cold storage for fifteen months, they suggested on June 11, 1934, that it should meet again. But they did not give it much time, for on June 27 Lord Londonderry in the House of Lords proposed an increase in the British Air Force. " We can no longer hope," he said, " that an international convention will solve the problems which agitate the whole of Europe. His Majesty's Government have, therefore, decided that they can no longer delay the steps which are necessary to provide adequately for the air defence of these shores."

He also said that " the abolition of military air forces is not a matter that we are likely to see achieved in our lifetime, nor indeed in the time of many generations yet to come." But this last statement, though recorded in the press, he caused to be deleted from the official report in Hansard.

When President Roosevelt succeeded President Hoover, the Americans made another proposition. In his message to Congress of May 16, 1933, the new President suggested the abolition of bombing planes, tanks, mobile heavy guns and poison gas. We took no notice.[1] He also suggested a series of non-aggression pacts, barring " resort to force ", as well as " resort to war ", and the acceptance, as the test of aggression, of the crossing of one's country's frontiers by the armed forces of another. We opposed, except in Europe, the renunciation of " resort to force ", and we opposed also the acceptance of this, or any other, definition of aggression. In practice, any definition might prove too rigid, we said.

The abolition of the private manufacture of arms

[1] Except that on March 13, 1934, when pressed by the Labour Party in the House of Commons, Sir John Simon characteristically stated that it was not true that the United States had " made the offer of agreeing to abandon all arms except those that were allowed to Germany under the Treaty of Versailles ". Yet, following up President Roosevelt's message, Mr. Norman Davis on behalf of the United States had said on May 23, 1933 : " we feel that the ultimate objective should be to reduce armaments approximately to the level established by the Peace Treaties. . . . In particular, as emphasised by President Roosevelt, we are prepared to join other nations in abolishing weapons of an aggressive character." And on December 28, 1933, President Roosevelt tried again. " Let every nation," he said, " agree to eliminate over a short period of years and by progressive steps every weapon of offence in its possession, and to create no new additional weapons of offence." The British Government made no response.

was proposed by France, supported by Poland, Spain, Denmark and other countries. It was opposed by the British Government.

Proposals were made for the limitation of budget expenditure on armies, navies and air forces. The British Government obstructed these proposals, raised difficulties of detail, and said that publicity of expenditure would be enough.

The British Draft Convention, presented in March, 1933, was both late and lame. It proposed reductions in the personnel of land forces for others, but none for us, and no limitation at all on colonial forces; certain limitations on the size of land guns and tanks; the reduction of all foreign air forces down to our level, and then a further proportionate reduction by all of us; no further reductions for the present in naval armaments. It made no reference to the private manufacture of arms,[1] nor to the private trade in arms, nor to budgetary limitation.

[1] No, we have no private armament firms! Asked, as were all other Governments represented at the Disarmament Conference, " what undertakings in the territory under the jurisdiction of your State are chiefly or largely engaged in the manufacture of arms and implements of war ? " the British Government replied as follows. " With the possible exception of certain firms manufacturing sporting weapons, and a few firms manufacturing aircraft (civil and military), there are no private undertakings in the United Kingdom which can strictly be described as engaged chiefly or largely in armament manufacture. Even the largest firms, such as Vickers-Armstrong, making armaments in this country devote only a portion of their time and output to this work. . . . Again, firms obtaining contracts for war materials one year may not do so the next year. It will be seen, therefore, that no useful purpose will be served by attempting to give a list of private undertakings such as is apparently required to answer this question." This astounding piece of evasive humbug should be compared with the very full and detailed replies made by other Governments, notably those of France and the United States (League of Nations Report, issued on June 3, 1933).

But, having presented this Draft to the Conference, the British Government showed no eagerness to secure its detailed discussion. The months dragged on, until on October 14, 1933, there was a public " show down ", and the Germans left the Conference. Sir John Simon then engaged in a public wrangle with the German Foreign Secretary, Baron von Neurath, as to their respective responsibilities for this most unfortunate event.[1]

I conclude that if, at the moment of writing, the Disarmament Conference is still alive, and if there are still hopes, however faint, that it may in the end achieve even a limited success, most of the credit must go to Mr. Henderson, its President, who has stuck to his post with typical British tenacity, and with inexhaustible patience and resource has held the Conference together. Several times, but for him, it might easily have broken up in discord and confusion. Several times he might have broken it up himself, and won easy cheers by resigning the Presidency in protest and disgust. But would such a break-up have helped peace ?

The British Government have a heavy responsibility for the failure of the Conference up to date. A real British drive for disarmament, which they have never made, would, particularly in the early days, have gathered a tremendous momentum behind it. And in those early days, for more than a year indeed, Germany was still ruled by pre-Hitler Governments and had not yet set all her neighbours' teeth on edge. The parties of the Centre and the Left in Germany were still

[1] No doubt both, by their previous conduct, had a large share of responsibility. But I note that " it is reported that one of Sir John Simon's colleagues, before he spoke on October 14, said that his coming speech ' would blow up the bloody Conference, and a good job too ' " (Special report on the Conference by Mr. W. Arnold Forster to the National Peace Council, February 3, 1934).

CROSS-CURRENTS OF HOPE AND FEAR 363

powerful, and still desired disarmament rather than rearmament. If, at the outset of the Conference, we had boldly accepted two principles, first, the all-round abolition, to be achieved over a short term of years, of all the weapons forbidden to Germany; and, second, the full implications of Collective Security, the odds are that the Conference would have succeeded, and the Nazi triumph of March, 1933, might not have occurred. Germans, other than Nazis and Nationalists, still hoped, as they had gone on hoping since 1919, for a sign from Geneva of the beginnings of general disarmament.[1] No sign came, until the burning Reichstag heralded the fiery dawn of the German Terror. Then followed German rearmament, rapid and uncontrolled.

I have argued that the British National Government are largely responsible for lowering the power and prestige of the League since 1931, and for discrediting the Collective Peace System. In further support of this contention, I cite two South American incidents. The first arose out of the small-scale but very barbarous war, prompted, it seems, by oil interests, and kept going by armament interests, between Bolivia and Paraguay. The official Commission sent out by the League reported that the capitals of both belligerents were thronged with agents of European armament firms. During a few months of 1932, British firms sent six tanks, 99 machine guns and two million rounds of ammunition to Bolivia, and sixteen million cartridges to Paraguay. Between November, 1933, and March, 1934, British firms sent 101 machine guns, with a quantity of other

[1] If Mr. Henderson had had his way, the Disarmament Conference would have met in June, 1925. This was provided for in the Geneva Protocol, which he negotiated under the first Labour Government, but which Sir Austen Chamberlain rejected. Had the Conference met in 1925, it should at least have succeeded, as a first step, in stabilising armaments at the levels of that time, and preventing subsequent increases.

arms equipment to Bolivia, and five million rifle cartridges to Paraguay.

On May 17, 1934, Mr. Runciman stated, in reply to a question in the House of Commons, that no application for licences to export arms to either belligerent during the present hostilities had been refused.[1]

The second incident arises out of another small war, between Colombia and Peru. On May 6, 1933, the Council of the League—Peru having been declared the aggressor—unanimously recommended that no member of the League should furnish supplies to certain Peruvian warships, which had passed through the Panama Canal in order to proceed up the Amazon and attack the Colombian forces in the rear. The Dutch authorities accordingly refused these ships supplies at Curaçao. But, on May 11, the British authorities at Trinidad gave them all they wanted. The British Government thus showed itself disloyal to the decision of the Council, of which it was itself a member.

All this humiliating narrative is an essential preliminary to the exposition of a positive international policy, by which the ever-worsening situation may yet be retrieved, before it has gone too far.

[1] Later, though very tardily, an embargo was imposed by a large number of countries, including ourselves, on the export of arms to both belligerents. But by that time both were well supplied.

CHAPTER XXXV

THE LABOUR PARTY'S FOREIGN POLICY

OUTSIDE this island, any British Government has certain special relationships—to the Dominions, to India and to the Colonies.

As regards the Dominions, if I may repeat what I have written elsewhere,

> the ties of common origin and language, the grip of common memories, the possession of common political institutions, the coming and going of friends and relatives across the seas, all these are bonds which unite us in a sense of friendly and intimate kinship. . . . There is no inconsistency between peace and friendship and co-operation with all the world, and specially intimate friendship and co-operation with the Dominions, just as in private life we may have many good friends, but a few best friends among them. In the wider field of international relations, the influence of the Dominions is on the side of peace. They can take a detached view of European problems and it is natural that they should look with disapproval upon European mischief-makers whose policies hold risks of war. They play their full part at Geneva in the work of the League of Nations.[1]

The second British Labour Government secured the assent of all the Dominions to a united British Commonwealth policy of constructive peace. The next Labour Government will seek to repeat this co-operation. And it will seek to settle, by practical negotiation and

[1] *Towards the Peace of Nations*, pp. 85-6.

willingness to arbitrate points in dispute, the stupid Anglo-Irish quarrel, which has been so clumsily handled by Mr. J. H. Thomas.

The Labour Party looks forward to the day when the United States of India will take their place, willingly and with full equality of status, among the British Dominions. We are dissatisfied with many of the details, and with the grudging and patronising temper, of the National Government's India Bill.[1] But this Bill, in spite of all its shortcomings, advances in the right direction. If Indians take it, frankly as an instalment, and work it successfully, further advance towards Dominion Status must come soon.

As regards the Colonies, a Labour Government would seek to make the principle of trusteeship for the native populations a reality, and to end economic imperialism. " The objective of the Colonial policy of the Labour Party may be summed up in the two words—socialisation and self-government. Steps will be taken to those ends, having due regard to the welfare and the stages of development of the peoples concerned."[2] There should be an extension and a strengthening, by international agreement among the various Colonial powers, of the mandatory system under the League.

I turn to the Labour Party's foreign policy proper. This was redefined at the Annual Conference at Southport in 1934. There was no change in guiding principles, but a restatement with a sharper outline.[3]

---

[1] See the Minority Report of the Joint Select Committee on the Government of India submitted by Major Attlee and his colleagues of the Labour Party.

[2] *The Colonies*, p. 4. In this policy pamphlet issued by the Labour Party, and approved at its Annual Conference in 1933, Colonial policy is discussed in detail.

[3] Appendix II to the *Report of the National Executive of the Labour Party for* 1934 (pp. 101–5), entitled *War and Peace*. Mr. Henderson's speech in support of this restatement has been published by the Labour Party under the title, *Labour's*

The Conference accepted this restatement, and rejected a series of alternative proposals, by overwhelming majorities. In consequence of these decisions, the Labour Party stands, with deliberate emphasis and without any shuffling or ambiguity, for the Collective Peace System. It stands, in other words, for the honest and energetic fulfilment by this country of all its treaty obligations, including notably the Kellogg Pact and the League Covenant.

On this little planet, rapidly shrinking under the continued pressure of revolutionary new inventions in means of communications, we are all members one of another, not only in warm moralising, but in stone cold fact. This densely populated little island in the North Sea can never hope to live unto itself alone. We can find no oasis, either of prosperity in a world impoverished, or of peace in a world at war. Another Great War could not be localised. Whatever may be said beforehand, we should in fact have hardly any chance, if this catastrophe occurred, of steering clear of it. Therefore, we must turn all our energies and all our powers, moral and material, to preventing its occurrence. And, to do this, we must be prepared to play an active and influential part in the life of the world community.

Isolation, preached by peers who, through wealth and luck rather than intelligence, control widely read newspapers, is an impracticable policy and, even if it were practicable, would be both foolish and wrong. If we seriously tried to adopt it, we should first have to resign from the League. By such an act, and by renouncing all influence over other nations, and by declaring that, whatever trouble happened, we should

Peace Policy—Arbitration, Security, Disarmament (price 1*d.*). This is a sequel to his pamphlet on *Labour's Foreign Policy* (price 2*d.*), and his speech at the Party Conference of 1933, entitled *Labour Outlaws War* (price 1*d.*).

keep out of it, we should bring joy to every gangster Government in the world, and dismay to every peace lover in Europe, and we should bring war much nearer. And if war came, some of our mentally unbalanced isolationist peers—we know their past records—would probably be the very first to start a hysterical clamour that we should plunge in.

The Labour Party rejects this impotent isolationist creed ; it proclaims instead a World Peace Loyalty. This implies for British citizens three primary duties. First, the duty to insist that any British Government shall settle all its disputes with other Governments by peaceful means, and not by force ; second, the duty to support wholeheartedly any British Government which honestly takes its part in collective action against a peace-breaker ; third, the duty to refuse to accept any British Government's claim to be using force in self-defence, if this claim is rejected by the Council of the League, or by any other properly constituted international tribunal, and, in that event, to refuse to serve or support a Government which, by its aggression, would have forfeited all claim to moral authority. In these conditions, war resistance would become the duty of all citizens.

The recognition of this threefold duty is both true patriotism and true internationalism, between which there is no conflict.

To make this attitude both plain and effective, a Labour Government would pass into law a Peace Act of Parliament, binding all British Governments to submit any dispute with another State to some form of predetermined peaceful procedure, never to resort to force as an instrument of national policy, and to report at once to the League and to comply with its injunctions, on the basis of reciprocity, in case of having to use force in self-defence. So far the Peace Act would do little more than reaffirm our existing treaty obligations under the Kellogg Pact, the League Covenant, the Optional Clause and the General Act of Arbitration. But this reaffirmation, in solemn statutory form, would be worth making, on two grounds. First, it would drive into the consciousness of public opinion the nature and extent of the peaceful obligations, which already bind us. Second, it would give these obligations an even more emphatic legal form, and might, perhaps, be so drafted as to render Ministers who disregarded them liable to prescribed penalties.

But the Peace Act would do more than this. It would empower the Government to apply any economic and financial measures which it deemed necessary in order to take its share in collective action to cut off relations with a peace-breaking State. No further legislation, but only a resolution of the House of Commons, should be required to give the Government such powers, if in its judgment the situation demanded them.

We are bound, under Article 16 of the League Covenant, to adopt such measures against " any member of the League " which " resorts to war in disregard of its Covenants under Articles 12, 13 and 15 ". Similarly, under Article 17, against a State outside the League guilty of like conduct. And under the Kellogg Pact, though this Treaty contains no provision for sanctions, it is difficult to resist the conclusion that any State which violates the Pact thereby becomes an outlaw, with whom the rest should have no dealings.

In my opinion, collective economic and financial pressure, or even the threat of it, if known to be seriously meant, would, in nearly all hypothetical cases, halt an intending aggressor in his tracks. The threat of it would certainly, I believe, have halted Japan in September, 1931, when her first tentative aggression in Manchuria began, had the British and American Governments acted together, though at later stages of this affair, as the militarists gained the upper hand in Japan and became flushed with success, a threat might not have been enough. Post-war experience shows that nearly every case of international tension, if handled firmly and authoritatively at the beginning, can be resolved without great difficulty. But, if handled weakly, it is apt to become increasingly intractable. In the Far Eastern affair, however, from the start the British Government was running hard —away from its treaty obligations. Had Mr. Henderson still been Foreign Secretary, there would, I think, have been a very different outcome. A wonderful opportunity was missed of demonstrating, not only to Japan, but to the world, the power of the Collective Peace System. And if Japan had proved her case against China peacefully before an international tribunal, and China had refused to make amends, effective international pressure could have been applied to China.

The potential force of these peaceful and bloodless pressures is, in the modern world, tremendous. Thus it has been argued that the stoppage of supplies of petrol alone would prevent an aggressor from going forward with his plans, since modern armaments on land and sea and in the air all move by oil.

General Smuts, among others, has advocated a " mineral sanction against war ". He points out that " the only two nations that could fight for long on their own natural resources are the British Empire and the United States. If they are firm in refusing to export mineral products to those countries that infringe the Kellogg Pact, no war can last very long ".

It has also been argued that a financial boycott alone would suffice.

> No credits ; no bills discounted ; no loans ; no possibility of buying anything within the territories of the countries that stood for peace, or selling anything to

them, until a satisfactory settlement approved by all those countries had been reached. Further, all enemy, i.e. aggressors', property would be liable to seizure in the territory of these countries. It is almost inconceivable that any country, even pushed to white heat by nationalist fury, would then dare to violate its engagements. The immediate practical results of doing so would be too serious.[1]

Were the United States to associate itself with such a system, even to the extent of declaring in advance that, if the American Government concurred with the Council of the League, or with the other principal signatories of the Kellogg Pact, in the determination of a peace breaker, it would do nothing to hinder the application by other States of such pressure, in the most appropriate form, against the guilty State, it would make the success of this method practically certain. If the United States went farther, and were willing itself to take part in the application of such pressure, there would, in almost every conceivable case, be complete certainty.

I regard as not less important than active British participation in the work of the League, the maintenance of the most friendly relations between the British Commonwealth and the United States, and a constant willingness on our part for frank consultation and whole-hearted co-operation on every question of common interest. And incomparably our greatest common interest is the maintenance of peace.

The United States has been taking a prominent part in the World Disarmament Conference, as in other international conferences of recent years, and has now joined the International Labour Organisation at Geneva. If the American Government should be prepared for any closer form of international associa-

[1] Lord Howard of Penrith in a letter to *The Times* of November 19, 1932.

tion, we should welcome their decision from the depths of our hearts. The absence of America from a League which an American President created, has been the greatest single source of weakness in international organisation since the war.

If ever gangster politicians in power in any country realise that, if they break the peace, they will have to count, in addition to other unpleasant prospects, on the active disapproval of the United States and on all the consequences of this, the world will have turned the corner. Peace will be secure, if not for ever, at least for this generation.

Recently, indeed, the Collective Peace System has received a great reinforcement. The entry of the Soviet Union into the League in 1934 is an event which may well change the future course of world history.

If the Collective System holds firm, as a dam against war, in the critical next years, there is some chance of building solidly behind it. The next Labour Government must take the lead in organising these building operations. What do they include ? First, an international convention for real disarmament ; second, the creation of an international police force and an international organisation for civil aviation ; third, the ending of private arms manufacture ; fourth, provision for peaceful change in existing treaties ; fifth, international economic co-operation on much bolder lines than hitherto. I will discuss these five points in order.

First, disarmament. The nations of the world are now spending on armaments more than £1,000 millions a year ; this country more than £100 millions a year, or more than £200 a minute. All over the world armament expenditure is mounting sharply. So, as a natural consequence, is the sense of fear and insecurity.

The next Labour Government will inherit a situation

THE LABOUR PARTY'S FOREIGN POLICY

which their predecessors will have bedevilled. But it may not be too late to retrieve it. The Labour Party " favours the total disarmament of all nations throughout the world and the creation of an international police force, and calls upon the British Government at the Disarmament Conference . . . to submit proposals for a large and immediate reduction in the expenditure of all nations on armed forces, for the general abolition of all weapons forbidden to Germany by the Treaty of Versailles, for the abolition of military aircraft and for the international control of civil aviation, for the suppression of all private manufacture of, and trade in, arms, and for strict international inspection and control of the execution of a Disarmament Treaty." [1] The Labour Party does not favour " disarmament by example " in this country alone. Proposals to this effect were overwhelmingly defeated at the Southport Conference in 1934, as on previous occasions. We can see ugly beasts prowling to-day in the international jungle. We do not fancy that they would become tame and friendly, if we alone threw away our arms. We have to clear and civilise the jungle, not to lie down defenceless in the midst of it. The disarmament of one nation alone will do nothing for peace. It may do less than nothing.

The Labour Party stands for the disarmament of all nations by international agreement, and is prepared, unlike the National Government, to make bold offers, conditional on like action by others, to scrap British arms.

How much disarmament can be got, and how much international agreement, only a strong British initiative can disclose, when it is made in an international situation, which we cannot now clearly foresee. But we should, at least, propose, as a first step, the all-round

[1] Resolution unanimously adopted at the Annual Conference at Hastings in 1933, and reaffirmed at Southport in 1934.

scrapping within a comparatively short term of years, and the complete cessation of new construction, of all weapons legally forbidden to Germany, so that she shall have no valid ground for alleging that she is still subject to differential treatment. We should also propose a large all-round cut in budgetary expenditures on armaments.

We must insist upon an effective system of inspection and control of the execution of any Disarmament Treaty by a Permanent Disarmament Commission. Every signatory must swallow its national pride and, without obstruction, let accredited foreigners come and poke about among its stores of arms and its arms factories. Inspection should be periodic, in every country, even if there be no complaint of infringement of the Treaty. This is a vital condition of security. If in any country inspection discloses forbidden weapons, or an excess of permitted weapons, these must be destroyed before disarmament proceeds elsewhere. If there is refusal to destroy them, or undue delay in their destruction, there is a strong case for the application of economic or financial pressure to the Treaty-breaking State.

How much international agreement is necessary for a Disarmament Treaty ? Best of all that it should be universal. We must strive our hardest for this. But, neither here nor elsewhere, should we make a fetish of unanimity. In respect of some forms of armament, a convention between a small group of the most heavily armed States, as in the Washington and London Naval Treaties, might be sufficient.

But, further, " the Labour Party is convinced that in the absence of a world scheme of pooled security, the policy of reducing national armed forces in return for international guarantees of security, backed by international armed forces, may be promoted by States within the League concluding agreements under

Article 21 of the Covenant."[1] We should form no exclusive alliances; we should make an offer to all nations to come in on equal terms. But, if some accept, while others refuse—particularly if many accept, while few refuse—it may be worth while to go forward with those who accept.[2] Those who refuse at first may change their minds later.

Both an international police force and an international control of civil aviation may begin in this limited way. We reject the fallacious argument, often used by reactionaries, that the collective organisation of security, and the obligations which it will impose on this country, will increase the scale of national armaments which we shall need to maintain. The truth is the exact reverse of this. In isolation we should need, if we follow this fantastic policy to its fantastic logical conclusion, national armaments sufficient to defeat a whole world united against us. In proportion as we abandon isolation and join a group, it is only necessary that the group, either by their individual armaments or by the collective armaments of the group as a whole, should be strong enough to defeat possible enemies outside the group. The more numerous the group, the fewer those who remain outside it, the lower the levels of necessary armament, either individual or collective, of its members. If we rule out the possibility of war with other members of the group, we need no longer arm against them. We should, indeed, enter into friendly discussion and bargaining with them, not to increase, but to reduce, our own expenditure on armaments.

[1] Major Attlee in the House of Commons on July 13, 1934. The same point is made in the statement on "War and Peace" accepted at Southport.

[2] This idea is developed in detail in a pamphlet on *Labour's Foreign Policy*, issued by the New Fabian Research Bureau (Gollancz, 6d.).

The creation of an international police force is a necessary condition of the abolition, and perhaps even of the substantial reduction, of national armed forces. The first step in this direction should clearly be the creation of an international air police force. I believe this to be already within the range of practical politics.

> Labour in power [says Major Attlee, in an admirable statement of the case] [1] should propose that all Air Forces should be handed over to international control, that all Air Lines with their personnel and fleets should be internationalised, and that all industrial establishments producing aircraft should be taken over by the League. The International Air Force and the World Air Service should have no national sections. Its members should be trained as a world brotherhood of the air. . . . The units of the Air Force and the aircraft factories should be distributed widely in as many countries as possible, so that no one State should, if evilly disposed, be able to seize more than a small fraction. This distribution is tactically possible, because of the superior mobility of aircraft, which would allow concentration at the place required long before aggressive action on land or sea could develop seriously. . . . Private aviation should be strictly controlled; in particular the fastest and most powerful planes should be in the hands of the international authority. It is my belief that such a force would never have to be used. Its superiority would be such that the threat of its use would be enough to deter any would-be aggressor.

A Labour Government

> would try to get a world organisation, but failing that it should try to bring about within the League a body

---

[1] In an article in the *Daily Herald* of October 16, 1934, entitled " No More War if Planes Police the World ". See also his pamphlet on *An International Police Force* (issued by *The New Commonwealth*, price 3d.). Also an article on " An International Police Board ", by H. R. G. Greaves, *New Commonwealth*, September, 1934.

of States which would agree to pool their security and create an International Air Force. If, as I think possible, two or three big powers and the great majority of the smaller powers responded to such an appeal, their collective strength would be too great for any militarist power to challenge with any hope of success. ... The menace of air warfare is so great and the danger from the continuance of national armaments so imminent that nothing but a bold and revolutionary policy can save the world.

As regards civil aviation, I quote a distinguished airman, famous in connection with the Flight over Everest, Air Commodore P. F. M. Fellowes. " The only solution from the civil side appears to resolve itself into the formation of an internationalised civil aviation company." Such a

> company, supported by the Governments of Europe, Great Britain and the Dominions, to own all aircraft in that area over a certain size, is quite conceivable. . . . The danger of flying has, like the risk in other dangerous sports, a uniting effect among those who fly, and this should promote a sufficient *esprit de corps* to cancel out any international friction. . . . There would no doubt be many difficulties to overcome, but none should be allowed to prove insuperable if by such means this danger to civilisation can be averted.[1]

An international service of civil aviation holds immense possibilities of rapid development. Once this is firmly established, it will be worth while to incur a large capital expenditure on lighted air routes, fully equipped with air bases, hotels, repair stations, radio-beam and meteorological services, etc. This will create a large amount of skilled employment in nearly every country. And it will be a grand adver-

[1] In a letter to *The Times* of June 21, 1933. See also *World Airways. Why Not ? A Practical Scheme for the Safeguarding of Peace*, with a foreword by W. Arnold-Forster (Gollancz, price 1s.).

tisement of practical and beneficent internationalism. Already the national sovereign State will begin to look petty and old-fashioned. Man will have started on the greatest flight in the history of the air, towards a single World Authority.

The Labour Party is pledged to the abolition of the private manufacture of, and trade in, arms. There is much more to be said in this case, than in that of disarmament, for unilateral action by this country alone. But it would be incomparably better to secure similar action by all countries. Otherwise the virtuous countries only pass the profits of this trade in death to those which are less virtuous. We should abolish these profits, not transfer them.

It would be contrary to human nature, if those who made arms for profit did not try to sell them, and did not both welcome, and seek to create, conditions favourable to increased sales. There is a mass of evidence regarding their operations, not in one country only, but all over the world. Private armament firms have sought to influence public opinion through the control of newspapers in their own and other countries. They have fomented war scares and spread false reports regarding the armament programmes of other countries. They have bribed, or attempted to bribe, Government officials at home and abroad, in the hope of getting orders. They, or their directors, have founded and financed so-called " patriotic societies ", in order to stimulate the clamour for more armaments. They have sold armaments to both sides in wars, and in impending wars, and played off one against the other. They have sent paid agents, well supplied with funds, to seek by false propaganda to defeat the efforts of international conferences for disarmament and peace. They have sold arms to countries which they have known might easily become in war time the enemies of their own.

We do not forget the British guns, sold for the profit of British armament firms, which killed British soldiers on the Western Front and in the Dardanelles ; nor the British torpedoes, sold for profit by the subsidiary of a British armament firm, which sank British ships and drowned British sailors in the Mediterranean sea. And we have noted that in November, 1932, Vickers inserted in a German newspaper a full-page advertisement of one of their tanks, though Germany, under the Treaty of Versailles, is forbidden to possess these weapons.[1]

Business, we know, is often dirty. This armament business is very dirty, and bloody as well. There have been innumerable exposures.[2] The latest has been furnished by the American Senate inquiry of 1934, in which not only American, but also British and other foreign firms and their agents have been the objects of most remarkable revelations.

It was disclosed, for example, that Vickers in England and the Electric Boat Company in the United States had a working agreement, as regards orders for

[1] Sir Herbert Lawrence, the Chairman of Vickers, when questioned on this incident by Miss Eleanor Rathbone at his annual meeting on March 26, 1934, explained that this advertisement was intended to be read in South America, where Vickers had " a number of clients " and " the English press is not well circulated ". Further asked whether there was any reason to suppose that Vickers' munitions and armaments were secretly being used for the rearmament of Germany and Austria, Sir Herbert Lawrence is reported to have replied : " I cannot give you an assurance in definite terms. But I can tell you that nothing is done without the sanction and approval of our own Government " (*Daily Herald*, March 27, 1934).

[2] See Mr. Noel Baker's admirable pamphlet, *Hawkers of Death* (published by the Labour Party, price 2d.). Also the two deservedly well-known pamphlets (issued by the Union of Democratic Control, 34 Victoria Street, London, S.W., price 6d. each), *The Secret International* and *Patriotism Limited*.

submarines, for dividing the world between them. The price of every submarine made by Vickers for the British Government included a commission to the Electric Boat Company. It appeared that, when Chile and Peru were on the point of war in 1929–30 over a boundary dispute, Vickers sold armaments to Chile and the American company sold to Peru, and both companies shared in each other's profits. The American company's representative in Peru, a certain Commander Aubrey, tried to get himself appointed one of Peru's delegates to the Disarmament Conference. He wrote to his principals, " I feel I can do something good for Peru there, as well as for the cause of submarines in South America."

A number of letters were produced, alleged to have been written by Sir Charles Craven, Managing Director of Vickers, to his American co-adventurers. One said : " Even in code it is better not to mention any names of ships, as I am rather afraid that such telegrams might get into the hands of our clients, and it would be awkward if they asked me about our agreement with you ". The " clients " were the British Admiralty ! Another said that certain Admiralty orders might have to be withdrawn " if Geneva or any other troublesome organisation upsets the large submarines ".

Sir Basil Zaharoff, the international armament tout from the Levant, whom Mr. Lloyd George made a Knight of the British Empire in 1918, and a Knight of the Bath in 1919, is all over the record. " I trust ", he writes to an American firm " that orders for submarines . . . will bring much business to your company, and you may count upon my little efforts always working in your direction." He was tout for Vickers as well.

Spurred into defensive action by these revelations, and by the rising tide of popular feeling in favour of the abolition of this form of private enterprise, the British National Government are appointing a Royal Commission to conduct an inquiry under three heads : the relative advantages of private and State manufacture of armaments ; the adequacy of our present Export Licence system ; and the question whether private armament firms stimulate the demand for arms " by means of improper pressure ". But we, or rather the private armament makers, are assured by Sir John Simon that it will not be a " fishing inquiry ", and by *The Times* (of November 23, 1934) that the Government are determined that there shall be no investigation of " the past activities of armament firms or the accounts of individual firms ". On these conditions, the third head of the inquiry will be sheer humbug.

On the first head we already have the conclusions of the McKinnon Wood Committee, which reported in 1919, when the lessons of the Great War were still fresh. Its members included representatives of the Admiralty, War Office, Air Ministry, Treasury and Board of Trade, and even two gentlemen who had been directors of private armament firms. They anticipated that " the country will insist on the production of all armaments being confined to government factories ", and they declared that " the disappearance of the large armament firms " would not " materially handicap production in the event of a serious war ". In the Great War the private armament firms had shamefully fleeced the taxpayers and made enormous profits out of their country's necessities, and the State had, none the less, been compelled to produce its own munitions in State factories on a gigantic scale.

On the second head of the inquiry it is obvious that the licence system does nothing to curb the foreign agents of armament firms or their methods of getting business. Licences are granted in ordinary times practically as a matter of course.

The Labour Party regards this whole inquiry as a waste of time, only designed to whitewash black practices, and make an excuse for inaction. The evidence already available is overwhelming. Our minds are made up. We hold that whatever arms are needed should be manufactured in Government arsenals and dockyards and, as regards the air, in international establishments.

Countries unable or unwilling to manufacture all the armaments, which under a Disarmament Treaty they are permitted to possess, should be entitled, subject to full publicity and international control, to import them from the Governments of other countries.

In this country our present State establishments could now manufacture by far the larger part, if not the whole, of our armament requirements. If these were reduced by a Disarmament Treaty, the task would be still easier. Any specialised armament plant in the possession of private firms could, if required, be taken over at a valuation, and the making of armaments by private firms thenceforward legally forbidden, and the prohibition enforced by Government inspection. Delimitation of armaments would be governed by the simple principle of " reserving to the State that part of industrial production whereby a product undergoes the first transformation which renders it unfit for pacific purposes and destines it exclusively for military use ".[1]

I turn to the so-called " problem of peaceful change ".

[1] This definition is taken from a Memorandum submitted to the Disarmament Conference on February 27, 1933, by the French, Danish and Spanish delegations. See, on the whole question, Mr. Noel Baker's pamphlet *Suppressing the Private Manufacture of Arms, The Objections Answered* (National Peace Council, 39 Victoria Street, London, price 2d.)

If we are to ensure the final settlement of all disputes by peaceful means, we must make some provision for peaceful change in existing treaties.

No treaty, or any other human arrangement, can stand eternally fixed. We must provide not only for declaring and enforcing the law, but for changing the law. Treaties are, in fact, continually being revised. The Treaty of Versailles, for example, has already been revised to an extent not generally recognised. Thus reparations, after years of folly and bitterness, were revised out of existence in 1932. The best procedure for treaty revision is friendly negotiation between the parties concerned. But it is often argued that in some cases, especially as regards certain controversial European frontiers, this procedure is inadequate, and that something more is required.

Many of the current claims for frontier revision, based on hysterical nationalist propaganda, when closely and impartially examined, are weak, and are growing weaker with time. Migrations, differential birth rates and other factors of adjustment are steadily weakening them. In general, time is on the side of the present frontiers. But some of the more modest claims are still strong. At present all the countries from which territorial concessions are asked stand very stiffly on the defensive ; the more so as a result of the present state of international tension.

I have written elsewhere that

> it is possible, and it is to be hoped, that, in time, public opinion will relax its present stiffness on this point. But it is folly to dream, at this stage, of important changes in frontiers otherwise than by war, and it is worse than folly to prefer war, with all its horrors and the hazards of its issue, to the itch of present discontents. The only practical and wise starting-point of immediate policy is to take existing frontiers for granted and to aim, not towards their revision, but towards their

obliteration.[1] Let justice be done within the present frontiers, let communication and trade and personal intercourse be facilitated across them, and the itch may be soothed. Then, in a happier and less inflamed future, frontier revision may come to seem both less impossible and less important.[2]

An essential preliminary condition of any serious consideration of frontier revision is, therefore, the restoration of a sense of neighbourliness and tranquillity on both sides of the line.

The Labour Party fully recognises the need for facilitating treaty revision in appropriate cases and circumstances. But some present circumstances are by no means appropriate. " This country should tell Germany ", said Major Attlee, speaking on behalf of the Labour Party,[3] " that if she wants a revision of the Peace Treaties, she must come with clean hands. Germany is demanding a number of adjustments, and there is even talk of her asking for a retrocession of some of her former colonies. In all those areas there are minorities and people of alien race. We should say, quite frankly, to Germany, that at present no one in this country would propose to entrust any

[1] " I was asked," said Mr. Henderson in his speech on foreign policy at the Labour Party Conference at Southport in 1934, " whether I agreed with Mr. Baldwin that our frontiers were now on the Rhine. I replied that my job was not to shift frontiers, but to abolish frontiers." The Conference greeted these words with prolonged applause.

[2] *Towards the Peace of Nations*, p. 46. See Chapter III of that book for a further discussion of this question, which I can claim to have studied in some detail, both at a distance and, in the case of some of the disputed frontiers, on the spot. I note that Professor Gilbert Murray, in his chapter on " Revision of the Peace Treaties " in *The Intelligent Man's Way to Prevent War* (Gollancz), is broadly in agreement with me on this point. See in the same book (pp. 342–62) Mr. W. Arnold-Forster's interesting discussion of " Peaceful Change."

[3] House of Commons, April 14, 1933.

minority to Germany, when she treats her minorities in her own country as she is doing."

Territorial change is primarily demanded, and resisted, on nationalist grounds. But it has also economic aspects, sometimes profoundly important, sometimes trivial.

No Socialist is likely to underrate the importance of economic co-operation between the nations, and the removal of the economic causes of war. Competitive profit-seeking in the sale of arms is only one degree more dangerous to peace than competitive profit-seeking by way of concessions and loans in backward countries, or by way of cornering supplies of raw materials which all nations need. War between France and Germany all but came, in 1911, over a struggle between French and German capitalists for the possession of the iron ore in the Atlas Mountains in North Africa. There are many like dangers in different parts of the world to-day. We must establish international control over such concessions and loans, and make an international plan for a fair deal in raw materials and other essential commodities. And, as already stated, we must strengthen and extend the mandatory system in Colonial territories.

Every advance towards Socialism in any national area is to be welcomed. But Socialism by national compartments is not enough. Nor can we afford to wait for its general achievement in this form. In some countries we may have to wait a very long time. We must use, without delay and to the utmost, all existing instruments of economic co-operation between nations, such as the Economic, Financial and Transport Sections of the League, and the International Labour Organisation. And we must be prepared, not only to strengthen and sharpen these instruments, but to forge new ones as well, which only Planned Socialist Communities can handle.

There is hope that, through these means, men will gradually learn the trick of working together and the lesson that private greed may be a carrier of deadly plagues.

But all such hope depends on the firm maintenance of peace meanwhile.

To-day we are all like sleep-walkers, who walk near the sheer edge of a cliff. That edge may not be quite so near as some think. But it is not far off. We must wake soon, or crash. If we let the next few years slip, as we have let slip these last years, then, I fear, our feet may slip too, and we shall fall into horrors too complete and too hideous to imagine.

There is but one way back from the cliff's edge. It leads towards world government, and a worldwide plan, for justice and plenty and peace. We must step boldly away from national sovereignty and capitalism, both too weak to bear our weight much longer. Someone must lead. Let us lead. Let a Socialist Britain, by her influence and her example, help to save the world from war.

INDEX

Abercrombie, Prof. Patrick, 267, 270, 289
Aberdeen, 282–3
Acceptance houses, 183, 207, 238–9, 308
Acquisitive Society, The (by R. H. Tawney), 93, 165
Addison, Rt. Hon. Christopher, 20, 286–7, 289–90, 307
Admiralty, 136, 380–1
Adshead, Prof. A. D., 274
Advisory Financial Council, 315
Afforestation, 160, 255, 262, 283, 295, 297, 302
Aggression, 360, 368
Agricultural land, 154–5, 157–159
Agricultural Marketing Act, 60
Agriculture, 22, 128, 157–8, 182, 236, 267, 286, 295, 307, 311
Air Force, 136
Air Ministry, 125, 381
Air transport, 118, 125–6
Alexander of Jugoslavia, King, 350
Alternative vote, 36
Amazon, 364
America, *see* U.S.A.
America Must Choose (by H. Wallace), 305
Anglo-Irish Treaty, 6

Anglo-Persian Oil Co., 307
Anglo-Soviet Trade Treaty (1934), 305
Arbitration, General Act of, 355, 369
Armaments, 218, 352–3, 370, 372, 382
Arms manufacture, 145–6, 360–1, 372–3, 378, 381
Arnold, Lord, 71
Arnold-Forster, W., 362, 377, 384
Asquith, Lord, 339
Attlee, Major Clement Richard, 169, 366, 375, 384
Aubrey, Commander, 380
Australia, 208
Austria, 189, 208, 379
Austria-Hungary, 351

Bailey, Prof. F. G., 289
Bailey, Mr. John, 287, 289
Bakelite, 137
Baldwin, Rt. Hon. Stanley, 348–9, 384
Balfour, Lord, 47, 358
Balfour, Mr. George, 332
Bank for International Settlements, 187, 203, 219
Bank of England, 169, 183, 186–7, 189, 191, 202–10, 212–16, 232, 234–5, 238–9, 263–4, 308, 315

INDEX

Banking, Banks, 182–6, 190, 196, 207, 231–2, 237, 263
Banking (by Dr. W. Leaf), 203
Banking Corporation, 234–8
Barclay's Bank, 233
Barnes, Major Harry, 271, 275, 277
Barnsley, 60
Barrie, Sir C. C., 120, 332
Beale, Sir John, 120
Beatty, Admiral Lord, 358
Belfast, 38
Belgium, 31, 208
Belgravia, 151
Bentham, Jeremy, 17
Berkshire, 289
Berle, Mr., 332
Bevin, Mr. Ernest, 125
"Big Five, The," 232–5, 237
Birmingham, Annual Conference of the Labour Party at (1928), 18
Black and Tans, 6
Blackett, Sir Basil, 195, 248, 259
Blatchford, Robert, 17
Board of Education, 324
Board of Trade, 311, 381
Bolivia, 363–4
Boothby, Mr. Robert, 228
Bottomley, Horatio, 210
Brailsford, Mr. H. N., 217, 329
Brazil, 217
Brentford, Lord, 10
Britain, 31–2, 104–5, 111, 114, 117, 150, 153, 183, 187, 194, 198–9, 201, 223, 252, 267, 286, 301, 305–6, 330, 347, 377
Britain's Industrial Future, 225
British Broadcasting Company, 102

British Broadcasting Corporation, 97, 102–4, 142
British Commonwealth, 305, 356, 365, 371
British Draft (Disarmament) Convention (1933), 361–2
British Electrical and Allied Manufacturers' Association, 107
British Museum, 292
Broadcasting, 102–4, 113, 141
Bryan, William Jennings, 193
Bryce, Lord, 78
Buckmaster, Lord, 44
Building Societies, 224–5, 228–9
Bulgaria, 208
Burns, Rt. Hon. John, 267

Cadogan Estate, 152
Cairngorms, 289
California, 107
Campbell-Bannerman, Sir Henry, 48, 50
Campbell Case, 18
Canada, 107, 115, 199
Canals, 118, 125–7
Capital levy, 327
Capitalism, 223, 244–50, 252, 254, 256, 312, 320, 326, 329, 337, 354, 386
Carlisle, 270
Cassel, Prof., 247
Central Banks, 187, 203, 208
Central Banks (by Sir C. Kisch), 208
Central Electricity Board, 108–12, 122–3, 142, 227
Chamberlain, Rt. Hon. Sir Austen, 48, 50, 339–40, 357, 363
Chamberlain, Joseph, 10
Chamberlain, Rt. Hon. Neville, 187
Channel Islands, 342

INDEX

Charing Cross, 274
Chelsea, 152
Chile, 208, 380
China, 370
Churchill, Rt. Hon. Winston, 21, 57, 75, 187, 258, 339, 348–9
Citrine, Mr. Walter, 161–2
City of To-morrow and its Planning (by Le Corbusier), 269, 273
Civil Aviation, Internationalisation of, 125, 359, 372–3, 375, 377
Civil Servants, 93, 313
Civil Service, 11–12, 14, 206, 313
Clark, Mr. Colin, 214, 223, 226, 257, 261, 274, 299, 301
Clay, Prof. Henry, 331
Cliff, Mr. John, 162
Clynes, Rt. Hon. John Robert, 24
Coal, 113, 115–6, 129–40, 146, 175, 255, 307
Coal and Commonsense (by the Labour Party), 133
Coal Mines Act (1930), 131
Coal royalties, 131–2
Coal treatment, 130, 133, 135–9
Coalmines Reorganisation Commission, 131–2, 147
Coastwise shipping, 118, 125–127
Cobbett, William, 274
Cole, Mr. G. D. H., 17, 231
Collective Peace System, 357, 363, 367, 370, 372
Collective Security, 363, 375
Colombia, 208, 364
Colonial Office, 13, 88
Colonial Service, 13
Colonies, 365–6
Columbia River, 115

Colwyn Committee on National Debt and Taxation, 342
Commissioners of Crown Lands, 156
Committee of Imperial Defence, 230
Committee on the Allocation of Parliamentary Time, 49–52, 54, 56, 58, 66
Commons, Open Spaces and Footpaths Preservation Society, 285
Communism, 5–6
Communists, 35, 248
Companies Act (1929), 210
Compensation, 169–77, 282–283, 337
Confiscation of private property, 168–9, 171, 173, 176–7, 237, 327
Congress, 32
Conservative Government, 45, 108
Conservative Party, 16, 19, 47, 303
Constitution (A) for the Socialist Commonwealth of Great Britain (by Mr. and Mrs. Sidney Webb), 78, 99, 330
Consular Service, 13
Control of Investment (by Colin Clark), 223–4, 226, 257, 261
Cook, Arthur, 114, 130
Co-operative Movement, 147, 315, 327
Co-operative Societies, 135, 147, 224
Co-operative Wholesale Banks, 237
Coppock, Mr. R., 274
Cornish, Dr. Vaughan, 289
Cornwall, 289

INDEX

Corporative State, 94
Cotton, 146, 307
Council for the Preservation of Rural England, 285, 289
Court of Appeal, 80
Courtaulds, 211
Courthope, Sir George, 120, 297
Coventry, 22
Craven, Sir Charles, 380
Credit Anstalt, 189
Crighton, J., 73
Cromwell, Oliver, 77
Crown, the, 9–11, 55, 72, 74–76, 78, 83, 149, 156, 204, 286
Crown Colonies, 217
Crown lands, 150
Cunliffe, Lord, 183
Curaçao, 364
Currency and Bank Notes Act (1928), 202, 209
Currency, Banking and Finance (by the Labour Party), 192, 204–14
Czechoslovakia, 31, 208

Daily Herald, 24
Dallas, Mr. George, 159
Danube Basin, 306
Dardanelles, 379
Dartmoor, 281, 289
Davenport, Mr. E. H., 211, 225, 227
Davies, Miss, 151
Davis, Mr. Norman, 360
Death Duties, 153, 157, 173–6, 266, 290, 292–3, 329–30, 335, 337–43
Defence of the Realm Act, 68
Deflation, 182, 197
Democracy, 27, 31–3, 45, 49, 67, 71, 99, 161
Denmark, 199, 208, 219, 361

Department of Scientific and Industrial Research, 135
Derelict Area (A): a Study of the S.W. Durham Coalfield (by T. Sharp), 132
Development Fund, 262–3, 265
Devonshire, Duke of, 72
Dickinson, Goldsworthy Lowes, 352
Dictatorship, 32–3
Diesel locomotives, 124
Diplomatic Service, 13
Disarmament, 358, 362–3, 372–4, 378
Disarmament Conference, 349, 356, 358–9, 361–3, 371, 373, 380
Distribution of electricity, 105, 109, 111–12
Dominions, 9, 31, 34, 40, 80, 199, 217, 311, 356, 365–6, 377
Dominions Office, 88
Donoughmore Committee, 63–64, 68
Dovedale, 289
Drake, Mrs. Barbara, 325
Durbin, Mr. Evan, 198
Durham, 130, 132, 134
Dying Peace, The (by Vigilantes), 357

Ebury Farm, 151
Economic Advisory Council, 314
Economic Consequences of the Peace (by J. M. Keynes), 3
Economic Planning, 154, 205, 243, 309, 315
Economics of Inheritance (by J. Wedgwood), 335–6, 342
Education, 321–3, 326

INDEX

Edwards, Mr. Ebenezer, 135
Edwards, Mr. Trystan, 274
Egypt, 217
Einzig, Mr. Paul, 186, 188, 189
Electoral law, 37, 40–1
Electoral Reform Bill (1931), 36
Electric Boat Co., 379–80
Electricity, 105, 107, 110–13, 122, 124, 127, 130, 140–1, 268, 272, 300–1
Electricity Commission, 106–108, 111–12
Electricity Supply Act (1919), 106–7
— (1926), 108–9, 115
Electrification, 107, 113–14, 121–3, 136, 255, 263, 294
Elements of Political Economy (by I. Fisher), 335
Ellerman, Sir John, 338
Emergency legislation, 68
Emergency Powers Act (1920), 68
Employment, 69
Engineering, 146
England, 3, 6–7, 38, 109, 289, 322, 379
Equality (by R. H. Tawney), 320–1
Essays in Persuasion (by J. M. Keynes), 261
Estonia, 208
Etchells, Mr. Frederick, 269
Europe, 3, 6, 31, 62, 67, 189, 294, 311, 349, 354, 359–60, 368, 377
Exchange Clearing Act (1934), 219
Exchange control, 219
Exchange rates, 198–200
Executive of the Parliamentary Labour Party, 83
Exmoor, 291

Fabian Society, 23
Fascism, 5, 169
Fellowes, Air Commodore P. F. M., 377
Feudal system, 149
Finance, 27, 181–2, 184–6, 190–2, 196, 202, 230–1, 262, 264–5, 312
Finance Bill, 52, 55–7
Financiers and the Nation (by T. Johnston), 73, 185, 237
Finland, 31, 208
Five-Year Plans, 114
" Flight of capital," 218, 238
Flour-milling, 147
Foch, Marshall, 358
Fokker, Mr. Anthony, 349
Food distribution, 147
For Socialism and Peace, the Labour Party's Programme of Action, 15, 141
Foreign loans, 217–18
Foreign Office, 11–14, 88, 188, 307, 355
Foreign policy of the Labour Party, 366
Forest of Dean, 289
Forestry Commission, 156, 286, 294–8, 311
Foundling Site, 286
Framework of an Ordered Society (by Sir A. Salter), 62, 248
France, 31, 183, 188–9, 199, 208, 311, 361, 385
Francis Ferdinand, Archduke, 350
Free trade, 303–4, 306
Frick, Dr., 358
Friendly Societies, 169
Fuel Research Board, 137

Gardiner, Mr. A. G., 339

General Council of the Trade Union Congress, 83, 85, 133, 167
General Strike (1926), 4–5
Generating stations, 105–12, 124
Geneva, 351, 355, 357–8, 363, 365, 371, 380
Geneva Protocol, 363
Geographical planning, 113, 128, 229, 267–8, 283–4, 302
George, Henry, 152
Germany, 5, 7, 35–6, 107, 121, 181, 183, 185, 188–9, 191, 208, 255, 311, 358, 362–3, 373–4, 379, 384–5
Gladstone, William Ewart, 10
Glasgow, 39
" Gold Group," 188, 199
Gold standard, 183, 187–8, 192–3, 198–9, 203, 216, 263
Government in Transition (by Lord E. Percy), 51, 57, 62
Graham, William, 94, 304
Great Britain, *see* Britain
Great War, 348–9, 351, 353–4, 367, 381
Great Western Railway Co., 119–20, 332
Greaves, Mr. H. R. G., 376
Greece, 208
Grenfell, Mr. David, 296
Grey, Lord, 353
" Grid," 108–12, 122, 124

Hadow, Sir Henry, 13
Hailsham, Lord, 108, 115, 177
Haldane, Mr. T. G. N., 114
Halifax, 270
Hansard, 47
Harcourt, Sir W. Vernon, 339
Hardie, James Keir, 17, 47

Hastings, Annual Conference of the Labour Party at (1933), 82, 373
Hastings, Dr. Somerville, 324
Hatry fraud, 210
Hawkers of Death (by P. J. Noel-Baker), 379
Health, 322, 324–5
Henderson, Rt. Hon. Arthur, 12, 14, 16–17, 22, 188, 352, 355, 362–3, 366, 370, 384
Hewart, Lord, 63
Hills, Rt. Hon. Maj. John Waller, 232
Hitler, Herr Adolf, 358
Holborn, 39
Holland, 7, 31
Home Rule Bill, 10
Hooley, E. T., 73
Hoover, President, 360
Hopkins, Prof. Gowland, 274
Hore-Belisha, Mr. L., M.P., 60
Horne, Rt. Hon. Sir Robert, 45, 120, 182, 332
House of Commons, 7, 11, 18, 34–5, 37, 39, 41–7, 51, 54, 59–60, 63–4, 67, 69–70, 72, 74–80, 112, 279–80, 296, 299, 332, 348–9, 360, 364, 369, 375, 384
House of Lords, 31, 37, 48, 56, 64–5, 69–71, 73–7, 80–1, 106–8, 129, 131, 280, 359
Housing, 221, 224, 254–6, 266, 269–70, 302, 309–10, 324
Housing and Town Planning Act (1909), 267, 276
— (1919), 277
Howard, Mr. Peter, 332
Howard de Walden Estate, 152
Howard of Penrith, Lord, 371
Hungary, 208, 351

INDEX

Hunsdon, Lord, 164
Hyde Park, 286

Imperial Chemical Industries, 136
Import Duties Advisory Committee, 59, 61
In Days to Come (by W. Rathenau), 148
India, 217, 365–6
India Office, 88
Industrial legislation, 325–6
Inequality of Incomes (by the Author), 334, 341
Ingleborough, 289
Inherited wealth, 334, 336–7
Institute of Chartered Accountants, 128
Insurance, 147
Insurance Companies, 224, 228–9
Intelligent Man's Guide through World Chaos (by G. D. H. Cole), 231
Intelligent Man's Way to prevent War (by Prof. G. Murray), 384
Intelligent Woman's Guide to Socialism (by G. B. Shaw), 336
International Air Force, 359, 376–7
International Labour Office, 371, 385
International Police Force, 359, 372–3, 375–6
International Police Force, An (by Maj. Attlee), 376
International relations, 347, 354
Investment, 222, 224–7, 230, 232, 261–2, 264–5, 314, 331
Investment Trusts, 228–9
Iraq, 307

Ireland, 6
Iron and steel industry, 133, 144–6, 307
Iron and Steel Trades Confederation, 144
Italy, 5, 208

Japan, 208, 356–8, 369–70
Jarrow, 144
Jennings, Dr. W. Ivor, 48, 276–7, 280
Jersey, 342
Johnston, Rt. Hon. Thomas, 73, 185, 237
Joint Stock Banks, 191, 203, 206–7, 210, 232–4, 236, 238
Jones, Mr. Joseph, 135
Jugoslavia, 208, 351

Kellogg Pact, 367, 369–70
Kent, 134
Keynes, Mr. John Maynard, 3, 190, 225–6, 261, 265–6
Kincardine, 282
Kisch, Sir Cecil, 208
Knott, Sir James, 342–3
Kreuger fraud, 210
Kylsant, Lord, 210

Labour and Education (by the Labour Party), 322
Labour and Government (by the National Executive of the Labour Party), 82
Labour and the Nation (by the Labour Party), 12, 18, 21
Labour Government, 13, 14, 60, 69, 72, 75–7, 82–3, 88, 99, 105, 123, 136–7, 140, 143, 147, 157–8, 168, 237–239, 252, 263, 266, 285, 292, 312, 325–6, 340, 366, 368, 372–3, 376

Labour Government, First, 363
— Second, 11–12, 19, 21–2, 26, 85, 125, 159, 163, 176, 216, 222, 256–7, 286, 355–6, 365
Labour Movement, 129, 162, 163
Labour Outlaws War (by A. Henderson), 367
Labour Party, 7–10, 15–17, 21–4, 26–7, 32–4, 36, 41, 44, 49–50, 63–4, 67–70, 72, 75–6, 83, 86–7, 93, 97, 105, 111, 117, 120, 126–7, 130, 132, 140, 145, 155, 158–9, 162, 167, 170–2, 175–7, 182, 184, 192, 194, 195, 197, 200, 212, 232, 234, 237, 254, 286, 303–4, 308–9, 322–3, 325–7, 355, 360, 366–8, 373–4, 378, 382, 384
Labour's Foreign Policy (by A. Henderson), 367
Labour's Foreign Policy (by the New Fabian Research Bureau), 375
Labour's Peace Policy (by A. Henderson), 366–7
Lake District, 288
Land, 149–51, 153, 155, 171, 173, 260, 267, 284–5
Land (The) and the National Planning of Agriculture (by the Labour Party), 155, 159
Land values, 152–4
Lansbury, Rt. Hon. George, 9, 12, 17, 45, 286
Laski, Prof. H. J., 73
Latvia, 208
Law and Custom of the Constitution (by Anson), 74
Law Lords, 80

Law relating to Town and Country Planning (by W. I. Jennings), 276, 280
Law Society, 128
Lawrence, Sir Herbert, 379
Layton, Sir Walter, 304
Le Corbusier, M., 269, 272–3, 347
Leaf, Dr. Walter, 203
League of Nations, 189, 218, 351–2, 355–8, 363–6, 368, 371–2, 374, 376, 385
League of Nations Covenant, 367, 369
Lee, Mr. Peter, 133–4
Lees Smith, Rt. Hon. H. B., 56, 78
Leicester, Annual Conference of the Labour Party at (1932), 105
Lenin, 114–15
Liberal Party, 10, 16, 19–21, 35–6, 303–4, 339
Life of William Clissold (by H. G. Wells), 336
Linnean Society, 292
Lithuania, 208
Litvinov, M., 352
Liverpool, 39
Lloyd George, Rt. Hon. David, 6, 20–1, 140, 339, 380
Lloyds Bank, 233, 332
Loan Funds, 222–3
Local Authorities, 13, 31–2, 44, 65–7, 79, 109–10, 112, 126–7, 134–5, 138, 155–6, 221, 224–5, 227, 254–5, 269–71, 275–80, 282–3, 285, 287, 290, 295, 301
Local Government Act (1929), 277
Local Government Board, 276
Location of industry, 299–300
Lombard Street, 184

INDEX

London, 18, 39, 66, 105, 118, 128, 135, 141, 151, 181, 184, 190, 202, 206, 211, 215–16, 219–21, 233, 264, 267, 270–1, 273–5, 299–300, 348
London and Home Counties Traffic Advisory Committee, 128
London and North Eastern Railway Co., 119–20
London County Council, 128, 271, 275, 286
London, Midland and Scottish Railway Co., 119–20
London Naval Treaty, 356, 374
London Passenger Transport Board, 128, 142
Londonderry, Lord, 131, 359
Long-term credit, 210–11, 231, 310
Lutyens, Sir Edwin, 274

MacDonald, Mr. James, 24
MacDonald, Rt. Hon. James Ramsay, 8, 17, 21–2, 24, 50, 63, 71, 83, 87, 163, 183–5, 257, 286, 314, 357
McKenna, Rt. Hon. Reginald, 234
McKinnon Wood Committee, 381
Macmillan, Capt. Harold, 248, 299
Macmillan Committee, 207, 215–16, 219, 226, 232, 236
Manchester, 39
Manchuria, 357, 369
Manufacture of arms, *see* Arms manufacture
Marconi Company, 102
Marketing Act (1930), 307
Marseilles, 350
Marshall, Alfred, 150

Marx, Karl, 7, 17
Marxism (by A. J. Williams), 7
Maurice, Gen. Sir Frederick, 274
Maxton, Mr. James, 60
Maxwell, Sir John Stirling, 272
Means, Mr., 332
Means to Prosperity (by J. M. Keynes), 266
Mediterranean, 379
Memorandum on Parliamentary Problems and Procedure (by the Labour Party), 63–4, 68, 75
Metropolitan Water Board, 227
Midland Bank, 233–4
Milk marketing scheme, 59
Millbank, 151
" Mineral Sanction," 370
Miners, 129–30, 134, 139, 164, 176, 297
Miners' Federation, 133, 135, 176
Mining industry, 130–1
Ministry of Agriculture, 157, 159, 311
Ministry of Education, 13
Ministry of Finance, 88, 204, 206
Ministry of Health, 13, 276, 311
Ministry of Labour, 13
Ministry of Transport, 125, 311
Modern Corporation (The) and Private Property (by Berle and Means), 332
Molotov, M., 352
Monetary policy, 192, 194, 261
Money, Sir Leo Chiozza, 153
Montagu Norman : a Study in Financial Statesmanship (by P. Einzig), 186

More, Sir Thomas, 272
Morris, William, 17
Morrison, Rt. Hon, Herbert, 20, 117, 121, 126, 128, 162–4, 313
Mosley, Sir Oswald, 5
Most favoured nation clause, 305
Murray, Prof. Gilbert, 384
My England (by G. Lansbury), 9, 12

National Agricultural Commission, 156, 159
National Council of Labour, 83
National Council of Labour Colleges, 7
National Electricity Board, 112
National Executive of the Labour Party, 48, 82–3, 133, 167
National Forests, 285, 294, 298
National Government, 32–3, 59–60, 68, 83, 85, 128, 131, 136–7, 142, 159, 184, 219, 222, 257, 279, 324, 356–7, 366, 373, 381
National Housing Commission, 310
National Income (by C. Clark), 223
National Investment Board, 147, 205, 212, 214–16, 218, 220–2, 225, 227–30, 235, 239, 301, 310, 314
National Liberal Club, 10
National Parks, 281, 283, 285–92, 294, 311
National Parks Commission, 156, 290, 291
National Planning (by C. Clark), 299, 301

National Planning Authority, 143
National Planning of Transport (by the Labour Party), 117, 170
National Playing Fields Association, 285
National Provincial Bank, 233
National Transport Board, 26
National Trust for the Preservation of Places of Natural Beauty and Historic Interest, 156, 249, 285, 287–8, 291–4
National Wages Board, 160
Nationalisation, 131, 237
Naval armaments, 356, 359, 361
Netherlands, 208
Neurath, Baron von, 362
New Fabian Research Bureau, 223, 375
New Forest, 286
New Industries (Development) Act (1932), 301
Niagara, 115
Nicolson, Hon. Harold, 13
Nobel Peace Prize, 355
Noel Baker, Prof. Philip, J. 379, 382
Norfolk Broads, 288–9
Northern Ireland, 301
Norman, Mr. Montagu, 181, 183, 186–90, 204, 208, 215
Norway, 78, 107, 199, 208

Office of Works, 293, 311
Oil, 131, 135–6, 255, 272, 307
Ontario, 115
Ontario Hydro-Electric Power Commission, 115
Optional Clause, 355, 369
Ottawa Agreements, 305
Owen, Robert, 17

INDEX

Paddington, 271
Panama Canal, 364
Paraguay, 363–4
Park Lane, 233
Parliament Bill (1911), 10, 31, 72, 75–6, 78
Parliamentary Problems and Procedure (by the Labour Party), 48
Parliamentary Reform (by W. I. Jennings), 48
Parliamentary time, 47–8
Patents and Designs Act (1907), 137
Patriotism Limited (by the Union of Democratic Control), 379
Payton, Mr. E. L., 226
Peace, 27, 69
Peace Act, 368–9
" Peaceful Change," 382–4
Peak District, 289
Peel, Sir Robert, 10
Pembrokeshire, 289
Pen-y-Ghent, 289
Percy, Rt. Hon. Lord Eustace, 46, 51, 57, 62
Permanent Disarmament Commission, 374
Peru, 208, 364, 380
Petrol, 135–6, 138
Plan or No Plan (by Mrs. B. Wootton), 244, 246
Planned Money (by Sir B. Blackett), 195, 248
Planning, 27, 69, 106, 110, 118, 138–9, 144, 154–5, 192, 212, 245–51, 266, 269, 276–9, 281–2, 284–5, 300–1, 304–5, 309, 312, 314
Planning Department of the Government, 214, 221–2, 230
Plural voting, 37, 39

Poland, 208, 361
Political democracy, 31, 37, 41
Political pacifism, 4–6
Political Quarterly, 44
Portal, Sir Wyndham, 257
Portman, Duke of, 151
Portugal, 208, 294
Post Office, 93–5, 142, 228, 235
Postmaster-General, 95, 102
Power, 116–17, 129, 160, 274, 299
Price level, 192–3, 195–9, 222, 261
Price movements, 243, 245–6, 250
Principles of Economics (by A. Marshall), 150
Private manufacture of arms, *see* Arms manufacture
Private Members' time, 65–6
Problem of Industrial Relations (by H. Clay), 331–2
Property or Peace? (by H. N. Brailsford), 329
Proportional Representation, 35–6, 79
Public Corporations, 94–5, 97–8, 104, 108, 157, 162, 229, 235–6, 307–8, 315
Public ownership, 27, 147, 152–3, 156–8, 167, 207, 236, 268, 285, 329, 331, 341
Public Ownership and Compensation (by the National Executive of the Labour Party), 167
Public Works, 255–60, 262
Public Works Loan Board, 164, 221
Purchasing Power and Trade Depression (by E. Durbin), 198

INDEX

Question (The) of the House of Lords (by A. L. Rowse), 71
Quotas, 305–6, 308

Railway Companies, 119–20, 124
Railway Trade Unions, 119
Railways, 118–23, 125–8, 169, 175, 255, 263
Railways Act (1921), 119
Rathbone, Miss Eleanor, 379
Rathenau, Walther, 248
Rationalisation, 144, 191, 248
Reconstruction, a Plea for a National Policy (by H. Macmillan), 248
Redistribution of seats, 39–40
Reflation, 197
Reichsbank, 208
Rendlesham, 294
Reorganisation of the Electricity Supply Industry (by the Labour Party), 105
Reparations, 183, 383
Research, 99, 137
Rhine, 384
Rhineland, 355
Rignano, E., 341
Rio de Janeiro, 217
Road Traffic Act (1930), 125
Road transport, 118, 121, 125–7, 138
Robson, Mr. W. A., 95
Roman Wall, 289
Roosevelt, President Franklin D., 14, 32, 97, 115, 199, 360
Rosebery, Lord, 339
Roumania, 208
Rowse, Mr. A. L., 71
Royal Academy, 292
Royal Institute of British Architects, 292

Royden, Sir Thomas, 120
Runciman, Rt. Hon. Walter, 8, 177, 329–30, 364
Ruskin, John, 17

Saklatvala, Mr. Shapurji, 5
Salisbury, Lord, 75
Salter, Sir Arthur, 61–2, 141, 217, 248
Samuel Commission of 1925, 131, 133, 135
Sandler, M., 351
Sankey, Mr. Justice, 93
Sankey Commission of 1919, 131, 135
Sarajevo, 350
Scandinavia, 31
School leaving age, 322
School leaving age (The) and Juvenile Unemployment (by R. H. Tawney), 322
Scotland, 38, 109, 116, 289
Second Chambers in Theory and Practice (by H. B. Lees-Smith), 78
Secret International, The (by the Union of Democratic Control), 379
Serbia, 351
Severn Barrage scheme, 116
Shanghai, 107
Sharp, Mr. Thomas, 132, 268
Shaw, Mr. George Bernard, 17, 336
Shepherd, Mr. George, 34
Shepherd, Very Rev. H. R. L., 274
Shipbuilding, 144, 146
Short-term credit, 231–2, 263, 301, 310
Simon, Rt. Hon. Sir John, 357–60, 362, 381
Slum (The), its Story and Solution (by Maj. H. Barnes), 271, 277

INDEX

Slums, 154, 303
Smillie, Mr. Robert, 135
Smoke abatement, 135, 272
Smokeless fuel, 136, 138, 272
Smuts, Gen., 370
Snell, Lord, 74
Snowden, Lord, 8, 17, 21–2, 84, 87, 152, 159, 163, 187, 257, 292, 339, 341
Snowdonia, 289, 294
Social equality, 69, 319–23, 325, 327–8, 342–3
Social services, 53, 60, 86, 266, 285, 321, 325–6, 330
Socialisation, 21, 27, 93, 97–9, 100, 105, 110, 133, 141–3, 146–7, 152, 154–5, 157, 159, 162, 165, 167–72, 174–6, 237, 255, 312, 325, 327, 332, 337, 343, 366
Socialisation and Transport (by H. Morrison), 117–18, 121, 127, 163, 313
Socialisation of the Electrical Supply Industry (by G. H.), 124
Socialised enterprises, 94–5, 97–100, 142, 162–3, 170, 172–5, 231, 235, 255, 262, 309–10, 313–14, 326–7, 343
" Socialised sector ", 255–6, 258, 327
Socialism, 7, 9, 16, 20, 23, 26, 31–2, 67, 69, 100, 108, 115, 117, 121, 141–3, 152–3, 156, 162, 168–9, 246–8, 250, 252, 254, 292, 312, 320–2, 326, 329, 331–332, 334, 347, 354, 385
Socialism and the Condition of the People (by the Labour Party), 192, 232, 254

Socialism, Critical and Constructive (by Ramsay MacDonald), 71, 184
Socialist Credit Policy (by E. Durbin), 198
Socialists, 11, 17, 77, 93, 141, 152, 181–2, 225, 232, 249, 256, 262, 268, 285, 294, 319–20
South Africa, 199, 208
South America, 199, 379–80
Southern Railway Co., 119–21
Southport, Annual Conference of the Labour Party at (1934), 15, 33, 48, 63, 167, 170, 177, 254, 322, 366–7, 373, 375, 384
Soviet Foreign Policy (issued by the Anglo-Russian Parliamentary Committee), 352
Soviet Union, 107, 110, 114–15, 200, 208, 249, 259, 305, 351, 355, 372
Spain, 208, 361
Speaker of the House of Commons, 72
Sprigge, Sir Squire, 274
Stabilisation, 195, 197, 199–200
Stalin, M. Joseph, 352
Standing Committees, 47, 52–53, 63–4, 66
Standing Orders, 47, 54, 56
Starvation in the Midst of Plenty (by Mrs. B. Drake), 325
State Forests, 295–6
State Planning Department, 99, 313, 315
Stock Exchange, 211–12, 215, 230
Stockholm, 156
" Super-Ministers," 86–7

Suppressing the Private Manufacture of Arms (by P. J. Noel Baker), 382
Supreme Economic Authority, 310–12, 315
Sweden, 6, 62, 107, 121, 195, 199, 208, 351
Switzerland, 31, 107, 121, 208

Tariffs, 303–4, 306
Tasmania, 107
Tawney, Prof. Richard Henry, 17, 93, 165, 320–2
Taxation, 167, 170, 175–7, 189, 229–30, 258, 262, 265, 311, 321, 326, 333, 335
Tea duty, 55
Tennessee River, 115
Tennessee Valley Authority, 97
Terms of transfer, 167, 171–2
Textile industry, 147
Thames, 349
Theory of Social Economy (by Prof. Cassel), 247
Thetford Chase, 294
Thomas, Mr. Brinley, 255
Thomas, Rt. Hon. James Henry, 12, 21–2, 88, 257, 366
Thorne, Mr. Will, 24
Tolpuddle, 291
Towards the Peace of Nations (by the Author), 355, 365, 384
Town and Country Planning (by Prof. P. Abercrombie), 267
Town and Country Planning Act (1932), 154, 276–82, 284–5, 290, 294
Town and Countryside (by T. Sharp), 268

Town Planning Act (1925), 277, 279–80
Trade depression, 19, 21–2, 110, 211–12, 222, 266
Trade Facilities Act, 221, 265
Trade treaties, 305, 308
Trade Union Congress, 83, 85, 133, 145, 167
Trade Unions, 16–17, 100, 121, 161, 163–5, 169, 299, 310, 312, 314, 325
Transport, 22, 117–18, 129–30, 140, 160, 231, 274, 277, 299–301
Transport, Minister of, 112, 126–8
Transport and General Workers' Union, 125
Treasury, 12, 21, 40, 59, 84, 88, 93–4, 98, 103, 109, 137–8, 150, 175–6, 204, 206–9, 211–12, 221, 236, 258–9, 263–5, 290, 295–6, 301, 311, 341–2, 381
Treaty revision, 383–4
Trinidad, 364
Trustee Acts, 221
Twelve Studies in Soviet Russia (by T. G. N. Haldane), 114, 249
Twenty-five Years (by Lord Grey), 353
Tyne Valley, 294

Ulster, 6
Unbalanced Budgets (by the Author and others), 255
Undistributed profits, 223–5, 227–9
Unemployment, 21–2, 88, 129–30, 138, 166, 168, 193, 211–12, 222, 230, 244, 248, 252–3, 256–7, 259, 266, 300, 303, 311, 322, 324, 326

INDEX

Unemployment benefit, 322
Unemployment Bill (1934), 51
Unemployment insurance, 159–60, 184, 222
Union of Democratic Control, 379
United Kingdom, 343, 361
U.S.A., 7, 14, 31, 34, 107, 115, 121, 181, 185, 194–6, 199–200, 208, 286, 311, 332, 350, 356, 360–1, 370–2, 379
University representation, 38
Unwin, Sir Raymond, 270
Up with the Houses! Down with the Slums! (by the Labour Party), 254
Utopia, 272

Versailles Treaty, 355, 358, 360, 373, 379–80, 383
Vickers-Armstrong, 361, 379
" Vigilantes ", 357
Viner, Prof. Jacob, 246

Wales, 38, 109, 116, 257, 281, 289, 322
Wall Street, 184
Wallace, Arthur Russell, 152
Wallace, Mr. Henry, 305
War, its Nature, Cause and Cure (by G. Lowes Dickinson), 352–3
War of Steel and Gold (by H. N. Brailsford), 217
War Office, 381
Washington, 14
Washington Naval Conference (1922), 358
Washington Naval Treaty (1922), 374
Webb, Mr. and Mrs. Sidney, 17, 23–4, 78, 99, 330
Wedgwood, Mr. Josiah, 335–336, 342

Weir Committee, 107–8, 122, 124
Wellington, Duke of, 10
Wells, Mr. H. G., 17, 336
Westminster, Duke of, 151
Westminster Abbey, 39
Westminster Bank, 203, 233
What happened in 1831 : a Record (by Sidney Webb), 23
What Labour has done for Agriculture (by G. Dallas), 159
Wheatley, John, 9, 46
Whyte, Mr. A. P. Luscombe, 152
Williams, Mr. A. J., 7
Williams, Mr. Francis, 229
Wilson, Field Marshal Sir Henry, 358
Wiltshire, 289
Wolverhampton, 270
Wood, Rt. Hon. Sir Kingsley, 142
Wootton, Mrs. Barbara, 244, 246
Worcester, 270
Workers' control, 161–2, 165
Workers' (The) Status in Industry (by the Labour Party), 162–3
Works Councils, 162
World Airways. Why not? (by W. Arnold-Forster), 377
World Economic Conference, 188, 199, 304
Wren, Sir Christopher, 267

Young, Rt. Hon. Sir Hilton, 279
Youth Hostels Association, 285

Zaharoff, Sir Basil, 380
Zinoviev, M., 8